STRIFE
in the
SANCTUARY

STRIFE
in the
SANCTUARY

RELIGIOUS SCHISM
IN A JEWISH COMMUNITY

Phil Zuckerman

ALTAMIRA
PRESS

A Division of Sage Publications, Inc.
Walnut Creek · London · New Delhi

For information address:

AltaMira Press
A Division of Sage Publications, Inc.
1630 North Main Street, Suite 367
Walnut Creek, California 94596 U.S.A.
http//www.altamirapress.com

SAGE Publications Ltd.
6 Bonhill Street
London EC2A 4PU
United Kingdom

SAGE Publications India Pvt. Ltd.
M-32 Greater Market
Greater Kailash 1
New Delhi 110 048
India

PRINTED IN THE UNITED STATES OF AMERICA
99 00 01 02 03 04 05 06 07   8 7 6 5 4 3 2 1

Library of Congress Cataloging-in-Publication Data

Zuckerman, Phil
    Strife in the sanctuary : religious schism in a
Jewish community / by Phil Zuckerman
        p. cm.
    Includes bibliographical references and index.

    ISBN 0-7619-9053-4 (alk. paper)
    ISBN 0-7619-9054-2 (pbk.: alk. paper)
    1. Judaism — Oregon — History. 2. Orthodox
Judaism — Oregon — Relations —Nontraditional Jews. 3.
Synagogues — Oregon — Membership. I. Title.
    BM223.O7 Z83 1999
    296'.09795.'41—dc21
                                98-40169
                                CIP

Interior Design and Production by Zachary Marell and Theresa Early
Cover Art by Stacy Elliott

Contents

About the Author

Phil Zuckerman grew up in Pacific Palisades, California, but considers Oregon his homeland. He received his B.A., M.A., and Ph.D. (1998) from the University of Oregon. He has recently had articles published in *Sociology of Religion* and *Journal of Jewish Communal Service*. His main areas of interest include the sociology of religion, Jewish identity, gender and sexuality, and the social construction of morality. He is currently a professor of sociology at Pitzer College.

A c k n o w l e d g m e n t s

My sincere gratitude goes out to the members of Temple Am Israel and Bayt Emett for allowing me the chance to get to know them and share their story. I would also like to thank the reviewers for AltaMira Press who helped with the earlier drafts of this book, especially Dr. Armand Lauffer. I am gratefully appreciative of Ezra Kopelowitz for his insights, Amatzya Mezahav for his unyielding glee, and Erik Hanson for being a great and supportive editor. I would also like to thank the wise and kind faculty at the University of Oregon for their perpetual advice and enthusiasm, especially Carol Silverman, Ken Liberman, Arlene Stein, and Marion Goldman. I am particularly indebted to my mentor, Dr. Benton Johnson, for his encouragement, prodding, and warmth and for teaching me so much about sociology, religion, and being human. I am grateful for my family, Grandma and Grandpa, Omi and Opi, Mom, Dad, and David, for their love. I would like to especially thank my daughter Ruby, whose smile melts me, and finally, I would like to thank my wife, Stacy, who is my everything.

Introduction

Sometimes members of a religious organization fight amongst themselves. Internal division arises and people belonging to the same denomination or the same congregation just can't get along or agree. Sometimes the differences are worked out so that compromise is attained, reconciliation is achieved, and the religious organization gets back to its original business of uniting the faithful.

However, sometimes things just don't work out that way. Congregants can't reach an agreement, compromise is unattainable, and internal division ends up tearing the religious organization asunder. This process, in which a religious body breaks in two, is known as religious schism (Ammerman, 1987). According to leading sociologists of religion Stark and Bainbridge, "Among the most common events in the history of religions is schism—a group of disgruntled members breaks away from a religious organization in order to found a new organization. When such groups leave, they rarely do so quietly or amicably" (1985:99).

While scholars have produced a plethora of historical accounts concerning major religious divisions (such as the split between Sunni and Shi'ite Islam or the rift between Protestant and Roman Catholic Christianity), and while there have been several sociological investigations of religious schism on the denominational level (such as the division of the North American Quakers or the schism of the Southern Baptist Convention), this study looks at how the process of religious schism actually occurs "on the ground." It explores the process of religious schism as it plays itself out on the micro, congregational level. It is an in-depth story of one individual congregation's breakup: the people involved, the issues at play, the tension, the conflict, the drama.

11

As a Jew, and one acutely aware of the current state of division that exists among Jews today, and having heard innumerable anecdotal tales about various Jewish congregations racked by internal strife, I decided to look at schism specifically within a contemporary Jewish American context. While no religious denomination is immune to schismatic strife, it appears as though American Jewish communities in particular suffer from internal division. And that division feels as though it is on the rise. It brings immediately to mind the relevance of a well-known Jewish joke— a joke that I heard, over and over again, from countless sources, while conducting my study.

Here's the joke:

A Jewish man has been shipwrecked on a desert island for fifteen years. When he is finally rescued, he shows his rescuers all the things he has built while stranded: a two-story bamboo hut, a spacious outhouse, a lengthy driftwood fence, fishing instruments, and his most proud production: two bamboo synagogues. One of the rescuers is puzzled. "But you're only one person—why *two* synagogues?" the rescuer asks. "Oh, well," replies the Jewish man, pointing to the second synagogue, "That one over there, that's the synagogue I *don't* go to."

The joke is a humorous way of dealing with this problematic undercurrent within contemporary Jewish life: congregations often fight, Jewish communities are often divided, and interestingly enough, a Jew's identity is often constructed largely upon which synagogue he or she *doesn't* attend.

This is the story of one Jewish community's division. A division in that the longstanding solidarity of a small Jewish community in Oregon gave way to strife and separation.

Oregon isn't a place with many Jews. Willamette, the third largest city in Oregon, is a beautiful metropolitan enclave nestled in the Chanook Valley, surrounded by verdant mountains and rivers, permeated by evergreens, health food stores, and public parks. Though wet and gloomy most of the year, the air is always fragrant.

Willamette is definitely a liberal town. While containing its fair share of nudie bars, deer hunters, and Rush Limbaugh fans, the overriding character of Willamette is one of progressive politics, bike lanes, and a striving for multicultural diversity despite the overwhelmingly white Protestant majority. Though most Oregon towns tend to be socially and politically conservative, Willamette is well known for its preponderance of tree-huggers and aging hippies. Generally speaking, most folks here like their berry beer micro-brewed and their tofu rare. And since the 1950s, there had been only one synagogue in this cozy town of few Jews, Temple Am Israel.

However, in the early 1990s, Temple Am Israel broke apart. This one congregation that had served Willamette's modest Jewish community for decades, harmoniously uniting them "under one roof," experienced in-fighting, factional division, and an eventual schism. Where there had always been one, suddenly there were two.

In his book *New Wine in Old Wineskins* (1988), R. Stephen Warner was confident that the one Presbyterian congregation he studied in Mendocino County was a "mirror" for American Protestantism in general, and that the community he analyzed was a microcosm of broader American religious trends. I, too, am confident that the congregational schism I shall describe is not isolated or unique but, rather, typifies, and is emblematic of, a general trend within American Judaism. Although the members of Temple Am Israel are relatively isolated all the way out in Willamette, Oregon, the issues that they struggled over are issues that face nearly all contemporary Jewish communities. The two factions disagreed over issues of gender equality, the Israeli peace process, inclusion of gays and lesbians, and a myriad of religious matters ranging from the acceptance of patrilineal descent to the appropriate wording of ancient prayers.

And aside from the Jewish particulars mentioned above, the issues that this community struggled and divided over are issues facing nearly every American religious community today. What denomination hasn't had to deal with the controversial issues of male/female equality or gay rights? Take the current tension among American Roman Catholics. In a recent study, sociologist of religion Christell J. Manning (1997:375) declared that "Roman Catholicism in America is becoming a divided church." And the very source of that division, according to Manning, is controversy over issues of gender. Take a national headline from a March 1,

1998, issue of *The New York Times*: "Baptist Group Ousts Church for Welcoming Gay People." A Baptist church in Dallas, Texas, was kicked out of the state's Baptist General Convention for ordaining a gay deacon and advertising an outreach program for gay people on its Web page. And a report from the Associated Press in May 1998:

> A doctrinal split is threatening to pull apart the World Council of Churches, the global assembly formed 50 years ago to unite Christianity. . . . [T]he dispute between the council's dominant Protestant denominations and its Orthodox Christian members involves issues that touch directly on the council's mission of inclusion: ordination of women and acceptance of homosexuals . . .

Indeed, to discuss the vast array of contemporary intradenominational conflicts surrounding questions of female equality and/or gay rights would take up an entire volume in and of itself. The point is that while this may be the story of one particular Jewish congregational split, it is clearly much more than that. It is an intimate illustration of a scenario that appears to be playing itself out in religious enclaves throughout the United States. Denominations and congregations everywhere are experiencing internal tension between liberal and conservative factions. And the result is often schism. This study is thus confidently carried out in the spirit of the sentiment expressed by Lynn Davidman (1991:71) that "well-done case studies of particular communities highlight trends and patterns that can be found in the larger society as well."

Temple Am Israel had been initially established as a "middle-of-the-road" synagogue affiliated denominationally with the Conservative movement. However, over the years, it grew more and more liberal and progressive in character. By the late 1980s, it was far to the left of mainstream Conservative Judaism in terms of prayers, rituals, and social activism. While still nominally affiliated with the Conservative movement, it had developed much more of a Reconstructionist-Renewal flavor.

A group of members of Temple Am Israel became increasingly unhappy with this liberal evolution and they eventually left. They broke away to pursue their own religious ends, which included the expressed desire to "get back to tradition." But it wasn't merely a return to Conservative Judaism that they sought. They decided to go much further—they decided to become Orthodox Jews. And those remaining at Temple Am Israel subsequently became even more liberal and experimental in their Jewishness. The split was thus a division between polar cultural and symbolic visions of Jewish life, a split between traditional, conservative, and Orthodox on the one side, and progressive, liberal, and innovative on the other.

And to make their differences all the more overt and their conflict all the more poignant, the breakaway group ultimately established its alternative congregation, Bayt Emett, directly across the street from Temple Am Israel.

In a large metropolitan area with dozens of synagogues, if one particular congregation has internal problems and a sectarian faction emerges and a schism results, the ramifications may not be as strong, nor the emotions so high. But when a schism occurs in a town with very few Jews and with only one existing synagogue, the rift is much more dramatic. It is much more profound and sociologically significant (not to mention communally traumatic) going from one to two, than from, say, thirty-one to thirty-two.

Since Temple Am Israel had been the only synagogue in Willamette, its split thus represented more than just the diversification of a growing religious community. It represented the breakup of a small enclave of Jews who, for decades, had sought strength and comfort in their unity and solidarity.

This division, in which a "middle-of-the-road" congregation broke apart and evolved into two congregations, one on the extreme conservative end of the political and religious spectrum, and the other on the extreme liberal end, provides a compelling illustration of what James Davison Hunter discusses in his important book *Culture Wars* (1991). Hunter has argued that American society is becoming increasingly divided internally over various political, religious, moral, and cultural issues. On the one side are people with an "impulse toward orthodoxy," and on the other, people with an "impulse toward progressivism" (p. 42-44). In short, right-wing, conservatively-oriented people versus left-wing, liberally-oriented people. While this division has always existed in the United

States, Hunter argues that it is increasing in its scope and severity and infiltrating nearly every religious denomination. As Robert Wuthnow (1988:133) corroborates, there is evidence of "a deep division in American religion: a division between self-styled religious 'conservatives' and self-styled religious 'liberals'," a division that is ever-growing.

Willamette's Jewish community offers a clear-cut example of this "culture war" paradigm. A moderate community that was once united is now divided precisely along Hunter's axis: in one camp (Temple Am Israel), progressive Jews who take a liberal stand on various social, political, and religious issues. In the other camp (Bayt Emett), Orthodox Jews who take a conservative stand on the very same social, political, and religious issues.

Rather than a mutually-respectful parting in which both sides gracefully recognized the rights and needs of the other group, the split in Willamette's Jewish community was quite painful, characterized by damaging gossip, severed friendships, divided couples, tense confrontations, and a myriad of personal attacks. Lenny Levitan was one of the early leaders of the breakaway, Orthodox faction. As Lenny told me while we sipped tea in his cozy living room with the latest Neil Young CD playing in the background:

> It was ugly. It was as ugly as you can ever imagine it to be . . . the community really divided . . . socially, just the whole—it was ugly. It was really, really ugly.[1]

Or as Yakov Tish, the recently-appointed rabbi of Temple Am Israel, quietly lamented, "It was very tragic. Very painful."

What had happened?

I had lived in Willamette for several years prior to the split, but had only been marginally involved with Temple Am Israel. When I returned to Willamette for graduate school after a year abroad in Israel, and learned about the congregational rift, I was shocked. Internal Jewish conflicts are of particular interest to me, especially after that year spent in

---

[1] Spoken words that are italicized come from recorded interviews. Spoken words that appear in quotations come from written journal notes or memory.

Israel. But in Israel, the tension seems understandable: hostile neighboring dictators, terrorist bombs, messianic fervor, crowded buses, and rude bank tellers. But what could possibly cause disharmony among Jews out here in tranquil, beautiful Willamette, Oregon?

I wanted to know what was fought over, what was so irreconcilable—in short, what it had all been about. And while there has been much discussion of macro division in the Jewish world (most recently over the declaration made by the Union of Orthodox Rabbis that the two largest branches of American Judaism, Reform and Conservative, aren't really Jewish), little is said about Jewish division on the micro level. While political strife in Israel and rabbinic debates over "Who is a Jew?" are certainly significant, it is the actual drama of neighborhood Judaism that composes the smiles and sweat of real Jewish living. And it was here, at this micro level, that I wanted to study Jewish communal conflict and struggle.

What are contemporary Jews fighting about? How does this division play itself out? What can carefully analyzing an individual congregation's breakup teach us about the nature of religious schism in general? Such was the continuous line of inquiry that prodded my investigation.

However, as soon as I began my study, I was confronted with a personally troubling question. It was posed to me while I was down in Los Angeles one weekend, visiting my parents. I had accompanied my father to his weekly Saturday morning coffee klatch at the local deli. Several longtime friends meet with my dad there weekly to eat pastries, kvetch, laugh, drink coffee, and show off their kids if one happens to be passing through town. As usual, the group was interested in my studies and how graduate school was treating me. One of my father's oldest friends, Beba, asked me, "So, *nu*, on what are you doing your dissertation?"

"A case of Jewish communal schism," I responded. "I'm looking into why Jewish communities fight and break apart. I want to know what the issues are that divide contemporary Jewish communities." Most of my father's friends nodded with interested approval.

"Oh, yeah," said Stu, enthusiastically. "My brother back in Jersey, he's very involved with the Jewish community. And he's always telling me about the problems at his synagogue. This group wants this, that group wants that—always a mess."

But Beba didn't seem too impressed with my research topic. In fact, she was downright disapproving.

"Why don't you write something *nice* about Jews?" the 68-year-old Holocaust survivor asked. "*Why write about our troubles?*"

Everyone scoffed at Beba's comment and encouraged me. But midway through my fieldwork back in Oregon, Beba's question began to peck at my conscience. After my first few months talking to the Jews of Willamette about their communal difficulties, I began to feel doubts inspired by Beba's question. Was I just gathering gossip? Was I just asking Jews to tell me what they didn't like about other Jews? Was I just digging up dirt, exposing in a detailed manner the ways in which Jewish communities have troubles?

Fortunately, the continual encouragement of my informants managed to eventually shrink such doubts. All of those I interviewed expressed the sense that I was doing something worth-while and important for the Jewish community at large. There seemed to be an implicit and uniformly-held understanding that in my probing of communal differences, in my search to understand why those differences caused division, I was enriching Jewish communal awareness. Now, when Jews seem increasingly divided, the time to probe such division on the micro level is ripe.

As Lynn Rosefsky, a controversial leader of the Orthodox faction, said to me at the end of her interview,

> This was a situation . . . that the lessons of the need for Jews to cling to one another was forgotten . . . when it gets to the point where Jews are pushing other Jews out of the nest—the world isn't big enough for that.

It is my hope that I write this story with the purpose of helping and healing. It is my hope that in exploring the sources and dynamics of Jewish communal division, a greater understanding of contemporary Jewish identity will result, and perhaps some insight will surface that other Jewish congregations will be able to learn from, or at the very least, relate to. I hope that by learning what happened to the Jewish community of Willamette, Oregon, other religious communities (Jewish or otherwise) will be able to better deal with similar situations. As I stated earlier, the issues that confronted the Jews in Willamette, and eventually divided them, are issues that face nearly all religious communities as they approach the year 2000.

But this study isn't all simply academic. It isn't just about facilitating greater sociological understanding of religious schism or probing the depths of contemporary Jewish congregational conflict. Beneath all that is a genuine and personal desire on my part to explore what it means to be Jewish. And this mixing of "academic" and "personal" motivations certainly has its consequences.

Sociologist Marshall Sklare recognized that "perhaps the most notable fact about the Jew in American sociological thought is that writing and research on Jews has been left so largely in the hands of Jewish scholars" (1993:159). This factor, according to Sklare, can bode both good and ill for American Jewry. On the one hand, having Jews study other Jews means that we are in "the fortunate position of being able to determine how [our] group is to be portrayed" (p.161). On the other hand, Sklare warns that Jewish sociologists studying their own can fall into "a self-serving ethnocentrism," or, in the case of "alienated" Jewish sociologists, there is the possibility of studies involving an overly "critical, alienated, and even deprecatory view of the Jewish community" (p.164).

Throughout my study, I often wondered into which camp I fell.

Barbara Myerhoff, a social anthropologist who spent several years studying a small Jewish community center for the elderly in Venice, California, noted her own struggle as an academic doing investigative work among other Jews. She writes, "I spent a great deal of time agonizing about how to label what I was doing—was it anthropology or a personal quest?"(1978:18) Her answer was, of course, both. So it goes with my investigation of Willamette's Jewish community. As a *sociologist*, I am interested in the social sources and processes of religious schism. As a *Jewish sociologist*, I am interested in the specific divisive issues that face Jewish communities today. And finally, as an *individual Jew*, I am interested in just what that identity actually means. What better way to explore my own Jewish identity than by talking with members of a community divided over the very nature of Judaism?

TWO CONGREGATIONS

Bad News on *Shabbes*—On the day that Yitzhak Rabin was assassinated, I was attending a special Saturday morning *Shabbes*[2] service at the small, newly-founded Orthodox synagogue in Willamette, Oregon.

If all the Jewish communities of the world metaphorically resemble a human body, Israel might be the heart, New York might be the *kishkes*, and Willamette's Jewish community would be located somewhere on the tippy-tip of the pinkie fingernail. And yet, however isolated and far away this northwestern community may be from the major centers of Jewish life, the horrible news of Rabin's death reached us quickly and shook us up greatly.

It was a typically gray and wet day when the details of the murder of Israel's prime minister traveled out to this tip of the Jewish pinkie. I was praying (or at least *trying* to pray) in the small sanctuary of the latest addition to that pinkie, Bayt Emett. The little room that served as the prayer sanctuary was stale and drab: stucco ceiling, cheap carpet, and thin walls. Fluorescent lights buzzed overhead, giving the room an anything but holy feel. The members of Bayt Emett had rented the space only a few months earlier; before that it had been a discount computer store. It still felt like the latter, despite the attempts at Judaification, like the Marc Chagall postcards taped onto the walls.

It was 12:30. I was hungry. I had been standing up and sitting down and listening to Hebrew recitations for hours. This particular Saturday was a special *Shabbes*, however, because several students from the local university were visiting. They had been invited explicitly by the new rabbi—Rabbi Sapperstein—to come and check out what it's like *davening* in a "real Orthodox synagogue." Thus, in addition to the fifteen or twenty male regulars, and the three or four women on the other side of the *mehitzah*, there were some new faces. I wondered if these young students,

---

[2] Hebrew and Yiddish words have been transliterated. Please see Glossary beginning on page 247.

only a few years my junior, felt uncomfortable amidst all the dramatic chanting of the traditional Jewish prayer service. Did they find it odd to be *davening* in an Orthodox *shule* in the middle of Willamette, Oregon? Perhaps not. Did they find the separation between men and women noteworthy? Perhaps not. Perhaps these young students weren't at Bayt Emett to observe and note sociological nuances, but rather—unlike myself— were simply there to pray. Maybe they didn't notice or care to ponder what I considered to be the curious incongruity of swaying, mumbling men draped in sheet-like *talliseem*, praying in a strict Orthodox *shule* stuck in the back corner of an Oregon strip mall, sandwiched between a tanning salon and Burger King.

It had been well over an hour since the rabbi had given his talk on the week's Torah portion. The rabbi's talk was the only part of the Sabbath service in English. He talked about Abraham, who had been given a promise by God that he would have as many descendants as there are stars in the sky. Rabbi Sapperstein had put more verve into this sermon than I had ever witnessed before. He raised his hands with fingers spread wide to illustrate the vastness of the stars in the sky, and he raised the pitch of his voice to emphasize God's promise to His people. He made a point to make eye contact with every member of the congregation, even the women. I attributed this improved speaking performance to the fact that there were six or seven visiting students present.

Rabbi Sapperstein's cheeks had a healthy reddish hue. He had a soft brown beard and grandfatherly eyes that were surprisingly warm and knowing for a man not a day older than 37. His Boston accent was endearingly thick, despite the fact that he had spent the last ten years in Jerusalem. Bayt Emett was his very first congregation.

His sermon had been followed by more Hebrew prayers, more chanting and recitations. Finally the Saturday morning service came to a close. It was time to sing "*Adon Olam.*" Irv Mendel, the old man in the back corner with the gorgeous salt-and-pepper beard, woke up from his slumber to join in. A few other men patted their hands lightly upon their knees as they sat upright and sang, invoking a muffled, struggling rhythm.

And then, rather than the song casually ending with the usual rounds of "Good *Shabbes*" and the friendly shaking of hands, the rabbi impulsively came and grabbed me and some other regulars and led us hurriedly to the front of the sanctuary and began dancing us in a circle.

He continued singing the chorus of "*Adon Olam*" with conspicuous energy, and soon there were a dozen of us, including most of the students, dancing and singing:

"Yum did-a dum-dum dye-dye, Yum did-a lum-dum dye-dye . . . "

It was quite out of the ordinary; usually "*Adon Olam*" ended with pleasant stretches and relieved yawns. And yet suddenly the singing had grown louder and several of us were whirling about in dance. Everyone smiled and greeted this novel show of theatrical enthusiasm with happy approval. The older men clapped in support and some of the women converged against their side of the *mehitzah* to watch this fresh show of *Shabbes* festivity. The visiting students loved it, exhibiting wide grins, and the rabbi obviously loved that they loved it, holding their hands firmly, spinning them round and round. It was the most joyous and lively *Shabbes* I had yet experienced there in many months of participant observation.

After ten minutes the dancing petered out and we made our way into the lobby, a plain room used for *kiddush* ceremonies and shmoozing after prayer services. However, on this day, the lobby wasn't looking so plain. During the final prayers, some of the women had assembled and decorated several tables full of food for a special Saturday lunch in honor of the visiting college students.

After the Hebrew blessings over the bread and wine were recited, everyone took paper plates and helped themselves to fruit, cookies, and *cholent*. Several small children ran about while others hung onto the long skirts of their mothers. Those women not attending to children made sure the food supplies didn't run out. Some women did both: attended to their kids and simultaneously managed to fill up the depleted bowls with more food.

After saying hello to many of the people there and exchanging a few words with the visiting students, I sat down next to a psychologist and we got into an intense discussion about Freud's Jewish identity. Amidst the crunching of potato chips and the psychologist's musings, I didn't pay much attention to the rabbi's brief after-lunch speech. He was saying something about the Torah, but I was more interested in the psychologist's take on Freud's *Moses and Monotheism*. My ears did prick up, however, when a man asked the rabbi a politically loaded question.

"So does that mean that Jerusalem should be a shared city?" The man who asked the controversial question was the husband of Nora, who was one of the women regulars at Bayt Emett. And he wasn't Jewish. This had proven to be mildly controversial: Nora had embraced Orthodox Judaism a year earlier and had been extremely involved in the congregation ever since, and her husband's reluctance to convert to Judaism, despite her pleas, was a conspicuous source of tension, of which the rest of the members of Bayt Emett were quite well aware. He was a rare visitor to Bayt Emett and he never came to worship services. But for some reason he was there that day—perhaps to take part in the special lunch. His question concerning the political status of Jerusalem immediately aroused my attention. I highly doubted if any of the regular members of Bayt Emett would have asked the rabbi such a question. Most of the members, including the rabbi, were decidedly right-wing when it came to Israeli politics. In fact, during one of the first conversations I ever had with Rabbi Sapperstein, he had attributed the very formation of Bayt Emett, and his being hired there, to the fact that the *other* synagogue in town had gotten "too left-wing."

So I listened eagerly to the rabbi's response.

His voice took on a serious tone. He confidently explained that God promised Jerusalem not just to Abraham or Moishe, but to *all* Jews. Jerusalem, he stressed, was to *be under Jewish control forever.* Such was *God's will.* "God gave the entire land of Israel to the Jews," he explained. "And we have the Torah, which is our receipt!" He then began addressing the topic of Jewish control over the city of Hebron. However, Ari, a young man who had just recently joined the congregation a month earlier with his wife and two infant girls, amicably interjected. "*Shabbes . . . Shabbes . . .*" Ari called out in a sing-song lilt, which was a gentle way of implying, "Let's not talk politics on our day of rest." The rabbi got the message and quickly curtailed his speech.

With the conclusion of lunch, the psychologist left, as did several others. I was about to depart myself, when I was beckoned by the rabbi to come back into the sanctuary and *daven minkhah,* the afternoon prayers. Because of Orthodox ritual laws, ten men are needed to conduct most prayer services properly, and that afternoon, I was that needed tenth man. So I obliged.

The women stayed in the lobby and cleaned everything up. They folded the tablecloths and wrapped up whatever food was left over, they rearranged the tables back into their proper positions, and they did their best to deal with their now obviously cranky children.

Once back inside the prayer sanctuary, I stayed in the rear of the room and was too tired to follow along in the prayer book. Finally it was over. I got up, stretched, and then walked out of the sanctuary, ready to go home.

But as I stepped into the lobby, I was faced with a scene that threw me. There was a strange solemnity in the room and a sight not easily made sense out of.

There, standing in the lobby of Bayt Emett, was the *other* rabbi. Rabbi Yakov Tish. And beside him was Leslie Edelmann, a prominent leader of the *other* synagogue in town. I was shocked. Standing there in the middle of Bayt Emett's lobby were two prominent leaders from Temple Am Israel, the liberal congregation, the very same liberal congregation that many families had left amidst hostile circumstances to form Bayt Emett. Why were they here? They were conversing in hushed tones with a few of the Bayt Emett women. As more men emptied out of the sanctuary and into the lobby behind me, Rabbi Tish and Leslie quickly departed.

The women turned to the men and explained. Thus the news was spread to the tip of the Jewish pinkie.

"Yitzhak Rabin has been shot."

"What? Is he dead?"

"Yes, he's been killed . . . "

"Was it Hamas? An Arab?!"

"No. . . the assassin was an Israeli, a Jew."

"A Jew?! I don't believe it . . . "

The words were repeated quickly, spreading through the room.

"An Arab?"

"No, a Jew."

"A Jew?!"

"I can't believe it . . . "

"Killed . . ? . . . Dead!"

After the initial buzz, everyone just stood there, dumbfounded. Faces lost their expressions. Beth, Ari's wife, burst into sobs. She began calling out for her husband, who was still back in the prayer sanctuary. Although Americans, they had lived in Israel for many years. "Ari!" she sobbed, as she made her way into the men's side of the sanctuary. "Ari!" she called again, leaving her two infant girls unattended on the lobby floor.

Everyone stood there blankly, wincing at her cries, unable to do much else. Few spoke. Some of the women went to tend to Beth's kids. Most eyes looked down into the floor, with saddened gazes, as if in that thin, cheap carpet lay the answer to why peacemakers get murdered. Some exchanged long-faced glances or shrugs of dismay. Beth got hold of Ari and everyone could hear her breaking the tragic news. "Oh, Ari . . . Rabin . . . Rabin . . . " she wailed. Ari responded with something inaudible, and she continued to sob loudly. Their two young children looked as bewildered and uncomfortable as everyone else. Nobody knew what to do or say.

Then Rabbi Sapperstein entered the lobby, and immediately a circle coalesced around him. All eyes moved up from the floor and onto him— looking to him for something: for guidance, for comfort, for a structural, rabbinic response to the shocking news.

He reached for a prayer book and read a Hebrew passage quietly, and with tenderness. The message of the text was that we can never fully understand *Hashem*, and that we simply must trust that *Hashem* has a plan. He let out a few sad sighs as he finished the passage.

And then he declared, rather briskly, that we needed to put this horrible news in the back of our minds because it was still *Shabbes*. This declaration was met with confused silence. Put the horrible news in the back of our minds—come again?

And yet the rabbi was being quite serious. He told us that we mustn't think about Rabin's shocking murder just now, for it was still *Shabbes*. He explained that joy is commanded on *Shabbes* and it was not proper to mourn just yet, but to continue on with the *Shabbes* festivities. I couldn't believe my ears. We had just been informed that the prime minister of Israel had been assassinated, and the rabbi was instructing us to continue on with our *Shabbes* joy and pretend like nothing had happened? Was this possible?

The rabbi continued in earnest. He explained that in traditional Judaism it is improper to tell someone bad news on *Shabbes*, even the death of a close relative; one is supposed to wait until *Shabbes* is over to share such news. Again he stressed that to have joy on *Shabbes* is a central commandment. It was my personal perception that Rabbi Sapperstein seemed more concerned about explaining why we should be happy on *Shabbes* than with reacting to the news of the assassination of the prime minister of Israel.

Despite the rabbi's explanation of *Shabbes* joy, the long faces remained. Wide-eyed dismay prevailed. Everyone was still stunned, most of all, the young students. The rabbi noticed this. He walked up to them with a warm smile on his face and tried to proceed as if nothing had changed from an hour ago, when we were dancing in a circle, singing "*Adon Olam.*"

"So," he asked the students, "what shall we study? Huh? How about a little *Gemara*? A little *Mishnah*? What do you say to some Talmud . . ?"

Shocked and sad, I quickly departed.

Looking back, I realize that my immediate indignation may not have been wholly justified. What I had perceived as gross insensitivity on the part of Rabbi Sapperstein may have simply been the result of my own biased misunderstanding and lack of familiarity with Orthodox Judaism. After all, what did I really know of traditional Jewish mores concerning joy on *Shabbes*? Indeed, when I shared this incident with a Jewish colleague, she was quick to point out that Rabbi Sapperstein's insistence on joy may have actually served as a profound lesson for his congregation; there is a long tradition in Judaism of celebrating in the face of tragedy and there is great spiritual value in holding fast to the joy of the Sabbath in the face of persecution, misery, and death.

The next morning the local Willamette paper ran a story about the Jewish community's reaction to the murder of Rabin. It featured a picture of Rabbi Sapperstein and other members of Bayt Emett lighting candles at a special service of mourning for Rabin—a special service of mourning that was held once *Shabbes* was good and over.

I don't know what happened that morning at the other synagogue in town, Temple Am Israel. I don't know how the news was handled there. But my suspicion is that maintaining *Shabbes* joy or studying Talmud was not the order of the hour.

That following Sunday night, a huge community gathering was held in the ballroom of Willamette's largest hotel. Hundreds, if not thousands, of Jews and other sympathetic community members came together to mourn the tragic death of Israel's bravest leader at the hands of a sound, intelligent, religious Jew. Speeches were made, songs were sung, and tears were shed.

Although I too was caught up in the sadness, in between singing and crying, I looked around at the crowd. I saw people from both Bayt Emett and Temple Am Israel. To the uninvolved observer, it probably looked like a united Jewish community. And on some level it was, for the most part, at least in this time of sadness. But it was also a split community, to be sure. This pinkie of the Jewish world had recently divided.

"The First Real Jewish Feminist!"

After eight months of participant observation at the Orthodox Bayt Emett, I headed directly across the street to the primary center of Jewish life in Willamette, Temple Am Israel. Although the physical distance between the two congregations, in terms of pavement, is quite small (a literal stone's throw away), the religious and cultural divide between these, the only two synagogues in Willamette, is quite expansive. It's almost analogous to the distance between Jerusalem and Tel Aviv: in terms of miles, not much, but in terms of religion and culture, almost a world. However, whereas the divide between the holy *harreydeem* of Jerusalem and the secular hedonists of Tel Aviv developed over a period of at least one hundred years, the divide between the Jews of Bayt Emett and the Jews of Temple Am Israel was less than nine months old.

Prior to the split, this had been one united Jewish community. No longer. It was now Bayt Emett on one side of the street (Orthodox, traditional, and pious), and Temple Am Israel on the other side (liberal, experimental, and progressive).

The first thing that comes to mind when thinking of Temple Am Israel is purple.

During the first weeks of my participant observation there, my eye was constantly aroused by the pervasiveness of purple: people wore purple *keepote*, purple *talliseem*, purple clothes. The curtains of the sacred ark, covering the small booth where the Torah scrolls are kept, were purple. I even noticed one man consistently wearing a pair of purple socks underneath his worn-out Birkenstocks.

Having spent over eight months *davening* at the rather drab Bayt Emett, where all one generally sees is men draped in white and black *talliseem*, the rainbow of color among the congregants at Temple Am Israel was the first thing that struck me. The second thing was the abundance of women. Over at Bayt Emett, on any given *Shabbes*, the men outnumbered the women by at least five to one. Indeed, although women's names make up half of the membership list of Bayt Emett, I never saw more than five or six women actually praying at the synagogue on any given *Shabbes*. So once at Temple Am Israel, I immediately noticed the abundance of women among the congregation. And not only were there relatively more women in attendance at the Temple Am Israel *Shabbes* service, but women were often the ones actually leading the religious activities: reading from the Torah, singing prayers, giving speeches.

At Bayt Emett, a woman's voice is never heard. Men do all the praying, chanting, reading, and speaking. Not so at Temple Am Israel, where women's voices permeate the *Shabbes* experience.

Rabbi Yakov Tish, the recently-appointed rabbi of the Temple, is a thin man with a soft brown beard. Most members of the congregation refer to him by the informal title "Rabbi Yakov," as opposed to the more formal "Rabbi Tish."

When I first started attending services at Temple Am Israel, Rabbi Yakov wore a green *keepa* and a green-striped *tallis*—and again—this non-traditional color choice struck me. Considering the reputation of Temple Am Israel as a "new age," vegetarian, and politically-active congregation, I wondered if Rabbi Yakov's green *keepa* and *tallis* didn't perhaps signify some symbolic form of Jewish identification with environmentalism or Mother Earth.

There was a hippie-like feel, a "casual Friday" feel about Temple Am Israel. Affluence didn't scream at you. Women weren't audacious vehicles for golden adornments. Men's necks weren't constricted by Italian ties. Instead, people wore jeans, cotton dresses, sandals. And lots of purple.

Riding my bike into the synagogue that first morning of participant observation I noticed that the cars and mini-vans of the parking lot boasted conspicuously-placed bumper stickers that read:

God Is Too Big To Fit Into One Religion
Defend Reproductive Rights
Visualize World Peace
Against Abortion? Don't Have One!
Question Reality
Wild Women Don't Get the Blues

The Temple isn't a large building, compared with other typical synagogues one finds in major American cities. It is humble, pale brown, and if one didn't notice the stone Star of David engraved on the side of the wall near the parking lot, one might not even know it was a synagogue. Inside, there is a large prayer sanctuary with low ceilings that are decorated with painted 1960s-style pseudo-Judaic-psychedelic patterns. The front wall of the sanctuary boasts small but beautiful stained-glass windows depicting traditional Jewish images, such as scrolls and candles. In addition to the prayer sanctuary, there is a kitchen, several classrooms, a playground for the children, a courtyard, an office, and a small library.

That first morning of my attendance at the Temple, there was a bat mitzvah. A girl of thirteen was being ceremonially welcomed as an adult member of the Jewish community. She would be reading a passage from the Torah, commenting on it, and leading various prayers all morning before family, friends, and the rest of the congregation.

As I entered the synagogue and looked for a seat within the well-attended sanctuary, I was overcome by beautiful music. Up at the front of the congregation was Rabbi Yakov, playing his cello. He was accompanied by a man with long hair, closed eyes, and an ethereal grin, who was playing a harp. They were performing an incredibly soft duet. Rabbi Yakov swayed from side to side. The harp player's dreamy grin persisted as his hands wove across the harp strings, cushioning Rabbi Yakov's mournful melody. About sixty people were in attendance, all sitting silently, listening to the performance. Some of the people up front had their eyes closed as they listened.

"This is a transgression," I immediately thought to myself. Having been over at Bayt Emett for the previous eight months, I knew: Jewish law forbids the playing of musical instruments on *Shabbes*. But my Orthodox sentiment soon slipped away as I was taken in by the beautiful tones. Within five minutes, I felt calm, warm, and open. The music continued softly and gently, and the whole synagogue felt peaceful, if not downright touchy-feely.

I had sat down next to a lesbian couple. And it was only after they handed me a prayer book that I noticed that Adam Axelrod was sitting directly behind us. Adam Axelrod—a member of Bayt Emett. And not just any member, but a founding member, and the current treasurer. What was Adam Axelrod doing back here in Temple Am Israel on *Shabbes* morning? Why wasn't he across the street, over at Bayt Emett? I could only assume that he must have had some personal connection to the young girl who was having her bat mitzvah.

The cello-harp duet continued, and I looked around at the congregation. Mostly baby boomers. A few older couples. Some children. Many of the women—like the men—were wearing *keepote* as well as *talliseem*. Colorful *keepote* and *talliseem*, to be sure. Men and women were sitting together, in sharp contrast to the setup over at Bayt Emett, where there is a men's section and a women's section, separated by a small wooden wall—the *mehitzah*. No *mehitzah* at Temple Am Israel.

I glanced through the prayer book, which was bilingual, printing English translations beside each Hebrew passage. As I flipped through the pages, my eyes fell upon the Ameedah, one of the most important prayers within Judaism. Although most of the Ameedah is prayed silently, parts are spoken aloud. This affirmation of God's loving-kindness and power traditionally includes a mention of the Jewish patriarchs:

> *You abound in blessings. Adonai our God. God of our fathers. God of Abraham, God of Isaac, God of Jacob . . .*

However, this version of the Ameedah in the Temple Am Israel prayer book was different. It had been changed, reworded. I read the following English translation:

> *You abound in blessings. Adonai our God. God of our fathers* and moth-ers. *God of Abraham* and Sarah. *God of Isaac* and Rebecca. *God of*

Jacob, and Rachel and Leah . . .

Here was the Ameedah affirming not only the Jewish patriarchs, but the Jewish matriarchs, too. Thus, women were not only prominently mixed in among the men in the pews of this congregation, but women were prominently mixed in among the men in the prayers, as well.

The musical duet concluded and the bat mitzvah *Shabbes* service officially began. Rabbi Yakov put away his cello, and took out a guitar. He invited the congregation to join him in song. The first song was in Hebrew, followed by a second song in English. The songs sounded like classic folk-rock, like the tunes of Cat Stevens or James Taylor. It was during the second song, the one in English in which the chorus lamented, "Teach us to treasure each day," that I first heard Adam Axelrod snicker. Or was it really a snicker? Maybe not.

More people steadily trickled into the sanctuary. Some of these latecomers wore suits and elegant dresses, standing out somewhat amidst the multicolored, casual apparel worn by most of the people in attendance. Their formal attire made me assume that they weren't local Willamettans, but probably relatives of the bat mitzvah girl, visiting from out of town.

After another folk-rock-Hebrew song concluded, the parents of the bat mitzvah girl were called up to lead a prayer. They were an awkward but kind-looking couple. By the nervous, smiling expression on their faces, it was clear that they weren't very comfortable in synagogue. They didn't seem too at home in this house of prayer. But they both wore a *keepa* and a *tallis*, as did their bat mitzvah daughter, who stood beside them as they pronounced the page number of the prayer to the congregation. The bat mitzvah girl was tall and thin, with a thoughtful face, big eyes and braces. It was obvious that she was more at ease with the morning's activities than were her parents. She stood there beside them and looked proud and dignified as they struggled—literally bumbled—through the Hebrew prayer. After the prayer was recited by the parents, the young girl promptly gave the English translation. I noticed that when referring to God, she said "Eternal One" instead of "Lord."

Some announcements were made, the friends and family of the bat mitzvah girl were welcomed, and then Rabbi Yakov led another song.

When it was time to say the *Sh'ma* prayer, we were asked to stand and give our attention to Leah, a handsome woman in her forties, who came up to the front of the congregation wearing a beautiful purple *keepa* and a large purple *tallis*. She took in a deep, powerful breath through her nostrils, exhaled out of her mouth with eyes closed, and then smiled out over the whole congregation with a look of exuberant inner peace. She acknowledged what a wonderful, powerful, and beautiful day this was and spoke of the honor that the bat mitzvah girl was bringing to her people. She then explained the importance of the *Sh'ma* prayer, telling us that it is the central prayer of Judaism, praising the "oneness of God, or the oneness of creation, or whatever." She said that it was best to recite the prayer not only with words, but with one's whole body. She then asked us all to join her in giving physical, bodily expression to the *Sh'ma* prayer.

As she said this, I heard Adam Axelrod sigh loudly.

Leah began demonstrating the body movements for the *Sh'ma* prayer. These were movements she had learned at a Jewish Renewal gathering last summer in upstate New York, led by Rabbi Zalman Schaechter-Shalomi. She went over the movements slowly, speaking with a supportive, cheerful voice. Upon the first words of the *Sh'ma*, we were instructed to raise our hands high, up to the sky. As the prayer continued, we were to breathe deeply, then exhale and lower our arms down to the ground to scoop up imaginary water. Finally, we were to raise ourselves up and sprinkle the imaginary water over ourselves and those around us, with love. She demonstrated the movements once again with the prayer, and then asked the congregation to give it a try.

The *Sh'ma* was thus recited. About half the congregation did the body movements, including the female couple next to me, who kindly sprinkled some imaginary water over me. The rest of the congregation recited the prayer in the traditional manner, standing still, without the physical stuff. As the prayer ended, I heard Adam Axelrod make a noise, like an annoyed click with his tongue against the back of his teeth. He then muttered something. I didn't catch the words exactly, but I could tell that they were an expression of sardonic amusement over the New Age body movements added to the *Sh'ma*. The two lesbians also heard Adam Axelrod's utterance; they exchanged annoyed glances with one another. They didn't appreciate his wisecrack.

More prayers ensued, followed by more songs. The prayer for peace was surprisingly inclusive: "Oh, Eternal One, bless all those in Israel. Protect all her people from hatred and war. Bless and protect Jews, Muslims, Druze, and Christians. Amen."

Finally it was time to read from the Torah. Rabbi Yakov asked the congregation to welcome Rabbi Anne Levin, a visiting rabbi from Seattle, who would be reading the week's passage from the Torah. He said that it was an honor to have Rabbi Levin in Temple Am Israel, for the day's Torah passage was about Miriam, and he knew of no other Jew alive who so much captured the spirit of Miriam as Anne Levin. Rabbi Levin, a blonde woman in her forties, came to the front and gave Rabbi Yakov a deep, lengthy hug. She then called up the bat mitzvah girl to be at her side. The two of them would share the reading of the Torah. Rabbi Levin would go first, the bat mitzvah girl second.

It was quite a sight: two women, one in her forties, the other thirteen, both wearing traditionally male garb (*talliseem* and *keepote*), standing at the Torah. It was quite a sight because at Bayt Emett, women don't come near the Torah. Indeed, for centuries, the Torah has been Man's Territory, exclusively. And yet here were two women, standing before a supportive congregation, about to delve into the most sacred writings of the Jewish people. Looking at Rabbi Levin and this bat mitzvah girl preparing to engage in one of the most honorable Jewish activities—the public reading of the Torah on *Shabbes*—I wondered: Was this progress or deterioration? Was this empowering of women within Judaism a needed improvement, or a desecration of heritage and tradition? I knew that the answer to such questions would be markedly different to the Jews of Willamette, depending on which side of the street they congregated.

After various members of the bat mitzvah girl's family were called up to recite the prayers before reading from the Torah, Rabbi Levin began. This was the heart of the service. She leaned over the Torah scroll and sang the ancient words in what sounded like a quasi-traditional cadence. Instead of chanting straight through the Torah portion, as is customary, she periodically lifted her head up from the Torah scroll and looked out at the congregation and commented (in sing-song English) after every few lines of Hebrew. So it went: several lines of ancient Hebrew, followed by a melodious English translation and interpretation.

This nontraditional form of Torah recitation was too much for Adam

Axelrod, who quietly—but staunchly—muttered, "Just read the Torah, already." Again, the lesbian couple exchanged annoyed glances with furrowed brows.

While the bat mitzvah girl looked on, Rabbi Levin continued in this manner: chanting the Hebrew, then interpreting and spontaneously commenting in sing-song English: " . . . And so we see Miriam here, Miriam the prophetess, leading her sisters and brothers in song . . . " followed by more ancient Hebrew and then, "Miriam represents to us water, which is really the source of all life . . . " followed by more Hebrew and then, "So this means that Miriam's space is sacred space and we must all dwell in *mahkome Miriam* . . . " The reading of the Torah continued this way for five minutes, and then Rabbi Levin paused. She took a deep breath and then declared, "It is so nice, so wonderful, to be in a congregation that acknowledges Miriam's spirit!" Many people throughout the sanctuary smiled and nodded at this statement, including Rabbi Yakov. But a few were a bit unsettled by this untraditional, constantly-interrupted reading of the Torah. Especially Adam Axelrod. He made a pointed comment expressing his irritation.

This last remark was too much for the lesbian couple. They were sick of his rudeness. The woman sitting directly next to me turned to address him.

"Do you mind?" she asked, pointedly.

"Huh?" Adam Axelrod responded, flippantly.

"Would you please be quiet. We're trying to listen!"

"Excuse me," Adam Axelrod muttered, without the smallest hint of compunction.

Rabbi Levin continued, reading the Hebrew, stopping to comment in English, and all the while smiling and beaming with joy. It was obvious that she truly loved the moment: the Torah, the congregation, the bat mitzvah, and the story of Miriam. After several lines of Hebrew that she read with exceptional verve, she stopped yet again, looked up at the congregation, and with her right arm raised in a proud, defiant fist, she exclaimed, "So you see—Miriam was the first real Jewish feminist!"

That was it. Adam Axelrod could bear no more. He guffawed loudly, stood up, snickered with all his might, maneuvered his way down the aisle, and stormed out of the back exit of the synagogue. Several people were distracted by his conspicuous departure, but the lesbian couple next to me looked relieved.

I could only assume that he was heading back across the street, back to Bayt Emett.

The service continued. The bat mitzvah girl read her portion from the Torah. She gave a speech. Rabbi Yakov made a speech. More songs were sung, more prayers recited. But all the while I was thinking about Adam Axelrod and his hostile exit, and Bayt Emett across the street. Was the tension I had just witnessed between Adam Axelrod and the lesbian couple a taste of the tensions that had existed in this congregation before the schism?

My Research Methods

In order to study the schism of Willamette's Jewish community, I simply got involved. I regularly attended religious services at both synagogues for over a year. I additionally conducted in-depth interviews with 46 people. Thus, my data consists primarily of my own observations while attending Temple Am Israel and Bayt Emett and the contents of my interviews.

Participant observation is a well-known method for collecting data in which the researcher closely engages in, observes, and records the activities and behaviors of a particular organization or culture (Babbie, 1992; Geertz, 1973; Clifford, 1988; Clifford and Marcus, 1986; Marcus and Fischer, 1986). Participant observation is particularly useful for studying religious groups (Ammerman, 1987; Roberts, 1984; Wilson, 1990), and there have been several excellent examples of participant observation within Jewish communities specifically (Danzger, 1989; Davidman, 1991; Harris, 1985; Kugelmass, et al. 1988; Myerhoff, 1978; Sered, 1992).

By personally, physically involving myself with the religious life of both Temple Am Israel and Bayt Emett—attending religious services, ceremonies, and congregational meetings, celebrating holidays, taking field notes, keeping memos and journals—I was able to gain an invaluable amount of insight into Willamette's Jewish community. It was also the way in which I was able to meet people and develop contacts that eventually made it easier to request interviews with particular individuals.

Prior to the eight months I spent at Bayt Emett, I met with Rabbi Sapperstein for coffee in order to explain my research intentions. While indicating that I was personally interested in experiencing Orthodoxy (having been raised as a secular Jew), I made sure to stress that I was primarily interested in doing sociological research on the recent split in the community and exploring the differences between his congregation and Temple Am Israel. He welcomed me and approved of my intentions. He said that even though I was going to be doing sociological research, he was confident that there was "another reason" behind my willingness to be part of Bayt Emett. He said that there was a clear trend of people returning to Orthodoxy and that this trend was part of a grand Jewish historical scenario. He indicated that we were in a very important, interesting time in Jewish history, and his overall implication was that there was something holy or mystical about this growth of secular Jews returning to tradition.

Once I began attending *Shabbes* services at Bayt Emett (which lasted for several hours every Saturday), I was quickly made to feel part of the congregation. The members accepted me almost immediately. They seemed happy to have me around. I was often given public honors during prayer services, such as being called up for an *aleeyah*, and I was regularly invited to various members' homes for *Shabbes* lunch after the service. Many friendships were established.

However, I sometimes felt deceptive in fostering such friendships. For example, one young couple repeatedly invited me to their home for *Shabbes* lunch after Saturday morning services and although they were extremely warm and served wonderful meals, I found their religious and political beliefs hard to swallow. For instance, they were certain that the Messiah was coming soon, that the Torah and the Talmud could predict future events, that Rabin's assassination was warranted (and predicted), and that Palestinians should be shipped off to Jordan en masse because Israel belongs to the Jews. They accepted at face value what I consider to be the most ridiculous and dangerous religious and political notions. That they could honestly and mundanely declare, over fruit salad and freshly baked *hallah*, that Israel had every right to kill Palestinian children, disturbed me immensely. But I never said anything. I simply sighed, nodded, and tried my best to be a nice guest. I avoided debating politics or religion with them, and instead, developed a nonconfrontational, friendly relationship with them because I wanted to interview them and study them and learn about their role in the community. However, such a situation left me feeling torn. On the one hand, I vehemently disagreed with almost everything they stood for. On the other hand, I was glad that they liked me and that they invited me into their home and that they would make great informants for my study. But the more they espoused their offensive rhetoric, and the more I withheld my true feelings because I was operating with ulterior motives, the guiltier I felt. After four or five lunches, I begin declining their invitations, offering a variety of random excuses. I think they ultimately felt somewhat snubbed. And in the end, neither were included as informants in my study.

However, most friendships that I established while at Bayt Emett were more genuine and are still maintained. One example is my relationship with Mike Fish. I became close with Mike while spending time at Bayt Emett, and he was one of the first people I interviewed. He was always very interested in my research and continually asked me for "updates." Although he's an Orthodox Jew and a central member of Bayt Emett, he sends his daughter to Hebrew School at Temple Am Israel, where I had her as a student. Largely because of that connection through his daughter, I still see Mike regularly and we enjoy each other's company, despite the fact that I no longer participate at his congregation.

Gaining entry at Temple Am Israel was even easier. For one thing, I knew several members from campus and other community contexts. Secondly, I had been raised in a Reconstructionist synagogue myself, and thus felt quite "at home."

As I had done with Rabbi Sapperstein, I met with Rabbi Tish early on in my participant observation and explained to him my research goals and sociological motives. He was quite supportive, saying that he welcomed such an academic investigation. He said that the rift between liberal Jews and conservative Jews worried him and that in the wake of Rabin's assassination we need to work on coming together as a people. He hoped that my research would help shed light on how to bridge our differences.

I developed many personal friendships while at Temple Am Israel (though I was never invited to any one's house for a *Shabbes* meal!), and towards the end of my participant observation, I began teaching 7th-grade Hebrew school there twice a week.

It is important to note that my participant observation began immediately *after* the split between Temple Am Israel and Bayt Emett had formally occurred. I started my involvement about one month after the sectarian Bayt Emett group left Temple Am Israel and rented its own synagogue space. This timing was somewhat problematic for my study; had I been involved with the community on a weekly basis *before* the schism occurred, I would have undoubtedly gained much better insight into the processes and communal dynamics of the schism. However, in terms of logistics, doing sociological fieldwork among a congregation *before* it splits is almost impossible. One would have to be quite lucky. The only way I can see this happening would be if a sociologist were studying a given religious community *for some other* reason (for example, looking at levels of religious devotion among members), and then an unforeseen rift were to suddenly arise, ending in schism. But unless this is the case, to study the sources of a schism before the schism occurs, is not feasible. The truth is, schisms are difficult to predict. Some situations may look like they are heading for schism, and then suddenly resolve themselves; the sociologist seeking to understand schism by studying such a congregation would have "wasted" at least a year's worth of fieldwork when the long-awaited outcome didn't occur.

Another possibility for studying the sources and dynamics of schism would, of course, be to study a congregation when schism appears almost completely inevitable to the astute observer, as Nancy Ammerman (1990) did with the Southern Baptist Convention. However, there is still a problem with this timing: when a split appears utterly inevitable, spurring the sociologist to get involved (after having recognized the event's inevitability), the major sources, occurrences, and divergent positions that facilitated and produced that conspicuous inevitability have already been germinating for some time. In other words, if a sociologist recognizes that a split is definitely about to occur, then in actuality, the fundamental sources and underlying causes of that split have already long been in progress.

In truth, the best a sociologist can do is to study a community as quickly as possible once the schism is recognized as inevitable, or has just recently occurred. The former was the case with Nancy Ammerman, the latter was the case in my study.

Since I began my fieldwork after the schism had actually occurred, the best way for me to understand what had happened and why it had happened, was by talking to those who were involved. Fortunately, I was able to jump into the community immediately, only a month after the formal separation had occurred. Thus, the memories were still relatively fresh.

While interviewing members of Willamette's Jewish community and asking them about their involvement in the schism, I sought out their personal, subjective perspectives. These interviews served two functions: they allowed me to gain an understanding of the historical development of the schism, but more importantly, they allowed me the chance to explore various pertinent and divisive issues with the congregants themselves, from both synagogues, which facilitated a fruitful exploration of the subjective Jewish identities of those involved.

I selected my sample of informants employing a nonjudgmental, purposive sampling method in which I solicited informants based upon my knowledge of their involvement in Willamette's Jewish community. I additionally employed a snowball strategy, in which informants were recommended to me by other informants.

The 46 informants that I interviewed ranged between the ages of 22 and 81, with 27 of them in their 40s. Twenty-one were from Bayt Emett (9 women, 12 men), and 25 were from Temple Am Israel (14 women, 11 men). A few members had ties to both congregations, but I placed them as members of one or the other congregation based on which one they regularly attended for *Shabbes* services.

The level of education ranged from completion of tenth grade to master's degrees, including 7 Ph.D.s and 2 M.D.s, with a large majority (75%) of the informants holding at least bachelor's degrees.

All informants were active members of Willamette's Jewish community throughout the period of division and all had been active members of the Jewish community for anywhere between two and twenty-five years prior to the schism[2].

---

[2] For a complete demographic breakdown of my informants (not including the rabbis) see Appendices 1 and 2 on pages 245 and 246.

Each interview lasted between one and four hours. Three of the interviews were conducted in informants' offices, one was conducted at my house, and all the rest at each informant's home. The interviews were tape recorded and then typed up for analysis.

All but three interviews (Rabbi Sapperstein, Rabbi Tish, and Rabbi Shibel) began with nine demographic questions:

1) age
2) where raised
3) occupation
4) education
5) political party affiliation
6) how many times married/divorced
7) occupation of parents
8) where parents from
9) religious affiliation of parents and while growing up

After these initial questions, I proceeded to engage the informants in more or less unstructured, friendly conversations. I wanted to know why they thought the community had divided, as well as their personal opinions on various issues that seemed relevant to the split. It was through the recollections of my 46 informants that I have pieced this story together.

There are disadvantages and advantages to this type of sociohistorical data collection. The disadvantage is that people tend to be quite subjective/selective in their memory. Asking 46 different people "What happened?" necessarily means I got 46 different answers. Some people recalled a specific incident, others didn't. Some people said the rabbi did *this*, other people said the rabbi did *that*. Thus, finding out what "really" happened was difficult. And this was precisely the advantage as well. People's individual historical accounts may not be "accurate" in the literal sense, but they are perfectly valid in the subjective sense—and that's what I was truly interested in: how people personally viewed the community's struggle, and what their subjective understandings were. In other words, finding out what "really" happened wasn't as important to me as was finding out how people felt and thought about what happened, how they constructed what happened in their own minds, and how they each perceived the story of this community's schism.

Informants were mailed transcripts of their interviews, and given the chance to amend or delete their testimony before I began working on my manuscript. I received four amended transcripts, from two women and one man at Temple Am Israel, and from one woman of Bayt Emett. They all elaborated upon their testimony by writing additional thoughts and comments to their interview manuscript.

I did have two people ask to have their transcripts deleted entirely. After receiving copies of their interview, a man and a woman, both from Bayt Emett, asked that their interviews be thrown out. The man explained his decision based upon l'shon horah ("evil tongue"), which relates to the teaching in traditional Judaism that prohibits gossiping. The woman didn't give a direct explanation for her desire to have her interview thrown out. I simply received a letter stating that she had been in a difficult emotional state during the interview, that it was a troubled time in her life, and that she wanted her entire interview deleted from my study.

Other than the four embellished interviews and the two withdrawals, I had no responses from the other informants concerning their interview transcripts.

Several contemporary ethnographers have employed a commendable strategy (in order to increase validity) that involves letting informants read the actual manuscript once it is completed, and allowing their voices to comment on the author's work as part of the finished publication (Rosaldo, 1986; Stacey, 1990; Lawless, 1992; Titon, 1988). With 46 informants, and a manuscript approximating 300 pages, for me to employ such a reflexive/reciprocal methodology was simply too costly and too time-consuming. Allowing them to amend their interview transcripts prior to completion of the manuscript was as far as I went in offering my informants the ability to have some power over their own representations.

Because of concerns of confidentiality, identifying characteristics of all informants have been excluded or changed to the best of my ability without compromising the integrity of their personal accounts. Most of my informants agreed to talk with me only if their anonymity was guaranteed. Since the schism had involved a lot of gossip and ill will, most people were reluctant to "kick up the dirt" again. Yet, at the same time, they were eager to "tell their side of the story." Therefore, in order to foster candid interviews, while at the same time protect my informants from further slander or embarrassment, I promised that all names would be changed.

However, two informants stated openly that they *didn't* want to be anonymous and preferred to be identified. The two were Yohanna Kohner (Rabbi Moishe's wife), and Lynn Rosefsky (who led the Orthodox group's insurgency). Both Yohanna and Lynn declared that they had nothing to hide and that they wanted people to know who they were. However, for sake of continuity, I went ahead and changed their names anyway. But nearly everything else about their identities remained the same.

Masking identities was sometimes difficult; a name change didn't always do the trick. That is, there were often things about an individual (for example, personal history or specific actions) that would render them recognizable to others in the community, even with the change of name. In such circumstances, I either did my best to change something else about them, or I "invented" a new identity altogether. This method of creating "fake" informants was done in the rare cases of those individuals who expressed the most extreme concern over their anonymity and insisted that they would only share their feelings and opinions if it was absolutely guaranteed that what they said would not be traceable to them specifically.

Thus, my masking of informants was like a continuum. On the one end were people whose identities were kept as "real" as possible, with only a change of name. On the other end were completely "invented" characters whose entire identities were fabricated so that the words they spoke would be completely untraceable. In the middle were individuals who had their names changed and perhaps some identifiable characteristics changed as well (such as occupation or hair color) but nothing too extreme. Most of my informants fell somewhere in this middle ground.

In discussing my research methods, a word on "objectivity" is necessary. This is a story of Jewish communal division, of quarreling factions, of opposing camps. It is a story of broken friendships and even strained marriages. It is a story of personality clashes, gossip, and misunderstandings. Can I—a Jew somewhat involved in Willamette's Jewish community—be objective in telling this story?

Absolutely not.

My understanding of "objective" is that which is "not influenced by personal feelings or opinions" (*American Oxford Dictionary*). As a human being, I simply cannot meet such criteria of objectivity. It is impossible. There isn't a human being alive who isn't "influenced by personal feelings or opinions."

I am *me*: interpreting, feeling, reacting, and responding. Every interview with an informant is more than just a cold collection of data; it is an intimate connection with another Jew that forces me to personally reflect on my own Jewishness. Every day of participant observation in synagogue is more than just time spent scientifically gathering field notes; it is a personal time for me to reflect on my own beliefs (or lack thereof), sing songs (or just hum along), and ponder the personal meaning of congregational bonds.

Every interview conducted, indeed, every experience that is part of this study, from attending religious services to reading academic journals, is rife with my own personal feelings and opinions. How could it be otherwise? I react to what people say, I react to social situations, I react to text. To be "objective" in a study of this nature is impossible. I am in complete agreement with Christian scholar Uta Ranke-Heinemann (1992:100), when she declares: "We never see a naked, objective fact, only interpreted facts, and in every act of perception we never stop interpreting." And as Judith Stacey (1990:36) rightly asserts, "Ethnographies are never factual records, but texts structured by the interests, privileges, commitments, quirks, and rhetorical strategies of their authors."

However, while I discard any claim to objectivity, that does not mean that I set out with the purpose of distortion. Taking sides or pushing my own views is not my goal. Bias is not my intention. Quite the contrary. I came into this study seeking understanding and knowledge and have sought, as best as possible, to be fair and honest. Nancy Ammerman (1990), a Southern Baptist who conducted a well-known study of the Southern Baptist schism of 1985, wondered about her own ability to be "objective;" could she, a Southern Baptist with emotions and opinions of her own, accurately study her own religious community's struggle? She writes:

> My involvement with the people I have studied has admittedly posed challenges to the task of objective and even-handed analysis. No analysis

is ever completely *objective*—both we and our informants are after all subjects . . . So while it is not objective, I hope it is even-handed. From the beginning, I have imposed rules on myself as a way to minimize the risks. Most basically, the questions I would ask about this conflict would be informed by sociological theory, not by any desire to prove one side right or wrong. This book is not an analysis of who was right and who was wrong but an analysis of why each side came to view the other as wrong and what they did once that had been decided (p.xii).

Ditto.

Rather than pretend to the reader that I am some mindless narrator, some plastic "objective" source relating a story in a purely value-neutral, agenda-free manner, I prefer to openly acknowledge my lack of objectivity, be frank about it, and in doing so, approach what I believe to be a more honest sociological method.

There are two "sides" in this drama, the liberal Temple Am Israel and the conservative Bayt Emett. The tendency to inadvertently portray one congregation as "good" and the other as "bad" is one I hope to avoid. What I want is to explore what they thought of each other and why the rift between the two occurred in the first place. However, since subjectivity is never truly overcome (even when a conscious attempted is made), it is hoped that by briefly explaining a little about who I am, I can account straightforwardly for any biases that will inevitably emerge, despite my best endeavors to remain even-handed.

My paternal grandparents were poor, socialist, Yiddish-speaking, atheist Jews from Poland. My maternal grandparents were wealthy, liberal, German-speaking, atheist Jews from Bohemia. My mother grew up in Los Angeles as a completely assimilated Jew celebrating Christmas, Easter, and Passover. My father grew up in the Bronx as a secular, Bundist, Yiddish-speaking Jew acutely aware of his Jewishness in all but the religious sense of that identity. I grew up in Los Angeles where I was bar mitzvahed at a Reconstructionist synagogue, attended and worked at both Episcopalian and Jewish summer camps, and eventually lived for a year in Israel after graduating from college. I am an atheist, extremely left-leaning politically, supportive of gay rights, supportive of feminist praxis, and I prefer egalitarian Judaism to gender-segregated Judaism. I also support

Palestinian statehood and the internationalization of Jerusalem.

I was 26 to 28 years old when I conducted this study and wrote this dissertation, pursuing a Ph.D. in sociology. And though my liberal politics and religious sentiments are much more in line with those of Temple Am Israel, I truly enjoyed the months I spent at Bayt Emett. There is something powerful and calming in Orthodox worship. And while I made many personal connections with members of Temple Am Israel, which were strengthened when I began teaching Hebrew school there midway through my study, I still consider many members of Bayt Emett friends as well.

Sociologist of religion Stephen Warner (1988:65) has noted that American sociologists compose "the least religious stratum in the most religious modern society in the world." He remarks upon the tendency of liberal sociologists studying religion (such as myself) to treat "liberal churchmen [sic] with respect and fellow-feeling but [dismiss] conservatives with contempt and incomprehension." I heeded this warning and tried my best to overcome such a bias. I wasn't out to disparage the Orthodox Jews of Willamette, nor glorify the liberal Jews. I simply wanted to get to know both groups—know their feelings, opinions, and stories.

I found every single informant, on both sides of the schism, thoughtful, open, and more often than not, genuinely friendly.

COMMUNITY FORMS

The House on University Street—Clyde Tish came to Willamette in the mid-seventies.

> *I grew up in Chicago, and when I was twenty-four . . . I knew that it was time for me to leave . . . I had been working in a rehabilitation institute for disabled children. I had been a political activist back in the sixties and I was living in a large urban commune . . . and it was time for me to go off by myself . . . Um, basically I looked at a map and—choonk!—Willamette was where I came.*

With two hundred dollars in his pocket, a sleeping bag, and his cello, he got a ride with a friend of a friend from Chicago to Willamette in an old VW van. En route they picked up a hitchhiker who was also heading to Willamette. The hitchhiker informed Clyde and his traveling companion that Willamette was the place that the reincarnated souls of people who had lived and died in the lost city of Atlantis were gathering. Upon arrival, Clyde didn't notice any overt signs of an Atlantis reunion. But he did quickly notice the ease with which people interacted with one another—a sharp contrast to the hustle and bustle of Chicago. He loved it.

> *I started working as a manager of a food co-op and playing the cello eight–ten hours a day. I just fell in love with Oregon. I really thought it was so beautiful here, the beauty of nature.*

It was a time when there were still plenty of thriving communes in the surrounding countryside, a plethora of various worker-owned grocery store cooperatives on many street corners, and a resilient spirit of political activism, which—like so many other things—had held out from the sixties.

Many of the Jews now living in Willamette first met each other in the 1970s as social activists involved in protests against a nearby nuclear power plant. For instance, when Julie Horowitz first came to Willamette, her connection with the Jewish community happened at one such protest:

> I came to Willamette in the mid-seventies and got involved in the sort of post-hippie, antinuclear, peace-oriented, communal-living world that was here at the time . . . one person who was involved in that . . . was Jeff Bronner . . . who later became extremely Orthodox in his practice. At that time he lived—as far as I could tell—a non-Jewish lifestyle. Anyway, at some event, at some vigil at the Federal Building in the rain, he started playing on his banjo and was singing 'Everyone 'neath the vine and the fig tree.' And I said, do you know the Hebrew words? And we sang it in Hebrew.

Back then, the Jewish community was even smaller than it is today. Temple Am Israel was the only synagogue in town, with about 120 families in 1975, though a far smaller number was actually involved with the congregation on a regular basis.

Since its construction in the 1950s, Temple Am Israel had been affiliated with the Conservative movement, which was then—and perhaps is still today—considered a "middle-ground" denomination, a compromise between Orthodox Judaism (which some perceive as overly rigid and strict) and Reform Judaism (which some perceive as lax and un-Jewish in its mimicry of Protestant religious services).

In the mid-seventies Rabbi Oliff was the rabbi. He was an elderly man, stern, and well-loved by the few involved Jews who bothered to come to the synagogue now and then. Clyde Tish became one of those few.

> I started getting more and more a really deep need to reconnect with Judaism, which I had had in great depth and richness in my growing up years . . . I came to synagogue, I spoke with Rabbi Oliff—olam shalom—and I told him that I needed to get back involved with my Judaism. At that point I had hair halfway down my back and was a real holy hippie. And I was working very, very hard with the cello and disability rights. But there was something that was just missing in terms of the soul food. So I came and

spoke with him . . . and I just started coming to shule *and studying with him on* Shabbes *afternoons, and we would often walk—I would often walk with him back towards his home after* shule *and we'd have arguments and, you know, it was wonderful. I really loved and appreciated him.*

For Clyde, this reconnection with Judaism was satisfying on several levels: his soul received its food, he was welcomed into a small, elderly community that appreciated his youthful eagerness (despite his counter-culture aura), and deep down inside, he was rekindling his boyhood experiences.

I was being able to call on tradition that I knew from my early childhood. I grew up in an Orthodox shule *with Habad teachers, Lubavitch teachers. My zaydeh was very learned. He was really quite a scholar . . . my grandparents were very strictly Orthodox . . . I felt very God-conscious as a kid . . . I remember very, very specific moments walking down busy streets and having that sense of knowing.*

For several months, Clyde was all alone in his Jewish involvement. He didn't know any other Jews in Willamette his age. He had no one to share *Shabbes* meals with. And he was the only person showing up at synagogue under the age of fifty.

Then one day, another young man wandered into the synagogue. Yoav. Like Clyde, Yoav had long hair. And also like Clyde, Yoav had been raised in an Orthodox home, had meandered away from his Judaism during the sixties, and had somehow found himself adrift in Willamette, Oregon, on a random Saturday in the mid-seventies, in Temple Am Israel.

A guy showed up at shule *one Shabbat morning, another young guy . . . and Rabbi Oliff asked him who he was and he said, 'Oh, I'm a musician' and Rabbi Oliff said, 'There's another musician over there' . . . so Yoav and I got to meet, and we had a wonderful time . . . I remember that day, after* shule, *we went over to this University Street park and we're playing on the monkey bars and we're singing trope and it was like 'Gevalt!' there's somebody else that knows trope that cares about this . . . Yoav had been through the sixties, just like I was. He was a musician who played guitar. So he and I started hanging out, a lot. This was like a brother, really, a brother. All of a sudden someone doing Shabbes with, learning with. It was incredible. And he had just moved up to Willamette from Marin County. It was really quite a shiddukh made in heaven.*

The two became best friends. They studied Talmud together with Rabbi Oliff. They explored the beautiful mountains and rivers surrounding Willamette. They drank kosher wine in the park near Yoav's apartment late at night and talked about life. They both supported one another in their mutual reimmersion into Judaism, feeling a mutual need to explore new ways through which to draw on this ancient tradition that would help them achieve that sense of awe and wonder they so craved.

In addition to sharing their Judaism, they shared their music. Clyde had his cello, Yoav had his guitar, and they both were blessed with smooth voices. As a duet they became quite polished and were soon playing the most coveted gig in town: Sunday mornings at Moma's Home-Fried Truck Stop. They developed a local following, and every Sunday, amidst herbal tea, marionberry scones, and marijuana, they'd play Hasidic folk tunes to a packed house.

Through their musical performing, Clyde and Yoav met more and more young people, and as it would turn out, more and more young Jewish people. Some of them were students at the University. Some of them were picking blueberries and living in the woods. Some were just drifting. They were young, disaffiliated Jews like Clyde and Yoav; young Jews who had cut themselves off from their parents' tradition during the sixties, but now found themselves, in the mid-seventies in Willamette, Oregon, thirsty for some kind of communal and spiritual connection. And the Judaism they saw emanating from this youthful, longhaired musical duo was just what they needed. Clyde and Yoav seemed tuned-in and hip, open and dynamic—the opposite of what most of these twenty-something Jews had experienced back home in their parents' Reform or Conservative synagogues.

Clyde and Yoav decided to get a place and move in together. They rented a blue house with several rooms in a quiet neighborhood on University Street. The house was old and worn, with creaky wooden floors, a fireplace, and a big backyard perfect for cultivating vegetables and herbs. It was only a few yards away from the Old Pioneer Cemetery, where some of the first white people to come to Oregon were buried amidst an old-growth forest resplendent with redwoods.

Several friends joined Clyde and Yoav, both men and women, and it became a thriving house of communally-oriented, quasi-Orthodox Jewish hippies. Few had the traditional childhood training that Clyde and Yoav had, but they all were eager to learn, to taste of this youthful, neo-Hasidic brand of Judaism.

So then Yoav and I . . . started living together with Rachel and other friends on University Street. We had a little house there and on Friday night we'd have Shabbes, *and thirty or forty people would show up. It was incredible. And we were very traditional in our approach, I mean really, everything. I was in my tearing toilet paper stage . . . very into it.[4] And we would have very strong* Shabbes. *People would come and we would sit there clicking our chopsticks on those* kiddush *cups until the middle of the night, singing* nigguneem, *having real strong* havdalahs *where* Shabbes *was very full until the end. It was deep. And so community was kind of happening there.*

Pete Ruskin, a dark and curly-haired hippie with water-blue eyes, was part of that community. As he recalled:

It was an amazing little shtetl . . . *It was a run-down dump of a little house and had incredible spirit. For me, it was the first real exposure to what is a more observant lifestyle and a more spiritual orientation . . . in a sixties retro kind of way . . . and there was a real sense of family and familiarity that started to grow in that group. It felt very nice. It was very warm, a lot of humor, an open, friendly kind of feel.*

One of the many young Jews of Willamette who found herself drawn to Clyde and Yoav's house for these spiritual, song-filled *Shabbes* evenings, was an 18-year-old student at the University, Lynn Appelbaum. The

---

[4] For observant Jews, work and/or creative acts are prohibited on the Sabbath. This prohibition includes the tearing of toilet paper when cleaning oneself after using the toilet. Observant Jews will therefore tear an ample supply of toilet paper the day before the Sabbath begins for anticipated use during the actual Sabbath.

daughter of a prominent neurosurgeon, Lynn, a third generation American, born and raised in Seattle, knew little of Judaism growing up.

We had a Christmas tree and when I was a little girl we had Easter eggs. . . . My parents had really negative attitudes towards religious Judaism.

Coming to Willamette at the age of 18 was the first time Lynn had ever been outside of Seattle. Pretty and sharp, with a sparkly smile, fiery eyes, and a quick wit, Lynn began dating soon after her arrival to campus. She lived in the dorms, and by her third week, had a steady boyfriend. Lynn had never given much thought to religion and didn't consider herself a believer, but her new boyfriend was deeply engrossed in the eastern teachings of a local Indian guru. Lynn was encouraged by this yoga-entrenched boyfriend to explore her spiritual side, and she became curious. However, her curiosity ended up leading her away from the new boyfriend, and into Temple Am Israel.

I started coming to services because I had a boyfriend who actually joined a . . . an ashram, I guess. It was that fat Indian boy—the guru—that was very popular in the mid-seventies. So he would meditate, and somebody in his ashram . . . had a Jewish catalogue, and he brought it to me because he knew I was seeking and I was asking a lot of questions. So he brought me the Jewish catalogue and I started reading it . . . and I ended up thinking and thinking and decided finally that I would go to services, because there was a synagogue here.

Lynn headed for Temple Am Israel. She had never been to synagogue before in her life.

I showed up there with a notebook to take notes, because I didn't know what to do . . . I didn't know how to dress—didn't know anything.

She wandered into the synagogue alone, not knowing anyone. She found a seat. Clyde and Yoav were sitting right behind her.

There was maybe like four people sitting in the sanctuary, and the rabbi was

*giving some kind of sermon, very informal . . . I started taking notes in the
service on his lecture . . . and Yoav leaned forward and tapped me on the
shoulder and said, 'You don't write—it's Shabbat.' So I was mortified—
turned ten colors of red—and tucked it under my seat.*

Clyde and Yoav were interested in this attractive young woman and
they invited her back to their house once the *Shabbes* service was over.
She was delighted.

*Clyde was wonderfully generous in inviting me back to his home on
University Street for lunch—I had other commitments and I was a little bit
nervous about the whole thing—but the whole walk home from the synagogue down to University Street was spent talking about how Judaism
was—American Judaism—was so centered on the Holocaust and the pain
of being a Jew. But what he was really into exploring in his group of friends
was how to put the joy back.*

Lynn immediately responded to Clyde and Yoav's enthusiasm and
warmth. She was interested in their thoughtful talk of creating a new, joy-
ful Jewish identity. She loved their communal home on University Street
and was intrigued by the special group of people hanging out there. That
very *Shabbes* afternoon they ate, drank, and sang songs well into the
night. There were guitars and tambourines, drums and recorders. More
and more people showed up, so that by midnight, Lynn found herself
dancing in a whirling circle to *klezmeer* music. Only twelve hours earlier
she had been a lone explorer stepping into a synagogue for the first time
with anxious trepidation. Now she was winding herself through a spinning circle of smiling faces and sweaty hands, singing songs in Yiddish.
She was hooked.
A month later she broke up with her boyfriend, moved out of the
dorms, dropped out of school altogether, and was living at Clyde and
Yoav's. She got a job cooking at night at a small restaurant and her days
were spent engrossed in her new Jewish commune.

*Oh, it was wild! It was actually very observant. Everybody was vegetarian,
so there wasn't any problems with kashrut. Everybody was kosher . . . It*

was just—you know—big group dinners and then long discussions and then lots of singing and nobody knew what they were doing except for Clyde and Yoav. But it was wonderful, and there was also—sort of typical for a group of people in their twenties—there was a lot of very heightened sexual energy, which kept the group—you know—really tight.

Along with Clyde and Yoav and a few others from that circle, Lynn began attending Temple Am Israel regularly. Most of the religious aspects of Judaism were still a bit foreign to her, and often hard to swallow. But she loved going to synagogue with her friends. And she also loved Rabbi Oliff, who was the "very image" of her grandfather.

He was a very straight Conservative rabbi and I just adored him. And we got very close, very slowly. And he'd be sort of protective of me and I remember reading—we came to the portion when Moses sees the burning bush—and I went berserk. I read it and I read it. I was being very dutiful. I was reading the portion every week. And I finally made an appointment. I came up to him after Shabbes, after the sermon, and I said, 'Can I come talk to you? I'm really confused.' So I came back one afternoon and I said, 'I don't get it. I just don't get it. I'm reading and I'm trying so hard and I don't get it.' I said, 'This bush is burning—it doesn't make any sense.' And he said, 'Tsk. You're taking it literally.' I said, 'You mean it's not supposed to be?' He said, 'Some people do, some people don't.' And from there on we were just very close.

The vibrant *Shabbes* gatherings at the University Street house were continuous weekly bursts of joy. Every Saturday Clyde, Yoav, Lynn, and several others would spend the morning attending services at Temple Am Israel and then they would come back home to prepare for and host the evening dinner, which would eventually lead to singing and dancing all night long.

And at the heart of this mini Jewish revival were Clyde and Yoav. They were the teachers, the song-leaders, indeed, the very role models for all these young Jews seeking community and joy. They were quite a charismatic pair. Many of the young women had crushes on one of them, or both of them. Including Lynn. Did she ever get romantic with Clyde?

I wanted to . . . all the women were in love with him, I mean, women were proposing to him.

But Clyde fell in love with another woman, Stacy, who would eventually become his wife. It was roughly during the period when Clyde was starting to grow more and more intimate with Stacy, that Lynn suddenly became disenchanted.

Finally I got so tired of it . . . it was just the same topics: how are we gonna be more spiritual, how are we—and it felt—there was a lack of productivity there that finally started getting to me . . . you know, from the time I woke . . . there were just long, intense discussions. And after a few months . . . I decided I had to get to Israel. I needed to define myself. And actually, my dream was to move there and find a soldier and have lots of kids and just sort of live in the land—this just wasn't satisfying my deepest needs of how to be a Jew . . . I decided that I really needed to try something else. And so Israel seemed about as extreme as I could go . . . I even had my passport application filled out, and I had given notice at my job. And I had a week left. And then Josh walked into my life. And that was it. And I never left. That's it.

Josh Rosefsky met Lynn Appelbaum at one of the big *Shabbes* dinners at the University house. They quickly fell in love and got married. The Rosefskys would later become one of the most important families in Willamette's Jewish community. But back in the mid-seventies they were simply a pair of young Jews, in love and open to the future.

In August of 1975, Rabbi Oliff died. His death brought sorrow to many, especially the several young Jews who had connected to Judaism, and to each other, under his grandfatherly tutelage.

Now that Willamette's small Jewish community was without a rabbi, it was up to Clyde and Yoav to keep things going. While the elders of Temple Am Israel sought to find someone to replace Rabbi Oliff, Clyde and Yoav essentially ran the synagogue. Their responsibilities included conducting services on Friday nights and Saturday mornings. These weekly Sabbath services, which had been standard Conservative fare, dry and steady, became festive and spontaneous under the helm of Clyde and Yoav. The duo brought their instruments and their spirits into the small synagogue, and while their neo-Hasidic-Jewish-hippie style was strange and different to the older members, they appreciated the willingness of these two young, *froom* longhairs to keep the congregation afloat. And while a few of the older regulars were flatly turned off by the songs and the loving vibe, many got pulled into the mood.

In the ensuing decade, Lynn and Josh would become upper-middle-class owners of a successful business, the house on University Street would disband, Yoav would move south to Ashland and become a Jewish Renewal rabbi, and Clyde would change his name to Yakov, get married to Stacy, and become a cantor.

And a year after Rabbi Oliff's death, a new rabbi came to Temple Am Israel, who would serve Willamette's rapidly growing Jewish community for the next eighteen years: Rabbi Moishe Kohner.

The New Rabbi and His Wife

I first met Rabbi Moishe Kohner in 1989, shortly after I moved to Willamette to attend the local university.

I had stopped by Temple Am Israel one afternoon to check out the sole synagogue in this town of over four hundred churches. There he was, trudging through the parking lot, his arms full of papers and books. I hesitantly approached him with that "I'm away from home and don't know anybody so I've come to the synagogue seeking something familiar" look in my eyes, and he immediately responded. He dropped all his books and papers (literally placing them on the moist concrete of the parking lot), and extended his hand with a smile. I was struck by this kind greeting. After all, he was a busy rabbi and I was merely some assimilated college kid. But he looked warmly into my eyes, listening intently as I told him about myself, and he seemed genuinely pleased to have made my acquaintance. There was a humility about his whole manner.

He was a huge man. He had the massive hands of a bricklayer and the shoulders of a linebacker. He was bulky and bearded and yet he exuded an aura that bombarded you with gentleness.

I later met his wife, Yohanna, at a peace demonstration that took place in front of Willamette's Federal Building during the Gulf War. She didn't exude the immediate warmth or humility of her husband the rabbi. She was rather coarse. Indeed, some people in the Jewish community found her hard exterior incredibly disconcerting. But many others, including myself, found her toughness endearing. It was quite apparent to me that beneath her hard skin flowed sweet blood. Rotund and hearty, she had engaged me in conversation as we stood on the street corner amidst the thousands of protesting students. She offered a brilliant analysis of the Gulf War situation. But although I was soundly impressed by her intricate knowledge of the Persian Gulf conflict, I was more intrigued by the big wad of chewing tobacco lodged in the rear of her left cheek.

Many people, as I would later learn, considered Yohanna the mastermind behind her husband. If Rabbi Moishe Kohner was all heart, Yohanna was all brains. Fluent in Arabic, Hebrew, French, Spanish, and English, Yohanna was born in Morocco to religious parents.

My father had the knowledge of a judge in terms of his Jewish education— of a Jewish judge. My mother knew a lot of Jewish traditions—folk traditions. She was not versed in Hebrew as was my dad, but she could rattle every single blessing and everything . . . their knowledge of Judaism expanded beyond their ghetto—which is called a mellah—*because they were active Zionists and they were training people and sending people to Israel until they were able to send themselves.*

Yohanna's grandparents were from the walled city of Sefrou. Her parents moved to the Jewish quarter of Fez, then Casablanca, and eventually, like most Jews of Morocco, finally made their way to Israel. Yohanna arrived there in 1964. Having been raised as a completely observant Jew, she maintained that Orthodox lifestyle while she was a student in Jerusalem.

My father and mother were practicing Jews, praying three times a day and observing the Sabbath very carefully and being aware of the Jewish calendar and the sense of Jewish time—something I grew up with . . . and even when we went to Israel, even when I was living alone as a student, I would not dream of violating the Sabbath or getting in a car and traveling on Shabbat or going to a store . . . I wouldn't—it wasn't that I had to make a conscious decision: do I do this act or don't I do this. It was just assumed.

Moishe Kohner grew up in Pittsburgh, playing stickball and watching "Howdy-Doody." Not only was Moishe's childhood world of Elvis, Little League, and Dad's new Chevrolet qualitatively different from Yohanna's Moroccan childhood world, but their Jewish family lives were equally distinct. Yohanna grew up in a kosher home that was completely observant, from the psalms her mother would recite while preparing *Shabbes* dinner, to her father's rigorous daily prayer schedule. Moishe, over in the land of TV dinners, grew up with very little in the way of Jewish tradition. Moishe's dad owned a radio repair shop and his mom was into Tupperware. Sure, his family knew they were Jewish, they knew about the Holocaust, but that was about it. Indeed, Moishe's folks had a slight suspicion of religion in general, and that included the Jewish religion. Thus, like most American Jews of his generation, Moishe was raised with a Jewish identity that consisted of little else other than knowing he was Jewish—whatever that meant.

But as he grew older, he decided to find out. He told his parents that he wanted to have a bar mitzvah. In the summer he went to a Zionist camp. In school he sought out Jewish youth groups. And the more he learned about his Jewish heritage and the more he tasted of its vast history and spiritual wealth, the more he craved.

In 1967, Moishe Kohner left his suburban, middle-class, nonreligious home in Pittsburgh and went to Israel by himself to help the country any way he could during the Six-Day War. He was twenty-two. However, as its name explains, the war lasted less than a week. Unable to contribute much to the war effort, Moishe moved to an Orthodox religious kibbutz, where he hoped to work the land and learn about religious Judaism. He was successful in the latter, learning the many traditions and observances of Orthodox Jews, but he was unfulfilled in the former. Instead of working the land, he was sent to kill baby chicks. As his wife explained:

They asked him to feed little baby chicks to their minks. They had a mink farm on this kibbutz. To make mink furs. And so he was supposed to take live baby chicks and grind them up and feed them to animals, and he was just—I mean, I think it really brought his humanity to the surface: 'What am I doing? Why am I doing this? Here I am in an Orthodox kibbutz and taking living animals and crushing them so that another animal will be turned into a coat—what is the value?'

Unable to reconcile his growing understanding of holiness with his job of crushing baby chicks in order to feed them to minks that would in turn be slaughtered to make fur coats, he left the kibbutz and decided to further his Jewish education in Jerusalem.

That's where we met. He was a student. He enrolled himself at Hebrew Union College to take classes, and then he volunteered at a hospital for socially disturbed children, and he came around one day to look for a friend of a friend—he came to our dorms . . . we explained to him that she had gone home, but he was welcome to stay with us. And he stayed for Shabbat. And we did Shabbat. We had a meal and we had, you know, the wine and everything. And so there he was, feeling very comfy. And he kept coming back. He just—the stuff that he craved so much was Jewish life. He craved it all his life . . . so he just kept coming back and the girls noticed that he was mostly talking to me.

Within a month they were engaged. Within three months they were married. It was the ultimate Zionist romance: an assimilated Jew from the United States, seeking to enrich his Jewish identity and deepen his religiosity, comes to Jerusalem. There he finds a young Jewish girl fresh from Morocco, seeking to find herself and forge some kind of life in her new world. Two young Jews from different corners of the great Jewish Diaspora—Pittsburgh and Fez—meet and unite in the restored capital of the newly emerging Jewish nation. And then leave.

He brought out the issue of going to the United States, and I was like—Oh, no! I came all the way from Morocco to Israel, now I'm going to the United States? 'Oh,' he said, 'it's just for a year or so.' Well, twenty-nine years later, here I am.

Although he could barely read Hebrew when they met, Moishe expressed to Yohanna his desire to become a rabbi. At first, she was skeptical.

He was not like anything that we knew. I mean, a rabbinical student is a man who covers his head and has a long beard and is constantly delving in books. And where was Moishe? Going from archeological dig to archeological dig. And the body of a Greek god. Very liberal. He smoked on Shabbat. He certainly was very open with his sex life. And this guy's a rabbinical student?

But she was impressed by his incredibly enthusiastic thirst for Judaism and once he won her father's approval, she supported him in his path to becoming a rabbi—even if that meant a Reform rabbi. After completing his rabbinic studies in Jerusalem and then Los Angeles, Moishe (now Rabbi Kohner) was hired as the new rabbi of the small Conservative synagogue in Willamette, Oregon. Temple Am Israel.

No sooner did we arrive in April than he was totally involved with getting a secretary, publishing a bulletin, picking up these bar and bat mitzvah kids and establishing a Hebrew school , . . . doing Friday night services. His first Saturday morning service—Moishe used to joke—there were two people: he and a non-Jewish girl. For two months—when we came to Willamette we were totally observant, we kept kosher, we did not travel on Shabbat—and he shlepped fourteen blocks, from 38th Street to the synagogue on Shabbat, on Saturday morning, to sit in an empty synagogue with this non-Jewish girl.

But Moishe was not discouraged. He worked and worked to improve the synagogue and build up Willamette's Jewish community. He made phone calls and convinced people to come in on Saturday mornings to read from the Torah. He organized Sunday brunches. He taught classes five days a week. He painted the walls. He had coffee with skeptical professors at the University and persuaded them to enroll their kids in Hebrew school. He fixed the binding on worn-out prayer books. He created a softball team to play in the church league. He organized weekly men's breakfasts. In short, he tirelessly sought to bring in Jews— whomever he met—to come and be part of the congregation. And he was incredibly successful. As Yohanna explained:

The thing that attracted all these unaffiliated people was the fact that their initial visit with him was: 'Oh, this is a rabbi? He's not like my rabbi in L.A. who, you know, charges a thousand dollars for a funeral. . . .' What they saw was a really outgoing, friendly person . . . that's what they saw. And he used to bring them home . . . whoever and whatever Moishe met on his way, he used to bring them home.

Yohanna helped Moishe in his efforts to create community. She taught at the Hebrew school as well as offering classes in adult education. She served on committees, organized traditional Moroccan festivities, started a women's group, and worked with Jewish students from the University. And she often had a hand in Moishe's rabbinic activities. As Temple Am Israel member Rachel Kantor recalled:

Once my parents visited. We said, 'Let's go to services' . . . We went there on a Friday night and there was Moishe giving a sermon and there was Yohanna completely berating him in the middle of it! It was like, what is going on?! Moishe was giving the sermon and Yohanna stood up and she said, 'If I had known that this is what you were writing when I was cooking dinner, I never would have..!'—I mean, it was like, oh my God! There was another time, one Saturday morning, when we were doing the deal about Elijah—the confrontation with the priests of Baal and all of the 300 priests killed and all that. Yohanna said, 'Those are priestesses!'—Moishe's up at the beema—and she said, 'Those are priestesses, Moishe!' and he said, 'You're kidding, right?' And she says, 'No, I'm not. I know!' And it was like—silence.

Soon after Moishe's arrival to Willamette, Clyde (who now called himself Yakov) underwent formal cantorial training and was hired as the synagogue's cantor. Yakov quickly looked to Moishe as his new companion in Jewish living. They were a complimentary team: Yakov the cantor, with his soulful spirituality and beautiful voice, and Moishe the rabbi, with his big heart and committed drive. Yakov, the gentle musician, and Moishe, the bulky softball player. Yakov attracted the ex-hippies and others seeking a less traditional approach to Judaism, while Moishe attracted the middle-class families and young professionals who began pouring into Willamette in the late seventies and early eighties.

Many of these new arrivals to Willamette account for their connection to the Temple as a direct result of their first impressions of Moishe. For instance, Charles Hoffman had been living with his wife, Jayme, on a commune on the Oregon coast. In the late seventies they left the commune, Charles cut his hair and got his law degree, and Jayme had a child and got her master's in landscape architecture. They bought a house not far from the synagogue, and thus, not far from Moishe's outreach. Charles had been raised in a stuffy Conservative congregation back in Michigan that had left anything but a good impression on him, and as a young adult, he had no intention of setting foot into any synagogue ever again. But Moishe changed that.

The person that really made the difference was Moishe Kohner. . . . He gave the community the enthusiasm and breath and provided the youth and energy that the congregation needed to attract young professionals like Jayme and me . . . He was just such a sweet person. So dedicated to what he believed— absolutely one hundred percent committed to the community and the growth of the community. You know, he'd go out and cut the lawn. He'd go out and take out the trash. Whatever it took to make the place a little bit nicer and a little more inviting, he would do it. And he did not have any of the pretentiousness of rabbis that I had grown up with.

Charles' sprightly wife, Jayme, concurred:

It was like all of a sudden we got real involved . . . and befriended Rabbi Moishe Kohner and Yohanna Kohner . . . and it became our community. Moishe was very approachable. I had probably never seen the inside of a Torah—let alone been allowed to touch one. And he called me up for an aleeyah—which I didn't have a clue what it was I was supposed to do, because of course I was raised in a synagogue where women didn't have that honor. And he just opened up a world of Judaism for me that I didn't know existed. . . . I would say that the fact that Charles and I have a Jewish home, and raised our children Jewish, is because of Rabbi Kohner. . . . I wouldn't have been affiliated, probably, if it weren't for him . . . Moishe was the mover and shaker in getting people involved.

According to John Meyers, who once held a term as the congregation's president:

Moishe, I would say, was the main mover . . . he was bringing young people who had been disaffiliated back into the fold. And professionals that were moving to Willamette—lawyers, doctors, were joining in large numbers. And also hippies. A lot of ex-hippies that had grown up and settled here. And other people—my wife included—who had had some bad experiences as a child related to her synagogue and so forth. And it was really Moishe that gave her—that created a synagogue which she could actually belong to and feel comfortable in.

According to Zack Norman, a soft-spoken man from Buenos Aires, who would become one of Moishe's closest friends:

Over and over I saw people who were Jewish, who had become sorely alienated from their Jewishness, coming back and showing an interest and a real admiration, first for Moishe and/or Yohanna, and then for being Jewish. He really helped a lot of people reclaim themselves.

Although Julie Horowitz had connected with several Jews within the community as a result of her political activism, she had never been drawn to the synagogue. But Rabbi Kohner managed to rope her in.

I had seen Rabbi Kohner out in the world, once or twice. I had been struck at a kind of simplicity and almost naiveté that I picked up from him. And I will confess I wasn't strongly drawn to it, until we went to the circus and ended up sitting behind them in these bleachers, and I watched him and his wife just getting off on the circus so much, you know, with such pleasure, such innocent delight in what was really a fairly hokey circus. Their kids were bored, my kid was bored, I was bored—and these two grown-ups were just eating it up with a spoon. So that was very impressive to me . . . I showed up at the shule one day and he happened to be on the street, he was probably walking away, walking home for lunch, and I sort of hailed him like a cab, 'Rabbi Kohner!' and he turned around and I said I want to join the synagogue and he immediately dropped everything he had been planning to do and came back in the building with me, signed me up, sat me down in his office . . . he immediately said, 'Would you like to be the youth group leader?' No thank you. 'Would you like to teach in the religious school?' No thank you. 'Well, will you do a haftorah? *' Okay. And then I started coming to the services.*

More and more Jews moved to Willamette throughout the early eighties, and under Moishe's constant enthusiasm, Temple Am Israel rapidly grew. Some who came were single drifters, having heard that Willamette was a special place. Others were middle-class families looking for a nice town in which to raise their kids. Moishe tried to welcome whoever came; whoever showed up at the *shule*, he warmly greeted and urged them to get involved. Although it was officially a Conservative synagogue, he welcomed Jews of all types, regardless of their level—or even lack—of religiosity. His vision was that Temple Am Israel should be more than just a house of prayer, but a community center for Jews to come and do whatever they wanted. His motto was: "If you want to do something Jewish, Temple Am Israel's the place." He instituted an official policy of openness and tolerance; after all, his was the only synagogue in town—if he wanted people to join, he couldn't be too judgmental or rigid. He had to be accepting of people's own diverse Jewish tastes and styles.

Caitlin Twain, who came to Willamette in 1982, recalled the texture of the community under Moishe's leadership:

Low-key congenial. And a real openness to variety and acceptance of variety. I was struck by how incredible the mix of people was that got along, and I attribute that directly to Moishe Kohner—being able to hold lots of people together and pointing out how common we were.

Moishe's acceptance of difference and variety even extended to non-Jews and intermarried couples: anyone that wanted to be connected with the synagogue was welcome. That approach greatly impressed David Decker, who wasn't Jewish and was married to a practicing Catholic. David had always felt drawn to Judaism, but he was reluctant to explore it, assuming that a rabbi wouldn't perform a conversion for someone already in a mixed marriage. But he was wrong. Moishe was open to

David's desire to become a Jew and happily converted him.

Among the people who steadily poured into Willamette throughout the 1980s were two women, Rhoda Fogel and Camille Vigeland. Both were converted to Judaism by Rabbi Kohner at Temple Am Israel.

Today they don't speak to one another.

Rhoda and Camille

Rhoda Fogel has a pointy nose and plum cheeks. She grew up in a small town in central Idaho, the daughter of Southern Baptists. Her first husband was a drug dealer whom she met while a teenager living in San Francisco. He beat her and sexually abused her, but she eventually managed to escape from his torturous domination. (Today, Rhoda is quick to point out, he is a Lubavitch Hasid.)

She found refuge in a commune full of Jewish hippies in Haight Ashbury, but after its collapse, she moved to Oregon, where she had a sister living outside of Willamette. She met John Cohen, a quiet, gentle book collector, who was Jewish. They started dating, and Rhoda explained to John that she had always felt Jewish herself. She revealed to him that she had a deep sense that in her past life she had been Jewish and had been killed in the Holocaust. She wanted to reconnect. Together they took classes at Temple Am Israel and Rhoda became close friends with Moishe's wife, Yohanna. Within a year, Moishe converted Rhoda to Judaism and presided over her marriage to John Cohen.

Camille Vigeland's involvement with Temple Am Israel, and her eventual conversion to Judaism, were a bit more complicated.

Camille Vigeland is small and white. She struck me as a strong spirit trapped in a fragile, delicate body. She expresses herself with tenacity and verve, yet her pale wrists are no larger than celery sticks. She was born and raised in a tiny town in Minnesota where all 400 residents were Lutheran, of Scandinavian stock. Her folks were third-generation Americans, with ancestors coming from Växjö, Sweden. Her first time outside of her home town was when she went to attend the University of Minnesota at the age of seventeen. It was 1967, and the antiwar movement was growing. Camille got involved in the protests against American military involvement in Vietnam. She also became a Quaker.

I went to University . . . during Vietnam. . . . Things were just building up, and I became a Quaker . . . they believe in absolute nonviolence. Absolute equality. And both of these are based on their belief that there's some aspect of God that dwells in each person. It's very compelling, actually. Plus, you know, they're very gentle people.

She met another young Quaker and they got married. Then they got divorced. Then she met another young Quaker, Victor, and they got married. However, this second Quaker husband happened to be of Jewish heritage.

I married the second time someone who was a Jew, born of Russian and Polish immigrant parents . . . he went to Quaker summer camp. So in fact I met him at Quaker meeting and we were married in Quaker meeting and never was Judaism ever mentioned anywhere along the line. And his mother, who's a widow, never mentioned—just didn't, you know—it just never came up. So we had one child. We had a second child. We moved here to Willamette and had a third child. And when the third child was born, his mom called up and said, 'I want you to take the kids to the synagogue and have them named.'

This was in 1982.

So she came to visit us and said, 'You really have to—you've GOT to take the kids to the synagogue and have them named!' So . . . we went here to Temple Am Israel and Moishe—much to his credit—said, 'You know, you can't just bring kids in here and get them stamped and leave again; this requires a commitment to raising them as Jews.' So I had a lot of talks with him about what that meant, and could I as a Quaker raise them as Jews, and you know, some of my core beliefs having to do with there's some aspect of God in every person and therefore you can't kill anybody and everyone's equal and dah-dah-dah . . . and he said, well, sounds pretty Jewish to him and that it wouldn't be an impediment and that was fine. So . . . Victor . . . . was not at all keen about this. However, he wanted his mother off his back.

You know, his attitude was: for Godsakes, anything to keep his mother quiet . . . so she came on maybe a Sunday—the kids were named on Thursday. She left Friday morning. And she died on Sunday. And I know in my heart that she . . . she knew her death was imminent, and that the most important thing to her was to see that those kids were Jews. I mean, she knew— it was one thing for her son not to be Jewish, but she didn't want her grandchildren not to be Jewish. There had to be a perpetuation of Judaism. There just had to be. And she and I had some talks about that and I think she knew she could trust me to raise them as Jews . . . the perpetuation of the tribe— you know, that tribal identity is just—it's visceral, it's in her blood. She needed to know that the line would not stop with her son. So it had tremendous impact on me. I mean I just—ah!—it was incredible.

After his mother's death, Camille's Quaker/Jewish husband Victor made it very clear that he wanted nothing to do with raising their three children as Jews. They had had them named in an official Jewish ceremony at the synagogue to please his mother, but now that she was dead, he wanted nothing more to do with the Jewish community. But Camille was committed. It was quite a situation: the husband (a Quaker who was the son of Jewish immigrants) wanted nothing to do with a Judaism, and yet Camille (a Quaker who was the daughter of Lutheran Minnesotans) was steadfast in complying with her recently-deceased mother-in-law's wishes to embrace Judaism. The couple could not agree and the marriage subsequently collapsed. After the divorce, Camille maintained custody of the children and quickly immersed herself in learning how to raise them as Jews.

First of all, I felt that the commitment I had made was not to my mother-in-law and not to Moishe—that it was really a commitment to God to raise these kids as Jews . . . so I got the younger two enrolled at preschool at Temple Am Israel . . . and that was the level of learning I needed to do— preschool learning. So I essentially learned right along with the kids. . . . The first thing we did—because it was easy, I mean, you didn't have to be literate to do it—was to start observing Shabbes . . . on Friday the kids and I would come home and we'd bake hallah and get the house ready and we'd really make Shabbat. And Moishe, all this time, was wonderful.

She took more and more classes in Jewish history and Jewish thought, she learned enough Hebrew to be able to following along with the prayers, and in 1987, she converted to Judaism. She met several others within Temple Am Israel who had also been converted under Moishe's tutelage, like David Decker and Rhoda Fogel. Acquaintances became friends.

Community Forms—With One Noted Exception

Lynn and Josh Rosefsky, who had fallen in love back at the old hippie commune on University Street, became good friends with Charles and Jayme Hoffman. They were approximately the same ages, as were their young children. They were both newly-successful professionals: Charles' new law career was taking off and Josh's new bakery was the best in town. Both couples were going through similar life transitions in the late seventies and early eighties: from hippie idealists, to pragmatic, successful professionals. Charles never thought he'd be a lawyer and Josh never thought he'd be a capitalist. Lynn and Jayme never thought they'd be content housewives, living in two of the nicest homes in the nicest neighborhood in town. Through their friendship they were able to share the excitement and worries of their new lifestyle.

When the bespectacled Josh Rosefsky moved to Willamette in the mid-seventies, he had intended to be a social worker. He had received his master's in social work back in Boston and had come out West to explore a new environment and work with troubled adolescents. But social work just wasn't what he had thought or hoped it would be. The work was all-consuming, depressing, and the pay was miserable. He realized that Willamette didn't have a decent bakery, and with some help from a relative, he went from idealistic social worker to budget-conscious entrepreneur.

He rented a small shop in South Willamette, only five blocks away from Yakov and Yoav's house on University Street, where he met Lynn just before the business took off. Hearing of the University Street co-op, he ventured over there one night.

I started to spend time with the people in that community. It was sort of this group of people about my age who were looking into Judaism for the first time, mixing it with a lot of New Age ideas and trying a lot of things out. I sort of kept an arm's length from a lot of it, but I was interested in having the social outlet . . . I was single, I had no attachments . . . two weeks before we opened the business, I met Lynn—formally met Lynn. And we hit it off right away. And ultimately this was it, and we were going to get married.

The marriage succeeded, as did the small bakery, which soon grew into a large bakery.

Initially, Josh wasn't too interested in pursuing an active involvement with Judaism. Like Charles, he had grown up in a straightforward Conservative synagogue, with his folks not particularly religious but observing the major holidays, and he wasn't so eager to involve himself with the Temple in Willamette. But Lynn was, and so they joined up, and that's where they met the Hoffmans. As Charles recalled:

Lynn and Josh and Jayme and I were VERY close friends. We used to get together regularly for Shabbat, and actually spent a fair amount of time together. And I still love Lynn's sense of humor, you know, because it's very much like mine.

As Jayme recalled:

Oh, Josh and Lynn. I mean—I got pictures, every Passover—our house or their house . . . I mean, Lynn and Josh and us have been doing Shabbats together since the kids were babies—Passover sayder and everything.

The Rosefskys and the Hoffmans became very involved with Temple Am Israel, working at the religious school, becoming board members, donating money.

Camille Vigeland and Rhoda Fogel also served on the board, as well as various other committees.

Julie Horowitz also became more active, as well as Jeff Bronner, the banjo-player she had befriended at an antinuke protest.

Tall and dark, Jeff Bronner grew up in Los Angeles, to nonreligious Jewish parents.

They were cultural Jews—still are. And I'd say that . . . they either didn't have any interest in the noncultural, religious area, or they were actively hostile toward it. I never knew what Shabbat was when I was real little. . . . Even though I came from a nonobservant home, they were very identified as Jews . . . they were sort of in the socialist, pinko-diaper crowd. And that was a very, you know, Jewish scene. Until they figured out what Stalin was up to . . . so they really passed on very heavily that I was Jewish, and I heard all the history of our family, constantly. So I always identified as being Jewish.

In 1979, at the age of twenty-three, Jeff moved to Willamette. He got into music, learning to play the banjo as well as the clarinet, and he became involved in the antinuclear movement, where he met Julie Horowitz. Once she got involved with the synagogue, Jeff followed suit.

I think I told somebody I wanted to go to a service. I think I told Julie. She came by and picked me up, Friday night . . . so anyway, I went there and she drove me back . . . and then I decided to keep Shabbat . . . not that I knew what that meant, by the way. But I knew that it meant that you didn't work . . . so I knew you weren't supposed to work and you lit candles. So over that year I'd start going to Shabbat a little more and a little more at Temple Am Israel.

Although Julie Horowitz and Jeff Bronner were great friends, they weren't romantically involved. Julie, a strikingly attractive woman with dark hair, dark skin, and iridescent green eyes, was from the Bronx. Her parents had both been brought up in completely observant, Orthodox homes. However, after her parents married, they broke from their Orthodox tradition and become two of the earliest adherents of the Reconstructionist movement. They were friends of Rabbi Mordechai Kaplan, the founder of Reconstructionist Judaism, and they became active participants in his new Jewish vision. Thus, Julie was raised as a complete Reconstructionist Jew. This meant that of all the women I interviewed, Julie was the only one who had been taught how to read and study Torah as a girl.

I grew up in the Society for the Advancement of Judaism, which is the mother-church of the Reconstructionist movement. And I was very interested, always—from my earliest childhood through my early twenties—I was very interested in Judaism. I was never really interested in the minutiae of observance, but I was very interested in the grappling of theology. I was completely fascinated by Kaplan's view. . . . My secular education wasn't entirely secular. I went to the Ethical Culture schools. So I was educated in the Jewish community's tradition, at Hebrew school, and at home, and in school in a secular humanist tradition, which had its basis in Judaism because Ethical Culture was started by a rabbi. A former rabbi. So I had a very wonderful grounding in values.

In her mid-twenties, she left New York and became a fulltime hippie/social activist, wandering the nation involving herself in worthy causes. She devoted herself to everything from helping organize labor in the Midwest to fighting against racism in the South. Her political activism became her spiritual path and she let go of Judaism for about ten years, until she found herself in Willamette, Oregon, connecting with Jeff Bronner, Moishe and Yohanna Kohner, and her eventual husband, Hugh Leon.

The child of Rumanian Jewish immigrants, Hugh grew up in Baltimore. His grandparents were Orthodox, but his parents were less observant. Like Julie, in his mid-twenties Hugh had drifted away from Judaism.

I had nothing to do with the religious aspect of Judaism for years. I saw myself as deeply spiritual—and my spirituality had nothing to do with Judaism—because I was so ignorant of Judaism as a spiritual phenomenon. My Hebrew school education was abominable. It was awful. It was deadly . . . so I was turning to other avenues to deal with my spirituality.

Hugh came to Willamette in the mid-seventies, but stayed clear of Temple Am Israel. Until he heard about Yakov and Yoav.

After Rabbi Oliff died, Yakov and Yoav took over the Temple as leading services, and I heard about these incredible people. I had met Yakov, and of course Yakov is so wonderful that I was intrigued with him leading the services. I went to services for about half a dozen times. . . . Moishe had just come to town, so I met him, and he and Yohanna came to my house for dinner. So here I was. I knew Yakov. I knew Moishe. I was very struck at what wonderful people they were . . . and I knew people that were involved at the Temple, but I just didn't see it as part of my life. Until I met Julie. We began dating in 1982, and one of her conditions in dating was that I would need to be involved in Judaism. And she brought me to the Temple and I got more involved.

The Hoffmans and the Rosefskys, Julie and Hugh, David Decker, Rhoda Fogel, Camille Vigeland, Jeff Bronner, Yakov and his wife Stacy, Rabbi Moishe and Yohanna. The community grew and grew. More and more people moved to Willamette, and more and more found their way to the synagogue.

Bruce and Amanda Wallin joined Temple Am Israel in the mid-eighties, after the birth of their first son. Amanda had been raised in a nonreligious home in Chicago, where High Holidays were observed, as well as Hanukkah and Passover, but nothing else. Bruce grew up in a small town in southern Iowa, the child of Presbyterians. But even before he met Amanda, he had always felt drawn to Judaism.

For some reason I developed a fascination and interest in Zionism and the history of the Jewish people, politically and culturally, when I was a teenager. And that led me to read a lot about Israeli politics and the history of the state of Israel and the history of the Jewish people. And I continued to pursue that interest in my twenties and thirties, following political developments in the Middle East and doing some reading about yiddishkeit. And then I married a Jewish woman [Amanda]. We didn't have a religious wedding, and neither one of us was interested in Jewish practice at that time. Then maybe three or four or five years after we were married, I decided that I wanted to convert to Judaism because I wanted our whole family to be Jewish. And I wanted to celebrate the Jewish holidays and participate in a Jewish way of life as a family. To do my part in continuing the Jewish tradition, by being a Jewish father to Jewish children.

Like David Decker, Rhoda, and Camille, Bruce was converted by Rabbi Moishe Kohner at Temple Am Israel. The Wallins sent their kids to the Hebrew school and they got to know the Rosefskys. Bruce and Josh became friends. They shared a mutual love of baking and cooking, and Josh helped Bruce open up a restaurant that, like Josh's bakery, became quite successful.

Most of the people involved at the synagogue weren't raised as religiously traditional Jews. There were a few exceptions: Yohanna had been raised in an Orthodox home in Morocco, and Zack Norman had grown up in a similarly traditional, Orthodox manner in Buenos Aires. But aside from these two foreign-born members, the congregation of Temple Am Israel had had no experience with Orthodoxy. They had all been raised as either Reform or Conservative Jews, or simply cultural Jews devoid of any religious trappings.

But then there was Lenny Levitan. Lenny was the only member of Temple Am Israel who came from an American Orthodox background.

Lenny Levitan, a charismatic man with well-carved cheekbones and fantastic eyebrows, had been raised as a completely Orthodox Jew. He grew up in Queens. His mother was a Holocaust survivor from Amsterdam and his father was a child of immigrants from Poland. Their household was fully observant, and Lenny was sent to a private Jewish day school, which he attended all the way through high school. Rabbi Meyer Kahane, the racist rabbi who founded the Jewish Defense League, was Lenny's ninth-grade Hebrew teacher.

Growing up, Lenny always wore a *keepa*, prayed regularly, and kept in line with his family's strict kosher diet. To this day, he's never eaten a cheeseburger. However, in his teens, Lenny did go through a period of rebellion.

Once I hit high school I became a troubled youth—as I guess my parents would put it, basically. I was kicked out of the first high school I went to— I was caught smoking cigarettes . . . This is early seventies . . . I was just a troublemaker. Basically I got kicked out of three different yeshivas for one reason or another. Well, what happened was I started hanging out—I became involved in the Jewish Defense League . . . and this is when the Jewish Defense League was just starting, and Kahane—there were some problems on the East Side of New York, these old people were getting mugged going to shule—back and forth from shule on Shabbes. So he asked for volunteers and we'd spend Shabbes there and we did it and it was very successful and I became part of that group and became a Meyer Kahane—not a groupie—but a follower of Rabbi Kahane. . . . So I got in with that crowd, and one thing led to another. I became, well—I wouldn't say I was violent, but I had—I hung out with that kind of group. . . . I was arrested a bunch of times on different situations with the Jewish Defense League.

In addition to his Jewish Defense League activities, Lenny slacked off on his religious observance. His parents were worried and thought he needed something that would straighten him out. They sent him to Israel, to a religious kibbutz. While on a break from the kibbutz, sunbathing on the beach in Tel Aviv, he met Ginger. She had been traveling through Europe with a friend and then, on a whim, flew by herself down to Israel for a week. She was also from New York. They were both twenty. Lenny never went back to the religious kibbutz, but traveled the country with Ginger, exploring Jerusalem, Tzvat, and the Galilee. He flew back with her to New York and within several months they were married. Their marriage was somewhat of a problem, because Ginger's family, though Jewish, was completely secular. And Lenny's parents insisted on a complete Orthodox wedding.

Ginger's family was totally, you know, from a totally secular environment—secular Jewish environment . . . they wanted mixed dancing and my family didn't want mixed dancing. So, we compromised. We had mixed dancing and our family rabbi refused to come and marry us. We had to get another rabbi—except everything else was very traditional.

To the dismay of Lenny's family, in 1979 they moved to Willamette, Oregon ("Who moves to Oregon?!").

We were headed to California, like every other New Yorker we heard that

California was the place to go. And Ginger had a friend of hers living in Willamette and we came here to stop for a visit and it was August and beautiful and we stayed. . . . We really loved it here. . . . I was a tree planter and Ginger worked for the dog pound. So we just rented a place in the country and we stayed.

They remained more or less unobservant and uninvolved with Jewish communal life, until their first child was born. Then they felt a pull to Temple Am Israel. For Lenny, going to a non-Orthodox synagogue was difficult.

I had never set foot in a Conservative or Reform shule until I came to Willamette . . . growing up it was like blasphemous to even think about going to a place that had, you know—I grew up in a place where they kind of made fun of Conservative and Reform shules. Not the people themselves, but just the way they operate . . . you know, it was a step closer to a church. It wasn't authentic Judaism.

But the Levitans had no choice since Temple Am Israel was the only synagogue in town. Although the congregation didn't meet his religious needs, Lenny did feel good about the people he met there and the friendships he made.

I didn't connect with Rabbi Kohner at all . . . but I connected very strongly with Yakov. He was the hazan at the time . . . I connected very strongly—and there was really—it was really a tight group of people who really . . . very warm . . . we'd show up at shule once or twice a month and we just really—it was a very nice place for Jews to get together and be Jews and it felt good.

Lenny began teaching Hebrew school at Temple Am Israel and was eventually voted onto the board of directors. The Levitans became good friends with Bruce and Amanda Wallin, Yakov and Stacy, Josh and Lynn Rosefsky, and the many other young couples who were active in the congregation.

The community was growing.

But there was one man out there in Willamette who would have nothing to do with Temple Am Israel. Like Lenny, this man was an Orthodox Jew. But unlike Lenny, he refused to compromise his traditional lifestyle or beliefs by being involved with a non-Orthodox congregation. Although he had been in Willamette since the early sixties, he had never once set foot in the synagogue.

This was Rabbi Abe Shibel: skinny and tall, with an Adam's apple like a granite meatball and white tufts of hair tiredly sprouting out of the back corners of his head. He wasn't a practicing rabbi—never had been. He was a physics professor at the University. Most people didn't even know he was a rabbi. But before delving into secular academics, he had been trained as a rabbi in New York and had graduated from Yeshiva University. Since he considered Temple Am Israel *treyf*, his only communal connection to Judaism was that he offered a weekly Talmud class at his home. Attendance tended to be sparse, usually only one or two students from the University.

However, Rabbi Moishe Kohner, when he first moved to Willamette, heard about this "closet rabbi" who taught Talmud, and sought him out. But their connection was not a successful one. As Yohanna Kohner recalled:

Moishe studied Talmud with Shibel the first few years that we lived in Willamette. Shibel is a horrible person. We had—we were on an emergency list for foster children. And one day, on Sunday afternoon, which is the time Moishe used to study with him, there was an emergency and we had to go interview a child who needed a home . . . there was a young lady who had died and there were kids, and—ugh! So Moishe called and said, 'Rabbi Shibel, I'm sorry, I'm not going to come to class because I have this emergency.' And Rabbi Shibel told him to go to hell. And Moishe said, 'I can't study with you if you talk to me that way.' So Moishe dropped out of this pseudo-Talmud class . . . so when you talk about the Willamette community, you should know that even though there was an attempt at harmonizing and bringing people together, there were always these sourpusses all over the place, and Shibel was one of them. Shibel was harsh. He was rude. He was judgmental. And he was—he actually broke away from the community . . . he set that example.

Chapter Three

THE COMMUNITY
BEFORE THE STORM

One Show in Town—Impressions of Willamette's growing Jewish community varied greatly among my 46 informants. I asked them how they felt about Temple Am Israel when they first became involved, what they liked or disliked, and how they would describe the flavor of the synagogue. There was an array of different responses. There were many who felt that the growing diversity of the congregation's membership was a strength; others saw it as a problem. There were many who felt that Rabbi Moishe Kohner's increasingly liberal approach regarding the structure of religious services was a fresh innovation; others saw it as a disappointing break from the Conservative structure that had been in place under Rabbi Oliff. There were many who appreciated Temple Am Israel's casual atmosphere; others felt that it was too loose, too informal. Upon this sea of diverse expectations and differing needs, Rabbi Moishe Kohner did his best to steer the ship of the community with sometimes greater, sometimes lesser success. The course was usually smooth but certainly not without its small storms, which would eventually give way to full-blown tempests.

Jocelyn Herzberg moved to Willamette in the 1980s and eventually served on the Temple's board of directors. As she recalled of her early impressions of Temple Am Israel:

Temple Am Israel definitely had a haymish *feel to it—which I liked . . . I didn't go to services that much myself . . . but I did go to one and somebody—I forget who—like didn't have their shoes on and kind of like wanted to dance around during one of the songs . . . and I thought, well, that's not my style. But I wasn't offended by it. I just thought, well, who would come to synagogue without their shoes on?*

Roger Diamond, who moved to Willamette with his wife in the 1980s, recalled:

The very first thing we noticed was dress. Coming from Salt Lake, which was a large, beautiful, architecturally recognized temple, and going to services was a semiformal event, you know, people dressed up for it. And then coming to Willamette—I remember one of our earliest attendances at services, Laura and I came away wondering whether we had hit 'dress-down day' or something. Very definitely remarkable in its casualness of dress and the very wide variety of dress and demeanor that the Temple tolerates.

Many noted the difference that having only one synagogue in town made on the character of the congregation. As Arthur Edelmann, a professor of literature, explained:

When I grew up—and I would say this is true for lots of those people—you went to YOUR temple. But there was another one. And not just one other one, but other ONES, in your neighborhood even, or in your area. So people brought all that experience to a place where there's only one synagogue—or as people used to say, only 'one show in town.' And that meant, either by design or in a de facto sense, that you kind of deferred to the one show. . . . Here, well, it was Jews, but it was not all 'people like you.' So I mean, I'm part of a university community, but there was a business community, a counterculture community—a this community, a that community—people who came in from the hinterland. You'd meet people or interact with people who were not part of your normal social world, and what you had in common was the synagogue. Personally, I felt that that was terrific. That was actually the thing I liked best about it—this kind of sense of feeling part of a community and the synagogue was the place you could go to feel part of the community. I liked that aspect of it. And what happened is that the community grew. . . . and then people said, 'This isn't like the synagogue I grew up in—it's most haymish, *it's comfortable, you don't have to get dressed up, only the rich people aren't in charge.' So that was the kind of broad character. I personally kind of liked the 'big tent' character—the 'one show in town' notion.*

According to Adam Lowy, who came to Willamette in the eighties:

Temple Am Israel was unique. It was definitely unique because it was really diverse. There were fairly straight, traditional people, older people—there were traditional people who span the whole gamut of religious affiliation. There were people from the University who kept to the themselves and were pretty elitist. There was also a sort of counterculture group . . . and there was—it was very diverse socioeconomically. . . . I think Moishe Kohner and Yakov really worked hard at trying to satisfy everybody. Theologically, Moishe was very flexible. He would do stuff that would set the hair on the back of some more traditional rabbis on end. I thought it was very positive . . . there was always the support for the diversity, at least, it was welcomed.

According to Marcello Bergman, who came to Willamette in the eighties:

What happened is that Rabbi Moishe enabled anybody who wanted to affiliate with Temple Am Israel to affiliate, regardless of their level of yiddishkeit. I mean, assuming they were Jewish—and in some cases even there he had many ceremonies and many ways of inviting non-Jewish partners of Jews into the synagogue. So it was a very big tent.

While booming as a community center, the structured religious flavor of Temple Am Israel, throughout the 1980s, was hard to pin down. Moishe tried his best to satisfy the variety of diverse denominational needs. On Friday nights he would offer a liberal, Reform-style service involving music and guest speakers. On Saturday mornings he would offer a traditional, Conservative-style service that was similar to the days of Rabbi Oliff. And every now and then, Yakov would lead a separate Saturday morning service in a back room of the synagogue that was of the Jewish Renewal bent, that is, a throwback to the old University Street days with tambourines and dancing.

This diversity of religious services that were being offered was disconcerting to some members who sought consistency in their congregation. They felt that the synagogue was "all over the place" in terms of its denominational identity. But others, like Charles Hoffman, enjoyed the experimental atmosphere:

> Oh, you could never predict what was going on there at any given time. You know, when I was growing up, services had—every service was a cookie-cutter service. This is the way you did it. The songs were all the same, the liturgy was all the same, the music was all the same. And there was a kind of experimental flavor that just pervaded Temple Am Israel. I remember being at one service . . . chairs were pushed back to the wall and everybody on their hands and knees, bending down and paying homage to an imaginary oasis in the desert . . . you know, just wacky. And there was sort of a sense of creativity.

As Caitlin Twain recalled:

> There we were with Orthodox, atheist, Zionist, anti-Zionist, every variety—and there we all were, as a sort of continuum, group, family . . . and definitely an attitude of getting along.

The eighties was thus a time when Temple Am Israel sought to fashion itself as all things to all people. And for a while, it was quite successful. An attitude of getting along, fostering community despite diversity, and placing a shared identity as Jews above all other differences, predominated. It seemed of utmost importance for the Jews of Willamette to be united. Thus, under the influence of Moishe Kohner, individual differences were downplayed, and solidarity was preached and, for the most part, practiced.

Although the variety of religious services offered (from Reform to Conservative to occasional Renewal) gave the synagogue a somewhat confused personality, the variety of religiosity among the congregants themselves wasn't actually all that diverse. Although everyone had their own particular tastes of the way a service should be run, most people involved with Temple Am Israel were either flatly nonreligious or mildly religious in the Reform or Conservative manner. The truth be told, most people didn't come to Temple Am Israel looking for God; they came looking for community. While there were certainly those who treasured the synagogue as a place to tap into their spirituality, the vast majority of those involved were there simply to be with other Jews. It was, for most people, a social and cultural center above all else. If people disagreed over how services should be run, it was usually based on their nostalgic memories of their childhood synagogue—"But we always did it this way. . . . " Very rarely—if at all—were the tensions over service structure based upon any deeply-held theological positions on the most meaningful way to commune with the Eternal One.

The only Orthodox Jews were the Levitans and Abe Shibel. Lenny and Ginger Levitan accepted the synagogue's non-Orthodox ways in exchange for the sense of community they received. Abe Shibel, with his fledgling Talmud class, would have nothing to do with the congregation. But aside from these three, there were no other Orthodox Jews in Willamette. So the few initial rumblings that did arise within the congregation tended to be less over issues of religiosity, and more in the realm of basic personality clashes.

One controversial personality that stood out was Moishe's wife, Yohanna.

According to Charles Hoffman:

Yohanna was—had a grating personality. You know, she could fly into rages. She felt very, very strongly—she was a very articulate person. She was not someone—she didn't suffer fools easily. And she alienated a lot of people. She just made a lot of people angry with her style.

Yohanna Kohner was often involved in bouts of disagreement. While she had her share of fans and friends, she also tended to anger and scare people. For instance, Janie Strickstein had a personal run-in with Yohanna:

I was in these talk groups with her, these women's groups, so I got to know Yohanna pretty well . . . . We would go to lunch together and stuff like that. And then we became bitter enemies. I mean, all of a sudden I was the worst enemy in the world to her. So Yohanna—she could be your best friend one minute and then she could hate you the next minute . . . But Moishe would sort of go trotting through it as if nothing was wrong, you know. He always had a smile on his face—that kind of thing. And then Yohanna would just be—ugh! She was a wonderful speaker. Very bright woman. Much brighter than Moishe. Much better thinker than Moishe was. But she didn't know how to talk to people. . . . She had a real hard time talking—her social skills were not terrific.

So what exactly happened between Janie and Yohanna? The incident was particularly shocking to Janie.

We were at this place that a group of women were together and it was like a talk group and Yohanna started talking about Moishe and her bitterness and feeling she was just tired of being a rabbi's wife and she was never looked upon dah-dah-dah. And I started to say something. I didn't—not even a word. And she stood up, screamed at the top of her lungs, had a knife in her hand, and all I could do was look at this knife! She had a knife in her hand and she threw it down on the floor, screaming and bellowing at me, saying, 'I am the rabbi's wife and you cannot talk to me like that!' She was totally out of whack . . . I stood up and walked out. I was crying. I was hysterical . . . I was worried about her, truly. I thought she was going nuts . . . But you see, that's the kind of erratic behavior that—I never talked to her again. She never wanted me to. I went up to Temple—at Temple one time I went up to her and said, 'Yohanna, don't you think we should talk this out?' And she took me, she took my arms like this, and whammed me against the brick wall of the Temple. I thought—holy! What's going on here? I said, 'Let go.' She let go. And she went into the Temple. And after that, . . . I never talked to her again.

While Yohanna managed to put people off on a fairly consistent basis, Rabbi Moishe Kohner himself was well loved by the community, maintaining an almost unanimously strong following of admiration and respect. Indeed, he was so gentle and calm, it was hard for me to believe that anyone could actually have a conflict with the man.

But someone did. There was one person in Willamette who just couldn't stand him: Lynn Rosefsky. As she explained:

I had been present at Moishe's first interview . . . and I remember he was unbelievably inarticulate . . . he was invited back to our house for lunch.

And we sat at this table. Yoav and Yakov, and I think Stacy was there, and Moishe and Yohanna. And I actually was very drawn to Yohanna. She's really crazy—crazy. Intense woman. But really on the mark. I like people who define themselves. I don't like mushy. I like the sharp. And she was wonderful. And he drove me nuts, from the beginning . . . so anyway, he was the candidate that was voted in. And when we got married we of course asked him to marry us. And up until about a month and a half before the wedding, that's the way it was. And then he came bumbling to us one day and said, 'Oh, I just looked at my calendar and I have something else to do on that day.' I wasn't surprised—but I was furious.

But it wasn't just his untimely cancellation prior to her and Josh's wedding that put Lynn off. She was utterly displeased by almost everything about Moishe. Lynn considered him an "ill-informed man" who "just didn't know his stuff." And she hated his sermons.

They always left me so angry . . . they were so unclear . . . I mean, he just didn't know how to write. He didn't know how to speak . . . we didn't have a lot of respect for his intellect. He was kind and he did wonderful things on a humanitarian level. And I respect him for that. But . . . I didn't trust him. . . . Not being raised with a rabbi, I didn't ever feel that rabbis deserved automatic respect. It's like, just because a doctor's a doctor and they're educated, doesn't mean that you have to respect their opinion or whatever. They're a human being. And I felt that he—I don't know—it just wasn't a fit.

Over the years Lynn stayed actively involved with the synagogue, even serving on the board of directors. But she could just never get along with Rabbi Kohner.

I was constantly challenging Moishe, in very rude ways. I would talk over him. I would basically—my body language was very dismissive.

As Josh Rosefsky, Lynn's husband, recalled:

Lynn . . . never liked him. From the moment he stepped on—she just thought—well—whatever she thought, I don't know what it was. But she really had a lot of problems with him. They had a real conflict from the very beginning.

This early personality clash was well known throughout the community. The vast majority of my informants characterized Lynn's antipathy toward Moishe as an endemic source of what would eventually result in communal division.

Rachel Kantor recalled being shocked by Lynn's often publicly-expressed dislike of Moishe:

I had always seen Lynn Rosefsky, you know, very pretty woman—had these children I saw here at preschool. I thought: nice lady. . . . I'm sitting there [in the Temple during a service] and she's like—it was the weirdest thing—I mean, her back was like ich! [imitates someone hunched and seething with anger] And it was like: what? And the venom that she put out was just like: huh? In fact, she did that on a Saturday morning after services to Moishe and I just wanted to go—she just started screaming—and Moishe, you know, was being—when Yohanna would yell at him he would just get, you know, quiet and calm—I think I only saw him one time in my life get mad at somebody. And she [Lynn] just was like—she was saying these things— she was like just being so disrespectful! Just putting him down as not even a person. And he just stood there. He just stood there.

As Judith Malka recalled of Lynn:

She was EXTREMELY hard on Moishe. And I don't know what she did, but I just heard that she was one tough cookie.

According to Camille Vigeland:

Lynn's a funny one. She had a personal issue with Kohner, and she—I think she really had a vendetta against him. And she is a very influential person— they were really big financial backers of Temple Am Israel.

As Hugh Leon recalled:

Josh and Lynn were very important people, volunteering a lot of time, money, and baked goods. They were very active community people. . . . They disliked Moishe's social philosophies and social progressiveness and his social activism. The Rosefskys were so negative about Moishe that they—at least on two or three occasions in the service—afterwards would come up to me and say, 'I can't imagine he said that!' and I would say, 'What?' and they would say something that I thought was either a neutral or normal or ordinary thing—and they would say 'I can't believe he would have said something so awful as that!'—so I mean, their experience of Moishe was kind of like—my experience of the Rosefskys' experience of Moishe was like a carte-blanche negating of anything Moishe had of value.

As Jayme Hoffman recalled:

Lynn, Lynn, Lynn . . . her difference with Moishe manifested itself in absolute lack of kavode for him as a rabbi, and she lost all respect for him. And she has her differences with Yohanna, as many people did.

As John Meyers recalled:

It's no mystery. Yeah, Lynn really ran headlong into Moishe. . . , I would say Lynn was really a prime mover in forcing the split . . . I would say that without Lynn, the split wouldn't have happened. She was a prime mover. Lynn's an intelligent, very capable—and a powerful person. And she was in a position—well, she was a catalyst for pulling in a lot of dissatisfaction.

"That Man Named Moishe"

Some rabbis dedicate their lives to accumulating knowledge, spending their days and nights soaking up thousands of years of recorded wisdom, delving through the deep pages of Jewish law and lore. Some rabbis dedicate their lives to fighting for justice, spending their days and nights immersed in social activism, advocating tirelessly for the rights of the oppressed. Rabbi Moishe Kohner was decidedly of the latter camp.

While he certainly enjoyed studying Torah and Talmud, Moishe's heart often called him away from studying in the *shule* and out into the streets: standing in picket lines, gathering signatures, joining committees, and speaking up for social causes. His commitment to social justice was his hallmark.

Moishe's compassion first asserted itself in social activism when he was a fifteen-year-old high school student in Pittsburgh in the early 1960s. Two black kids, freshmen like Moishe, were getting periodically harassed by a pack of older white kids, seniors. The black kids were being heckled, spat upon, and repeatedly beaten. Although many of the other white students felt sorry for them, none were willing to defend them in the face of the pack of seniors.

But Moishe was so pained by this all-American brand of evil that he couldn't help getting involved. Even though some of the white mob of seniors included respected members of the football team (which Moishe hoped to soon join), and even though Moishe didn't personally know the two black boys, he came to their defense one day when they were leaving school, waiting to catch a bus. Seven white seniors circled the black boys and began the taunting. Moishe came upon the scene, put down his books, entered the center of the circle, stood by the black kids, and put up his dukes. He was spat upon, and took a few blows, but his broad shoulders and thick hands served their purpose. As one of the older boys went to punch one of the black kids, Moishe intercepted and knocked the white boy square in the face. He took several blows in return, but was able to hold his own. The mob soon petered out.

Moishe had had his first taste of active social justice.

When he was eighteen, he moved to Philadelphia to go to college. He wasn't an exceptional student, but he enjoyed the freedom and broadening of college life. And he was well liked by his fraternity brothers.

At the conclusion his first year, he decided to stay in Philadelphia and attend summer school. But all his fraternity brothers went away and he was left all alone in the three-story fraternity house. It was lonely. Across the street from the fraternity was a place with lots of people. It happened to be a mental hospital. Moishe didn't care. He wanted some company. So he moved out of the fraternity and rented a room in the mental hospital for the summer.

Although he met many nice people there, he was deeply disturbed and impressed by the horrible conditions within the hospital and the inhumane ways the patients—often young children—were being treated. He quickly began volunteering his time helping out with the care of the mentally ill. The patients loved him and felt comfortable around him and he soon came to see problems in the way the mentally ill were not only treated, but defined. Many of these patients were not completely incapable of helping themselves. Many of the children had been misdiagnosed. But they were all being treated like animals in one big prison-like facility that was understaffed, underfunded, and unable to properly care for its patients' individual needs.

While continuing his studies, Moishe became more and more involved in helping the mentally ill. While his fraternity brothers were having beer-drinking competitions, Moishe was writing letters to his congressmen. While his fellow-students were experimenting with marijuana, Moishe was soliciting donations from private businesses to help fund the mental hospital. By the time Moishe graduated from college, he had led in the establishment of a halfway house/community care program for mentally ill children and disturbed runaways.

And in 1967, he flew to Israel to help the Jewish homeland defend itself against its neighboring enemies. There he met Yohanna, and soon decided to become a rabbi because, according to his daughter, Dalia, he wanted to be in a position to continue helping people.

When Moishe and Yohanna (along with their three children), arrived in Willamette in the mid-seventies, the Jewish community needed a leader. Moishe filled that role, tirelessly working to build up the congregation. But his energies were not limited to Temple Am Israel. His social activism extended into the wider Willamette community. He joined organizations committed to conserving energy. He joined an organization called Clergy and Laity Concerned (CALC), which fought for justice in Central America. While on the board of CALC, Moishe worked constantly to send humanitarian aid to the victims of U.S.-sponsored death squads in El Salvador, Honduras, and Guatemala. Moishe also joined the local NAACP. He also joined several ecumenical councils, connecting with ministers and priests from a variety of Christian denominations. He and Yohanna also volunteered to serve as emergency foster parents. He became a board member of the Willamette Human Rights Commission.

But Moishe's compassion and social activism weren't merely public. He didn't just serve on committees, chair boards, and lead marches. His home was the heart of his social activism.

Moishe and Yohanna's home was a place of refuge for people with nowhere else to go. Dalia, their eldest daughter, told me that there wasn't a time she could remember while growing up when there wasn't someone staying in their house: a bum, a drug addict, a poor family. "Our home was basically a homeless shelter," she recalled (in half-proud, half-bitter tones).

Moishe and Yohanna would see someone looking needy, perhaps asleep on a bus bench, and feel that it was their responsibility to help the person. Or people would come to the synagogue with nowhere to go. Moishe would call the homeless shelters, and when there were no vacancies, he saw no other choice but to take the unfortunates back to his own home. Turning them out into the street was simply not an option. Sometimes they would just stay for the night. Sometimes they would stay for three months. They would sleep wherever: the living room couch, the floor, the kitchen.

For several weeks they housed a man who had escaped from the Branch Davidian compound in Waco, Texas. For two months they had a man dying of AIDS living in their backyard. For a month they housed an Ethiopian immigrant. For another month they housed a four-person family that had come from the disbanded Rajneesh Puram commune in eastern Oregon. A heroin addict with her infant stayed with them for weeks at a stretch, on and off, many times. Often the people were mentally ill and had fallen through the cracks of the system. Moishe and Yohanna would care for them. In the 18 years that Moishe served as rabbi in Willamette, over 200 people found refuge in his home.

And in addition to his building up of the congregation, his community activism, and his constantly open home, Moishe was actively concerned about the country he was to visit year after year after year: Israel.

Something terribly unjust began coming to light in Israel in the late eighties. The Jewish state began violently repressing Palestinians seeking liberation from Israeli occupation.

For Moishe, love of Israel meant love of justice, and when Israel began beating, torturing, and shooting Palestinian civilians (often children), he knew something was terribly wrong. Moishe realized that the only path for Israel was the path of peace and reconciliation with her Arab cousins and that Israel could not survive if that survival was based upon the systematic humiliation and perpetual oppression of millions of Palestinians. Moishe not only knew that it was simply wrong to inflict such gross brutality on the Palestinian people—because such brutality violated the Jewish ethics of social justice—but he also knew that it was simply in Israel's best interests to end the occupation. He knew that a free, democratic nation cannot function while simultaneously acting as a military dictatorship over millions of people. Thus, his advocacy for peace came from both an acknowledgment of the humanity of the Palestinians, as well as a love for the Jewish state.

Long before Rabin shook Arafat's hand on the White House lawn, Rabbi Moishe Kohner began actively advocating a two-state solution for Israel and Palestine. He became an outspoken voice for Palestinian human rights. He gave sermons, he wrote letters to the paper, he contacted legislators. He invited Palestinian refugees to speak in the synagogue. His best friend in town, Ibrahim, was a Palestinian, and the two of them spoke out constantly throughout the community and the state, talking about peaceful coexistence and the right of both Jews and Palestinians to a homeland. He formed a group, the Interreligious Committee for Peace in the Middle East, in which Muslims, Christians, Jews, ministers, and priests advocated for a two-state solution. He organized a tour of Israel and Palestine entitled "Witness for Peace," in which the group witnessed the refugee camps of Gaza and the West Bank hospitals full of wounded Palestinian children, as well as peace-oriented kibbutzim, Israeli settler outposts, and government agencies.

One member of Temple Am Israel, who joined Moishe on this "Witness for Peace" tour of Israel and Palestine, was Zack Norman. Zack was deeply impressed with Moishe's social activism in the Middle East, and recalled this story:

> I was fortunate to go with Moishe to Israel on a 'Witness for Peace' tour. . . . We spent about two weeks in Israel. Five days at Givat Haviva . . . trying to make bridges between Jewish Israeli and Arab Israeli youth, through encounter groups, information, education. So that's where we were based.

And we did a lot of tours. We went to Ramallah . . . Nablus. We went to Gaza . . . Hebron . . . we went to one of the Gush settlements—it must be around Hebron, I think. It was one of these ardent American-Israeli—every woman having eight kids. They were an enclave of Jews surrounded by . . . well, anyway . . . we all went. We were in two buses, U.N. buses marked 'U.N.' And the driver was Palestinian, as was usually the case . . . all of us went into the settlement . . . and we had tea and we spoke . . . and I happened to go back to the bus to get something—maybe I left my camera or something. And the driver was sitting by himself. And I said to him, 'You want to come inside?' and he said, 'No, it's . . . '—he's Palestinian—'it's not safe.' And we got to talking a little bit . . . and he said to me, basically, that he's afraid of Jews. 'It's dangerous—you can't go among Jews.' He said, 'But there's one Jew'—he's learned—'who is okay.' Who's that? 'That man named Moishe.'

Zack was deeply moved by this encounter and he continued to harbor a great respect for Moishe's compassion for the suffering of the Palestinians, and his social activism on their behalf.

But Moishe's involvement with peace earned him a fair share of heated criticism, too. There were many in the Jewish community who viewed his advocacy of peace with Palestinians as anti-Israel, if not downright anti-Semitic. He was even labeled a traitor by some, a betrayer of the Jewish people and the Jewish state. It was believed by some in the community that the Anti-Defamation League as well as AIPAC (The American Israel Public Affairs Committee) placed Rabbi Moishe Kohner on the top of their lists of Jews gone bad. Indeed, I was personally shocked when the head of the Anti-Defamation League in Seattle told me in no uncertain terms during a phone conversation that Rabbi Kohner was to be considered a troublemaking anti-Semite for his public criticisms of the Israeli suppression of Palestinian human rights. While various clashes of personality had been simmering for some time, Rabbi Moishe's stance on peace in Israel was to become the first major source of overt division in Willamette's Jewish community.

DIVISION BEGINS

Initial Theoretical Considerations—As soon as I began my study of the schism of Willamette's Jewish community, I sought out previous research on the subject of intrareligious division. What had other sociologists discovered about religious schism? I was sure that there would be plenty of existing theoretical and empirical sociological studies analyzing and explaining the sources and processes of religious schism. But I was wrong. There wasn't much. For instance, the impressive *Encyclopedia of Religion and Society* edited by William H. Swatos, Jr. (1998) doesn't even include "schism" as an entry. As top sociologists of religion Liebman, Sutton, and Wuthnow found while conducting their own investigation of the subject:

> Issues of denominationalism and sectarianism have long fascinated soci-
> ologists . . . but they have paid little attention to schisms. While schisms
> have been recognized as a major source of new religious denominations,
> empirical research on the determinants of schisms remains sparse. . . .
> Given the theoretical and practical significance of religious schisms, we
> anticipated finding a large body of published literature on the subject.
> However . . . our own exploration of the major journals, books, denomi-
> national histories, and unpublished papers netted only a few studies
> (1988:343).

Indeed, there is little out there. However, what has been written on the sociology of religious schism—though minimal—is quite interesting. One book in particular that I got a hold of quite early in my research, a book that is the essential cornerstone of all subsequent sociological studies of religious schism, instantly grabbed my sociological imagination: Richard Niebuhr's *The Social Sources of Denominationalism* (1929). Niebuhr posited what would become the seminal sociological theory concerning religious schism, namely, that internal religious division is never *just* about religious matters, but always about something else, something *social.* That is, while two religious factions may claim to be fighting over purely religious matters, when you dig beneath the surface of the stated argument, you can find other factors at play, social factors, that are the true underlying causes of the ostensibly religious conflict.

It must be noted from the outset that Niebuhr was not looking at schism per se, but rather, the multitude of divergent Protestant denominations within North America. He wanted to know why there were so many different Protestant denominations and what the reasons were behind their entrenched differences. Through this groundbreaking sociological investigation, Niebuhr provided the basis for the traditional sociological model that ever after would be employed to explain religious schism. As stated above, Niebuhr asserted that religious division is seldom just a matter of religious opinion. Religious division, he argued, was not merely a matter of conflicting creeds, not simply attributable to a "divergence of opinion between men as to the manner of their soul's salvation" (p.11). Rather, "social forces" tend to be the underlying, determining sources of religious differences. In short, "the division of the churches closely *follows* the division of men into castes of national, racial, and economic groups" (p.6, emphasis added). By showing that various people join various denominations based largely on their ethnic, racial, national, or class identity, Niebuhr was able to illustrate "the sociological rather than . . . theological character of schism" (p.164).

I found Niebuhr's sociological insight fascinating and exciting. He was declaring that while divided religious members of a given denomination might fight over seemingly religious matters (for example, the wording of a prayer, the nature of God, the best way to attain salvation), these fights are actually determined or conditioned or caused by nonreligious factors—preexisting social factors that, once discovered, help explain the underlying, "real" root of the religious division.

"I intend to examine the underlying social sources of this case of religious schism," I confidently declared to my former employer, Eric Kline, the owner of the best used book store in Los Angeles. I was in L.A. for the winter break and had stopped by to pay him a visit. He had inquired about my research on Willamette's divided Jewish community.

"It's the sociological aspects of the schism that I am most interested in," I continued.

"What were they fighting over?" Eric asked.

"Lots of things. The Arab-Israeli conflict, gender issues, gays and lesbians, the wording of prayers. It was a typical liberal versus conservative division. But those were just the surface issues. I want to get beneath those and find out what the *real* sources of the division were."

"What do you mean?"

"Religious schism is never *just* religious," I explained, full of sociological confidence. "There's always something else going on in such religious disputes. For example, class. You'll find that often class predetermines any given religious schism—the rich are on one side, the poor on the other. Or education—the ones with a higher level of education will be on one side, those with a lower level of education on the other. Studies have shown that even though people assert that their differences are purely over religious matters, there are often other things going on. I have my hunches about Willamette's Jewish community. I'm sure I'll find some underlying, preexisting social division there."

"But maybe there isn't anything 'social' going on," Eric countered. "Maybe it was a purely ideological split. Isn't it possible that the two groups just disagreed?"

I scoffed. What a sociologically naive presumption! I preceded to explain to Eric all about Niebuhr's classic book and the few subsequent studies of religious schism that always found some underlying social division predetermining religious schisms.

However, as things would turn turned out, Eric was actually closer to the truth than I was.

Controversy over Israel

Like the rest of the American Jewish community at large, the Jews of Willamette throughout the late 1980s and early 1990s were divided over the Israeli-Palestinian conflict.

Many Jews saw Israel as the perpetual victim of Arab terrorism: a small, struggling nation surrounded by enemies out to destroy her. They viewed the occupation of Palestine (West Bank, Gaza Strip, and East

Jerusalem) as a necessary safeguard. But there were other Jews who were horrified by the images they saw on the nightly news, images of Israeli soldiers opening fire into crowds of rock-throwing Palestinian children. They were shocked by the reports of systematic torture of detained civilians, tear-gassed pregnant women, and the bombing of U.N. refugee camps. They felt that Jews—of all people—should understand the bitterness of oppression and the humiliation of being stateless, at the mercy of an unsympathetic, occupying power. For them, the occupation of Palestine was wrong. Such was Rabbi Moishe Kohner's position. He felt that the occupation of the West Bank and Gaza Strip needed to cease and that Palestinians should be given an independent homeland.

Some of Willamette's Jews supported Rabbi Moishe's vision of a two-state solution. Others did not. Some saw Moishe's activism on the matter as heroic and brave. Others felt he was simply irresponsible and naive.

As John Meyers, who served as congregation president in the late eighties, explained:

Moishe felt Israel was on a misguided moral course. And he felt a moral, a personal moral need to try to get it on a better course. . . . He brought us into these issues and he forced us to confront a lot of moral issues we wouldn't have otherwise—which is probably one of the most important issues of a rabbi. And he really brought us into these issues and made us aware of them. He became absolutely dedicated to the Palestinian cause. He felt that the future—not for the Palestinians, mind you, but for Israel—Moishe was fundamentally and centrally a dedicated Israeli, and he felt that if Israel had a future in the world, it had to make peace with its Arab brothers and sisters. And that's where he was coming from . . . and . . . he dragged a lot of the community, kicking and screaming, to that point. I mean, that was an enormous divisive issue . . . a lot of people felt that he was undermining the state by being critical.

As Julie Schoenberg recalled:

He thought there should be peace in the Middle East, and that we should go to any length to be neighbors with the Arabs . . . and of course, when you have only one temple, you're going to have people on both sides. And the people on the other side felt very alienated, because this is our rabbi saying things, you know, we are emotionally, defiantly against. So it caused a lot of inner schism. That one thing caused a lot of conflict, his stand on Palestinians issues.

One member of the congregation who fundamentally disagreed with Moishe's position was Bruce Wallin. Bruce had been converted to Judaism by Moishe in the mid-eighties. His conversion had had a lot to do with his wife and her desire to raise their children in a completely Jewish home. But even before his marriage to Amanda, Bruce had always felt drawn to the Jewish people. As a teenager he was greatly moved by what he learned about the Holocaust, and he became a strong Zionist, immersing himself in the history and ideology of Jewish nationalism.

Bruce's first feelings of unhappiness at Temple Am Israel came about in response to Rabbi Moishe's pro-Palestinian stance:

Various things happened . . . that led me to become alienated . . . there was a hypercritical view of Israeli politics and Israeli military ventures and an exaggerated sense of sympathy and concern for the Arabs. And not enough concern for the security of the state of Israel . . . a politically correct double standard. That is, wanting the Israeli people to behave in some sort of utopian kind of political fashion while at the same time they're being confronted by several barbaric nations with their goal being the destruction of the state of Israel. I thought it was ridiculous. So I wanted to distance myself from Temple Am Israel.

As Bruce's wife, Amanda, explained:

Moishe kind of mixed up his religion and his politics and used it to—he used his position as the rabbi of Temple Am Israel—to make political statements. And it was uncomfortable because not everybody held those political statements. If Moishe wanted to say something as Moishe, that's one thing. But when he writes a letter to [Congressman] DeFazio on Temple Am Israel stationery, purporting to be the voice of the Jewish community . . . and I think it was brought to a head over Israeli politics. You know, Moishe was a big peacenik, and not everybody in this community was.

Bruce Wallin and Josh Rosefsky had their businesses in common, Bruce with his popular restaurant and Josh with his popular bakery. But they also held similar views in common concerning Israeli politics. Josh was just as unhappy as Bruce with Moishe's activism on behalf of Palestinian rights. Josh, who was a large financial contributor to the synagogue, as well as a member of its board of directors, felt that Moishe's position caused definite division within the congregation:

The only real bump along the way in the eighties was the rabbi became very outspoken in support for Palestinians. . . . They had a Palestinian flag up at Temple Am Israel during some youth conference—and this was during the days when the Palestinian flag was illegal in Israel. So it was a red flag— literally—to everyone . . . and he would just make—blurt out these statements of support or condemnation of Israel's government. Um, that was probably the only really sore—the only real area of tension. . . . He would be interviewed by the media and make statements that represented the Jewish community. That really bothered people. He wrote a letter to Senator Packwood—Packwood was very supportive of Israel. And he also wrote a letter to [Congressman] Peter DeFazio, and representing the community, condemning Israel. And it really bothered people that he did this . . . I didn't like it. I thought it was wrong.

Charles Hoffman was Josh Rosefsky's best friend, but he disagreed with him politically. Charles favored Moishe's advocacy of a two-state solution. But he acknowledged that Moishe's peace activism had a controversial impact upon the community:

Moishe . . . would not differentiate his personal positions from that of the positions of the synagogue. And that tended to get him into some hot water. So he started staking out some very, very strong positions on Israel and Peace Now. . . . Well, there were some people in the community—and probably Josh and Lynn felt quite strong about it . . . there were people that really took a view of Israel that right or wrong, we had to support it. And Moishe didn't believe that . . . so Moishe would engender a lot of hostility over this particular issue. . . . I feel the genesis of the schism was Moishe's strong feelings about Israel and about Israel's obligation towards negotiating . . . land for peace.

Charles' wife, Jayme, explained:

There was a group of folks who felt absolutely ideologically at odds with the rabbi . . . those people with family in Israel, the real Zionist folks, you know, 'Israel right or wrong'—always Israel—and you wouldn't give back an inch of that land. And so there were very heated arguments. And he stood his ground.

Rhoda Fogel agreed with Moishe' position, but recalled the resistance he encountered:

There were some people who—along the way—didn't really like Moishe. They didn't like his politics. They didn't like that he and Yohanna were so supportive of the peace movement in Israel. They didn't like it that his best friend Ibrahim was a Palestinian . . . and they came up in every single congregational meeting that I ever went to. People would get up and start yelling about 'Your wife's a goddamn feminist!' or 'Shame on you—talking to those Arabs!' or, you know, that kind of stuff. Lots of personal attacks.

On one particular Israeli Independence Day (Yom Hatzma-ute in Hebrew), Rabbi Moishe's decision to attend a Palestinian gathering instead of the traditional Temple Am Israel celebration was met with major disappointment and derision by many members of the congregation.

As Rachel Kantor recalled:

I remember this one time it was the Yom Hatzma-ute—Israeli Independence Day—celebration. And where's Moishe and Yohanna? They're over at Palestinian thing [laughs]. And someone said, 'I think that's going a little too far.'

Lenny Levitan recalled:

It was Israeli Independence Day . . . we did this whole event . . . and some kind of Arab group—they were having a celebration. A Palestinian celebration that same exact night. So Moishe shows up at Temple Am Israel for five minutes, wishes it the best, and he says he was going to go there and spend the rest of the night over there. So that really pissed us off. We said, 'What?! This is the rabbi of our shule—how dare he do this?!'

Laura Diamond, who left Utah and moved to Willamette in the late 1980s, recalled her own feelings:

The first Yom Hatzma-ute that I was here, there was a Palestinian flag next to an Israeli flag in the synagogue and that was earth-shattering to me.

Laura was able to find comfort and solidarity with people like Bruce Wallin and Josh Rosefsky, who shared her political views regarding Israel. As she explained:

Part of my relationship with Bruce and the Rosefskys were that I could just be rabidly Zionistic with them . . . so yeah, we were all—we were much more right of center politically in terms of Israel.

Of course Lynn Rosefsky, Josh's wife, had never liked Moishe. And his position on Israel was just one more point of contention. As she recalled:

Talk was constantly about how can he be—how can he be so out front in giving so much attention and energy . . . to these Arabs . . . and we're so— we're so pained by what's going on in Israel, and what we need is to hear clear support from our rabbi. And he couldn't do it. He couldn't do it . . . the level of hurt—people felt so betrayed.

The Rosefskys, the Wallins, and the Diamonds were some of those most angered by Moishe's politics regarding Israel. Arthur and Leslie Edelmann were also opposed to Moishe's position. They joined the Rosefskys in creating a pro-Israel group that wrote letters to legislators and took out ads in the local paper supporting Israel.

But many others within the congregation found Rabbi Moishe's peaceful intentions appropriate.

Josh Binder, a longtime board member who eventually left Temple Am Israel to join Bayt Emett, was initially supportive of Moishe's politics:

I don't think the bad rap Rabbi Kohner got was altogether justified, and that was his very strong outspoken efforts to promote peace in the Middle East, which were—the people who were very hawkish for Israel found very, very irritating, and led them to accuse him of all kinds of treason. I thought he was right, and I don't think, in truth, he ever was treasonous towards Israel. He was always pro-Israel, there was no question. But he did want to put all the pressure he could towards forwarding the peace process and he profoundly believed—and ultimately to a large extent I think it's true—that you can't have peace without justice for the Arabs.

Julie Horowitz, who had always been a liberal political activist, was quite sympathetic to Moishe's public espousal for a two-state solution:

Way back before it was the mainstream, middle-of-the-road, sane point of view, Moishe was advocating for—as a member of the Interreligious Committee for Peace in the Middle East—advocating for a two-state solution to the Israeli-Palestinian conflict. He had the great epiphany in recognizing that Palestinians' longings for national sovereignty were exactly the same as the Zionist yearnings of the Jews. And I got it. I got on board with that pretty fast. I felt that there was no other way to look at the situation, and I worked with Moishe.

Julie's husband, Hugh Leon, was also supportive of Moishe's activism on behalf of peace and he became of member of Moishe's Interreligious Committee for Peace in the Middle East. As Hugh explained:

I think Moishe's—the political stuff about Israel stirred up a lot of people who are ardent Zionists, or thought they were Zionists, or very narrow-minded Zionists . . . and when Moishe and Yohanna spouted their views, people who were against them were so caught up in dehumanizing the Palestinians, and the glorification of Israelis, that . . . I think it was really a matter for them of racism, maybe. . . . So I think the issue of Israeli politics and Moishe was possibly a catalyst for some people to not like him. . . . I suspect they were upset with Moishe's views about Israel and entertaining that Palestinians were human beings and maybe had their own rights and it was possible to have a two-state solution. They wanted to exclude the Arabs and Palestinians. Moishe wanted to include them. I know the Rosefskys—at least Lynn in particular—was horrendously freaked-out about Moishe's politics. And any allusion that Temple Am Israel might be supportive of Palestinian needs really bothered her and Josh.

Susie Kohner, Moishe's younger sister who moved to Willamette in the early nineties, recalled:

I remember that somebody in the congregation . . . I think it was Josh Rosefsky, had the bumper sticker 'God is a Zionist.' And I mean, I knew what that meant in terms of politics, . . . it was taking a stand that anybody who's talking about negotiating is wrong and taking a stand against God. . . . I recognized that Moishe and Yohanna were taking a stand that was very hard to take in the congregation. There were hardly any rabbis around who were able to—or willing—to speak out about the Middle East.

Judith Malka found Moishe's position and activism on behalf of peace both noble and righteous. And she had a deep-seated suspicion of those in the community who opposed Moishe. She felt that the Jews who disagreed with him—and that included not only the Jews of Willamette but the politically established national Jewish organizations—were set on causing trouble for him:

Moishe's stand on Palestinians was always an issue . . . and then there was the issue of the Packwood letter—the letter to [Senator] Packwood. . . . Packwood gave a talk in which he sort of said, 'I feel like I am a Jew'—of course, he was very happy to get Jewish money—'I feel like a Jew, and as a Jew' . . . and he took a very hard, right-wing stance on Palestinians. He said, 'I support Israel on this, this, and this.' Well, Moishe wrote him a letter in which he said, 'You don't speak for my congregation; you don't speak for Jews.' He wrote it to Packwood's office. Packwood—this is my feeling about what happened—is that Packwood then sent this letter to AIPAC. I feel this. The letter found its way back to this community. Various people in this community received the letter that Moishe had written . . . and we later learned that AIPAC had a hit list of people—this came out—that AIPAC had a hit list of people. This later came out that AIPAC had a hit list. And there were a lot of people who, out on the left-wing about Israel, were on that hit list. I believe they tried to get Moishe in trouble. So they sent it to— members of this community who were pro-AIPAC received it and then began giving Moishe trouble. . . . And that was a very tense, unpleasant thing. I think that was really the beginning of some trouble in the community. . . . I think it was the beginning of big trouble.

During Temple Am Israel board meetings, the Israeli-Palestinian issue was constantly debated. During religious, fund-raising, and Hebrew school committee meetings, the Israeli-Palestinian issue was a source of perpetual contention among those with opposing politics. Sometimes friends would disagree, often vehemently. Moishe's activism was continually attacked by some and defended by others. People talked. People gossiped.

Things got ugly when some supporters of Moishe accused his detractors of insensitivity, inhumanity, and racism. How could they defend Israel's atrocities? Weren't the Palestinians human beings? Things got ugly when detractors of Moishe accused his supporters of being misguided liberals, anti-Israel, or even anti-Jewish. How could they defend terrorists out to destroy Israel? Didn't Israel need support at such a critical time, and not criticism?

But what about the Palestinian child shot in the eye in Nablus?

But what about the Israeli child maimed by the bomb on the bus in Jerusalem?

With each passing incident involving Israeli soldiers and Palestinian rock-throwers, with each passing incident involving Hamas bombs and Israeli schoolchildren, sides were clearly marked within the Willamette Jewish community. And this division would only widen.

The Temple Starts to Change

Temple Am Israel began to change in the late eighties and early nineties. Most obviously in terms of size: from a small, humble congregation in the fifties and sixties, through growth in the seventies, it then truly boomed in the eighties.

According to the *American Jewish Yearbook*, in 1968 there were 240 Jews in Willamette. In 1996, there were 3,000. When Moishe Kohner arrived in the mid-seventies, Temple Am Israel had 118 families. By the early nineties, that number had grown to 350. Growth meant many things. It meant an ever-increasing budget for the synagogue, more programs, a growing Hebrew school. But it also meant more diversity and a loss of communal intimacy. With more and more people joining, the congregation's tight-knit feel inevitably diminished and people began to coagulate into their own groups, their own circles. Mother Growth inevitably gave birth to Baby Cliques.

Another change was the ever-expanding openness to, and involvement with, the greater Willamette community, forged by Rabbi Kohner. It was Moishe's belief that the Jewish congregation should not be ghettoized, but rather, should become a well-established fabric within Willamette's wider religious and cultural quilt. In addition to his own personal involvement with various ecumenical and interreligious councils, Moishe opened up the doors of Temple Am Israel—widely—to the rest of the community. He invited Buddhists to come in and share teachings on meditation. He invited Native Americans in to share their beliefs and traditions. He invited a Baptist Gospel choir from the only black church in town in for a goodwill concert.

Another change came in the style of worship services. Before Moishe Kohner, the synagogue ran as a traditionally Conservative synagogue. But throughout the 1980s, with a growing congregation whose members sought diverse forms of worship, Moishe adopted a "we can accommodate anything" policy. This meant that Temple Am Israel departed from its strict Conservative tradition and incorporated other denominational styles, namely Reform Judaism. There was also the occasional Jewish Renewal service—usually held in a back room, led by Yakov—that was more experimental and hippie-like. But the congregation also began feeling out another form of Judaism: Reconstructionism.

One of the most involved members of the congregation was Julie Horowitz. She was close friends with Moishe and Yohanna, she served on various synagogue committees, and she was a regular participant in Saturday morning services, often leading prayers and reading from the Torah. Julie had been raised as a Reconstructionist Jew and her parents had been close friends of Rabbi Mordechai Kaplan, the founder of Reconstructionist Judaism. Through her involvement in the congregation, and her personal ties, Julie began to introduce Reconstructionism to Moishe, urging him to incorporate into the synagogue what she believed was a beautiful and timely vision of Judaism.

As Julie proudly recalled:

Moishe was beginning to talk like a Reconstructionist. He wasn't saying God 'He' anymore. He had suddenly recognized that God was perhaps beyond genitalia, and that to assign a gender to God was limiting and at some level even idolatry . . . um, and I have to confess, I think I had a strong effect on Moishe in this area. Because when I first came into the shule he was saying 'God of our fathers' instead of 'God of our ancestors' . . . he was still saying 'Lord.' And I took him aside one day and I said, 'Are you aware that Lord is a male noun?' . . . because I couldn't handle it . . . I was a feminist . . . and I kind of shlepped Moishe along this path.

Yohanna, Moishe's wife, also began to learn more about Reconstructionist Judaism. She agreed with her friend Julie that Reconstructionist Judaism held valuable insights, primarily in the area of gender equality.

Moishe's embrace of Reconstructionism manifested itself primarily in holding services in which prayers were altered so that they would be completely gender-neutral. In other words, God was never referred to as *He*. The terms *Father* or *Lord* were replaced with *Parent* or *Guardian*.

Additionally, also stemming out of his newly-forming Reconstructionist perspective, Moishe made some changes in whom the synagogue would recognize as a Jew. First, Moishe recognized and welcomed into the congregation intermarried couples. His policy was that the non-Jewish spouse must hold no other religious beliefs that conflicted with Judaism, that the family needed to provide a Jewish environment at home, that the children must be raised and educated as Jews, and that the non-Jewish spouse should be involved with the Jewish community. But complete, official conversion of the non-Jewish spouse wasn't required.

In addition to welcoming intermarried couples, Moishe began a policy of accepting patrilineal descent. Traditional Judaism only recognizes matrilineal descent: a person is Jewish only if his or her mother is Jewish. But Moishe felt that Jewish identity should also be recognized through the father, and thus he accepted as full Jews those whose fathers were Jewish, even if their mothers weren't.

So by the early nineties, Temple Am Israel was a hodgepodge of denominational styles. There were the more liberal Friday night Reform services. There were the more traditional Saturday morning Conservative services. And then both of these were slightly altered to fit the Reconstructionist concept of gender-neutrality in prayer. And finally, Yakov Tish would lead an occasional Jewish Renewal service in a back room of the synagogue.

Yakov also went through some changes in the late eighties. He had come to Willamette as a longhaired cello player named Clyde. In the early eighties he was trained as a cantor and changed his named to Yakov. By the late eighties he got the urge to tread even farther on his Jewish path. He began studying intensely under the tutelage of Jewish Renewal Leader, Rabbi Zalman Schaechter-Shalomi, and he eventually received his *smeekha*, becoming a full-fledged Jewish Renewal rabbi in 1989. This meant that Temple Am Israel now had two ordained rabbis, which gave Moishe even more free time to pursue his community activism. And there was plenty of activism to be engaged in, for in the late 1980s and early 1990s, Oregon became the leading state in the unbridled political persecution of homosexual Americans.

"If There Is a Jew, There Is a Homosexual"

In the mid-eighties, a group formed in Oregon called the Oregon Citizens Alliance (OCA). An organization consisting primarily of white,

Protestant fundamentalist Christians, the OCA sought to outlaw abortion, limit funding to day-care centers, stop the expansion of state-funded parental leave, and, most importantly, ban civil rights protection for homosexuals. It was this last cause that gained them the most notoriety and the highest degree of political success.

In the late eighties, the OCA began sponsoring city and state ballot measures that would make it impossible for homosexuals to claim that they were the victims of civil discrimination. In other words, if a man was fired from his job for being gay, or a woman was evicted from her apartment for being a lesbian, such individuals would not be able to seek justice: the OCA sought to make it impossible for any homosexuals to seek legal redress if they were discriminated against because of their sexual orientation. In addition, the OCA's ballot measures sought to make it illegal for any public school to teach about homosexuality, hire or maintain on the payroll any homosexuals, or have any books about homosexuality in their libraries. Although their statewide measures failed to pass, in 1992 and 1993, 26 of their city and county antigay initiatives passed throughout Oregon, including measure 20-08, which passed in Huckleburn in 1992. Huckleburn is Willamette's sister city, directly on the other side of the McKenzie River.

In addition to sponsoring antigay ballot measures, the OCA sought to persecute homosexuals on a variety of other fronts. They lobbied to keep homosexuals from becoming foster parents. They fought to keep homosexual elements out of public sex education programs. They produced antigay videos and distributed them to churches and schools all over the state. Unbelievable as it may seem, they even published and distributed a book claiming that the Holocaust was perpetrated by homosexuals.

Many people became active opponents of the OCA, and leading that fight was Rabbi Moishe Kohner. For Moishe, the OCA stood for nothing short of traditional intolerance and bigotry. Not only was his own sister, Susie, a lesbian; not only was it his stated goal to make Temple Am Israel a congregation explicitly welcoming of gay and lesbian couples; but in the final analysis, Moishe saw the OCA as an inevitable threat to Jews and any other minority. If they were going after homosexuals today, whom would they go after tomorrow? Moishe knew his history well enough to know that groups like the OCA were dangerous and needed to be resisted.

Through his work in the Willamette Human Rights Commission, as well as Clergy and Laity Concerned, Moishe began publicly speaking out against the OCA. And as with all of his social activism, he didn't limit himself to the public sphere, but brought this cause right into the synagogue. He began giving sermons on gay rights, writing letters and sending home mailers on gay rights, and he actively forged a policy of openness towards gays and lesbians within Temple Am Israel. For too long gay and lesbian Jews had been alienated from Judaism, and Moishe wanted to bring them back in. He wanted Temple Am Israel to be an example of inclusivity, welcoming all members of the Jewish people, regardless of their sexual orientation.

As Yakov Tish explained:

Moishe was very up front in a public way around gay rights, . . . very much involved in that work in a public way: press conferences with other people, . . . a High Holiday sermon on the subject of gay rights. He was direct about what he saw as an issue of human rights. And he was not shy about expressing—he was very courageous, actually. And he took a lot of hits for it. He really did. . . . It was definitely a real challenge for many in the community.

For many people, Moishe's activism on behalf of gay rights was inspirational. As Shira Deener recalled:

He spoke out against the OCA . . . for me, that was Moishe's gift. That was the strength he exhibited: an issue he believed in he took a stand on . . . he had guts. And I felt like those were the things that kept me supporting him . . . he had guts. The whole OCA thing was up and he was in support of any gay couples and that our door was open and that anybody who came in was welcome . . . and I agreed with the stand he took. I thought it was great. And I remember thinking also that that was appropriate for a clergy to do. That's one of the ways you lead your community—is to take a stand. And he had the guts to do it. The tensions in this town were extreme at the time, and there was a "STOP THE OCA" sticker on the door of Temple Am Israel.

Kathy Preminger cited Moishe's fight for human rights as the main reason she was so happily involved with the synagogue:

On Rosh Hashanah, Moishe made what I thought was a wonderful sermon around fighting the OCA and he talked about the importance of—how pleased he was going to be when the first child of a lesbian couple was on the beema. And all of a sudden, this temple was becoming a place where, well, first of all, I could join it—I could REALLY join it—not just write checks and send my kids—because it was a place of social activism. It was a place where people stood up for the progressive issues that I believed in. And for me, that was the only issue . . . I would never have gotten involved if the political, progressive things hadn't been the main thing.

I wondered if all the members of the congregation shared Shira's and Kathy's admiration for Moishe's position. I wondered if perhaps Moishe's activism on behalf of gay rights had been a controversial element in the community's eventual split. However, most of the people I spoke with said that the homosexuality question wasn't much of an issue in the schism. Few expressed any personal feelings indicating that they disagreed with Moishe's stance. Unfortunately, due to the nature of my research, I didn't know if people's reluctance to talk about gay rights was because they actually didn't feel it was important, or because they weren't comfortable telling me what their real feelings were on the matter.

Unlike Israeli politics, which generated overt controversy, the gay rights issue was not so openly debated. Those people who might have been uncomfortable with Moishe's position certainly didn't make their objections as publicly known as they had concerning the issue of Israeli-Palestinian peace.

But there were a few people whom I spoke with who did insist that the gay rights issue was a decisive factor in dividing the community. According to Yohanna Kohner:

It was a big issue. It was an incipient, insidious issue.

Yohanna told me a story about how, when a traveling exhibit on Anne Frank came to town, several members of the synagogue committee responsible for the exhibit wanted to add a small display about the OCA and the political attack on homosexuals in Oregon. However, the inclusion of homosexual persecution in the exhibit was resisted by others within the congregations. As Yohanna explained:

When we had the Anne Frank exhibit, that brought the issue of homosexuality—again—to the floor. Because we wanted a little display on the wall about the homosexuals in Willamette and the issues and the OCA. And Leslie Edelmann wouldn't have it. And Moishe went over her head. He called New York. He called the Anne Frank administration and he said 'We have a Jewish Federation member here who says we can't have the display.' And they called her and they said, 'You wanna quit or you wanna be taken off your role?' They said, 'In Amsterdam there is a display on the homosexuals, in New York there is a display, in every town we go there is a display. If there is a Jew, there is a homosexual. There's going to be the display.' She was furious. She was absolutely and totally furious and she was absolutely determined to get him out of this town—and me, too. There were a lot of people like that. There were a lot of people who could be his friend, be his congregant . . . and then because he took a stand on behalf of humanity—the Palestinians among them—or the homosexuals, he was perceived as broken or warped or destroyed or invalid.

This connection between Moishe's activism on behalf of Palestinians and homosexuals was mentioned by others. Rhoda Fogel pointed out that the same people who disagreed with Moishe's position on Israel also disagreed with his activism on behalf of gay rights:

They didn't like it that he actively worked on peace issues—not just in the Middle East, but locally. They didn't like it that he was vocally outspoken in support of gays and lesbians. They didn't like it is that his sister was a lesbian.

According to Janie Strickstein:

Moishe was very verbal in the community about it . . . as far as the gay and lesbian rights were concerned. I think that came about, number one, when his sister—and I think it also came about with a lot of the whole women's rights, you know, that whole business. Moishe's whole program was to get people to feel comfortable and move them into the synagogue. But he alienated people in doing it, too. There were a lot of people alienated.

"You mean by the welcoming of gays?" I asked.

Oh, definitely . . . now, as far as me personally, I didn't have any problem one way or the other. I think any gay or lesbian person . . . what they do privately is their own business.

Rachel Kantor recalled hearing negative remarks regarding Moishe's activism on behalf of gay rights:

This woman who was in charge of the gift store said, 'I wish he wouldn't wear that beanie of his when he goes and marches in these gay and lesbian advocacy parades, you know, representing us!"

Marcello Bergman admired Moishe's activism on behalf of gay and lesbians, but noted that others did not:

Clearly one of Moishe's greatest moments was when he led the fight against the OCA, which again, is something that—if you probe deeply enough—I think you'll find is one of the reasons why Bayt Emett split off.

"Can you tell me more about that?" I asked.

Well, you'll need to hone your interviewing skills up to get some people at Bayt Emett to reveal their antipathy. I've only heard about it third- and fourth-hand, but about how someone has said, 'Oh, well, gays just run Temple Am Israel.' This was someone from the Bayt Emett..

I asked Bruce Wallin, who resisted Moishe's peace activism on behalf of Palestinians, if he was bothered by Moishe's pro-homosexual stance and whether or not it was a source of division. Bruce replied:

Homosexuality was just one issue in the whole multicultural-Native-American-racism-lesbian—uh—diversity . . . it was a joke. It just became a joke. That if there was any kind of leftist political trend going on, you could be sure that Temple Am Israel—you know what side Temple Am Israel would be on. . . . It was like a 'Saturday Night Live' routine, like a comedy—it was a parody.

But what Bruce Wallin saw as comical knee-jerk liberalism, Moishe took seriously. He truly wanted homosexuals to feel comfortable at Temple Am Israel, and so when a lesbian couple indicated to him that they might want their child bar mitzvahed at the synagogue, Moishe was totally open to the idea. However, others weren't. Judith Malka, who taught at the Hebrew school for over a decade, recalled:

Moishe began to take a fairly heavy stand on lesbians and gays and we began to see many more lesbians coming into the community . . . he gave a High Holiday sermon in which he talked about the fact that there would be—I think he was saying to welcome gays and lesbians into the community, and that very shortly we would have a bar mitzvah of a child from—who was living in a lesbian household . . . he said we're even gonna have this kind of thing, and we should be more open and be thinking about welcoming people like this in our community. That shook people up, you know.

I asked Lynn Rosefsky whether the homosexuality question was an issue. She recalled:

It was lesbianism. It wasn't homosexuality. I mean, it was VERY specific. . . . I don't know what you've heard, but there—Moishe actually—okay, I do know what you're talking about. There . . . there was a woman who was becoming a leader in the community who was a lesbian, a professional in town. And her partner—I don't know if her partner's Jewish—but they were gonna have their child . . . they were gonna have the bar or bat mitzvah, and it was about two years down the road, and so there was this preparation for—more redoing of Temple Am Israel's bylaws . . . and that was going to be pushed . . . because they were changing all kinds of practices, and things that were okay, and so that—that lit the fire. That was the extreme thing—

*the idea that this was on the agenda . . . and it was going to be another com-
promise away from, you know, what Judaism is supposed to represent.*

Lynn's husband, Josh, characterized the homosexuality questions as
part of the early disintegration of the unity of the congregation:

*That was another sort of bump along the road. . . . Rabbi Kohner gave a
talk at one of the High Holiday services in which he tried to finesse the issue
of homosexuality. He said that the statement in Leviticus that a man should
not lie with another man as a woman, didn't really mean—that it just said—
it talked about roles—and he sort of tried to give his own interpretation of it.
And it was sort of met with universal: what is this guy trying to say? Nobody
really respected it. And it just lowered his respect in the community.*

Most Jews in Willamette are not affiliated with the synagogue at all.
Of those who are members of the congregation, most don't regularly participate. But nearly all will show up for High Holidays. Rosh Hashanah
and Yom Kippur are the two days out of the year when almost all of the
members of Temple Am Israel come to synagogue. Thus, the High
Holidays are the most important days of the year, especially from the perspective of the rabbi. It is during the High Holidays when the rabbi has
the greatest opportunity to speak before, and influence, the majority of
his congregation. Rabbi Moishe did not shy away from controversial subjects during the High Holidays, but rather used his pulpit to strengthen
Jewish commitment, express Jewish ideals, and explore what he considered to be the important and relevant issues facing the community.

On Rosh Hashanah in 1992, Moishe felt that it was the appropriate
time—with as big an audience as he ever would have—to speak out about
gay rights. He spoke about the homosexuals within the community; he
called on the congregation to resist political attacks against homosexuals;
and he sought—through some creative interpreting of Biblical text—to
present Judaism as inherently tolerant of differences, including different
sexual orientations. Many were impressed with his courage and were proud
to be members of a congregation whose leader was willing to take such a
public stand against the OCA. However, others were angered. One of those
who was most offended by Moishe's gay-rights sermon was Lynn Rosefsky:

That was infuriating. He gave a sermon on Leviticus 18 [laughs]—I can actually quote the Bible! [laughs]—And it was kind of unbelievable, because what it was doing was—it was very obviously setting the stage for this issue . . . about this couple and their child. And he started it off . . . with how to justify—how actually, if you look at the Torah—if you really study the words, there's justification. The same words that outlaw homosexuality, that everybody accepts outlaws it—you can actually see it as an acceptance of a particular kind. And what that had to do—he always pulled such straws out of the air—was it was the consciousness of the individual. I think the statement in the Bible is that it's a sin for a man to lie with a man as if he were a woman. But if the consciousness—he said —is that he is a man lying with a man, it's okay. We walked out of there—I was not the only angry person that night. Because I was usually the only one that was blowing steam out of my ears on the High Holidays. I remember Josh and I actually walking home, from several services . . . and I was FUMING. Just at the SHEER INTELLECTUAL STUPIDITY—the bunk that was communicated. . . . This time it was—oh, I could have started a riot I was so outrageous—it was so outrageous. And the parties were so clearly drawn. There were people coming out of there saying, 'That was great, that was so great!' It was just—it was horrible. It was just so horrible.

Lynn wasn't the only one angered by Moishe's High Holiday sermon. Camille Vigeland also took objection to Moishe's position. Yohanna recalled this incident:

Moishe made a sermon during High Holidays. And in his sermon he simply said that, 'Ten years from now I could easily have two mothers with a child to bar mitzvah.' He said, 'Our society is transformed and therefore we will have these people.' Camille Vigeland rolled her body . . . she came tumbling down the aisle, and in the process of coming down you could see a whole transformation in her body. By the time she got to Moishe, her nose was twisted, her eyes were screwed-up, and her whole face was held as if she had been hit with a baseball bat. And she bullied him: 'You mean to tell me that you're going to educate these homosexual children?!' And he said, 'Yes. They are our children. . . . I'm going to educate those children.' And Camille said, 'Well, I can't have a rabbi who educates with homosexuality!'

And Moishe said, 'My own sister is a homosexual.'

Camille, who went on to leave her position on the board of Temple
Am Israel and join Bayt Emett and eventually practice completely observant Orthodox Judaism, remembered the situation somewhat differently:

Oh, there was a huge flap about homosexuality. It happened—it was right
around High Holidays . . . it's the homosexuality thing. Yeah, Leviticus.
And the rabbi gave the most amazing sermon that essentially said, 'We can
just forget this mitzvah because, you know, it's the twentieth century and we
don't want to hurt any one's feelings, so we'll just ignore this one.' They
read it but they said it doesn't really mean what you think it means, and we
can change it now because times are different. . . . It was during the whole,
you know, homosexuality and civil rights and the OCA or whatever—look,
there's a civil code and there's a religious code. And in terms of civil code,
everyone should have equal rights. There should be no discrimination for any
reason. But in terms of the religious code, you know, there's—there are
things that are—the Bible was meant for all time, the Torah was given for
all time . . . well, the rabbi wasn't for that. I mean, it was really the thing
to do to be an absolute champion of homosexuality. Because the rabbi's sister is an outspoken lesbian. And very active. So he kind of jumped on the
bandwagon . . . so anyway, I met with him privately afterwards . . . I was
on the executive committee of the board . . . and he said, 'So what did you
think of my High Holiday speech?' and I said, 'Well, to be honest with you,
I don't like you standing up at the pulpit and telling my kids that they can
kind of pick and choose among the mitzvote. Because I think that's a problem with Judaism and that's why we've got assimilation in such alarming
numbers, is that people somehow think they're so smart that they can just
decide what's relevant today and what's not. . . . You know, don't be telling
my kids that they can just decide on their own what's'—he went nuts. He
told me that, um, I'd become a religious fanatic, and you know, he was
embarrassed that he had ever converted me . . . and I was becoming just as
bad as all those other, you know, Orthodox nutsos, and . . . I really—he
just went off the deep end.

"How did that make you feel?" I wondered.

Pretty bad. I thought, you know, I don't get this. This is the guy that con-verted me, for goodness sakes, and I figure I'm living a life that's consistent with Jewish ethics and Jewish history. And here's a rabbi telling me that I'm—I'm irresponsible, I'm a fanatic.

But by this time, there was much more involved in this tense dispute between Moishe and Camille, to be sure. Their differences were not sim-ply over the issue of gay rights. Camille was part of a steadily-forming movement within Temple Am Israel that was at odds with Rabbi Moishe Kohner and his supporters, a movement that would ultimately develop into another separate synagogue across the street.

Chapter   Five

ORTHODOXY

The Aleynu and Then Some

It is our duty to praise the Master of all, to ascribe greatness to the Molder of primeval creation, for He has not made us like the nations of the lands and has not emplaced us like the families of the earth; for he has not assigned our portion like theirs nor our lot like all their multitudes. (For they bow to vanity and emptiness and pray to a god which helps not.) But we bend our knees, bow, and acknowledge our thanks before the King who reigns over kings, the Holy One, Blessed is He. He stretches out heaven and establishes earth's foundation, the seat of His homage is in the heavens above and His powerful Presence is in the loftiest heights. He is our God and there is none other. True is our King, there is nothing beside Him, as it is written in His Torah: 'You are to know this day and take your heart that HASHEM is the only God—in heaven above and on the earth below—there is none other.'

Therefore we put our hope in You, HASHEM our God, that we may soon see Your mighty splendor, to remove detestable idolatry from the earth, and false gods will be utterly cut off, to perfect the universe through the Almighty's sovereignty. Then all humanity will call upon Your Name, to turn all the earth's wicked toward You. All the world's inhabitants will recognize and know that to You every knee should bend, every tongue should swear. Before You, HASHEM, our God, they will bend every knee and cast themselves down and to the glory of Your Name they will render homage, and they will all accept upon themselves the yoke of Your kingship that You may reign over them soon and eternally. For the kingdom is Yours and You will reign for all eternity in glory as it is written in Your Torah: HASHEM shall reign for all eternity. And it is said: HASHEM will be King over all the world—on that day HASHEM will be One and His Name will be One.

— Aleynu Prayer

Traditional/Orthodox version

It is up to us to offer praises to the Source of all, to declare the greatness of the author of Creation, who gave us teachings of truth and planted eternal life within us.

It is up to us to offer praises to the Source of all, to declare the greatness of the author of Creation, who created heaven's heights and spread out its expanse, who laid the earth's foundation and brought forth its offspring, giving life to all its peoples, the breath of life to all who walk about.

And so, we bend the knee and bow, acknowledging the sovereign who rules above all those who rule, the blessed Holy One, who stretched out the heavens and founded the earth, whose realm embraces heaven's heights, whose mighty presence stalks celestial ramparts. This is our God; there is none else besides, as it is written in the Torah: "You shall know this day, and bring it home inside your heart, that THE SUPREME ONE is God in the heavens above and on the earth below. There is no other God."

And so we put our hope in you, THE EMINENCE, our God, that soon we may behold the full splendor of your might, and see idolatry vanish from the earth, and all material gods be swept away, and the power of your rule repair the world, and all creatures of flesh call on your name, and all the wicked of the earth turn back to you. Let all who dwell upon the globe perceive and know that to you each knee must bend, each tongue swear oath, and let them give the glory of your name its precious due. Let all of them take upon themselves your rule. Reign over them, soon and for always. For this is all your realm, throughout all worlds, across all time— as it is written in your Torah: "THE ETERNAL ONE will reign now and forever."

And it is written: THE EVERLASTING ONE will reign as sovereign over all the earth. On that day shall THE MANY-NAMED be one, God's name be one!

—Aleynu Prayer
Modern/Reconstructionist version

Well into the early 1990s, although the Israeli-Palestinian conflict and the issues of gay rights generated controversy, Rabbi Moishe enjoyed wide popularity among his congregants. Many were continually drawn to him and positively affected by his gentle charm. Many were pleased with the successful growth of the congregation under his leadership. Many were inspired by him and joined him in his constant quest for social justice.

However, it is important to realize that most people who pay their membership fees to the synagogue, and are thus technically considered "members," are not actually very involved with the congregation on a persistent basis. At best, they have a child enrolled in the Hebrew school; at worst, they show up to the synagogue once a year during High Holidays, and that's it. Thus, even though a majority of members expressed satisfaction with the synagogue, most of them weren't really all that involved.

Within the inner circle of Temple Am Israel, within that relatively small group of highly-involved, perpetually-active members, satisfaction wasn't secure. Among those members who donated the most money, served on the important committees, served on the board of directors, and attended prayer services on a weekly basis, serious disappointment began to emerge.

At the turn of the decade, some important members of Temple Am Israel began feeling unhappy. Even though they still realized that Temple Am Israel was only a small congregation in the middle of Oregon, the sole synagogue in Willamette, and that the Jews of this community ought to stick together and support one another despite their differences, the impetus towards solidarity began to wane. Dissatisfaction began to grow.

The grievances of this handful of unhappy members were varied. For instance, a few people had personal, idiosyncratic falling-outs with Moishe. Mike Fish, a doctor in town, shared this story:

When I was in private practice in Huckleburn, I had a transcriptionist who worked for me, who turned out to be a very odd, odd person. And some-body who—when I described this person to a psychiatrist who's a friend—the psychiatrist said, 'Oh, I recognize the problem there, she has what's called borderline personality disorder.' She started to, um, leave notes for me along with the transcription, and finally she started adding notes that got longer and longer and more convoluted and . . . really turned odd. She start-ed to refer to me by a pet name that she had created for me . . . it was just, it was kind of bizarre. Then she started following me around—I mean, lit-erally—following me around. And there was one time when I came to my car and there was a lipstick kiss on the mirror. There was another time when she left a note on the front door. Sally [his wife] started to worry that she was going to snatch the kids. It was really—finally I had my attorney tell her to, you know, she had to stop—cease and desist—she had to go away and never be heard from again, and he threatened her sufficiently that she stopped. But before that even, she decided that her maternal, uh, fraternal grandfather was Jewish and that she was Jewish and she decided she was gonna join the synagogue, join Temple Am Israel. And she actually showed up at Simkhah Torah. It was pretty horrible, because I was telling my parents about this horrible episode and how it looked like it was over now and . . . they were out visiting and Sally and I and the children and the parents, we went to Temple Am Israel and there she was. And ugh! We all kind of retreated to one of the back rooms and then left. But . . . Moishe's response to this when she said she wanted to, you know, explore her Jewish roots and join the congregation, he . . . he . . . he . . . opened her—I'm sorry, he welcomed her with open arms. And you know, both Sally and I went to explain to him exactly what was going on—that she really—she really wasn't well. And he just said, 'Well, I just couldn't deny anybody a chance to, you know, become Jewish.' And he just totally . . . totally . . . he blew it. I mean it was a horrible thing.

Here was an instance where Moishe's warm welcoming of all who sought involvement with the congregation—this time an unstable woman with a history of stalking—clearly served to alienate committed members of the congregation; Mike and Sally Fish.

But only a few people spoke of such personal strains. Moishe, for many of those affiliated with the synagogue, remained well loved. Of course, several people had personal fights with his wife, who was notorious for losing her temper, spitting, and getting wickedly drunk at the yearly Purim celebrations.

And in addition to those few people who had bad personal experiences with either Moishe or his wife, other matters began causing disgruntlement. Some people didn't like the politics of Temple Am Israel; they felt it was too left-wing. Some people were unsatisfied with the form or services; they felt things had gotten too "loosey-goosey" and they wanted to get back to more traditional prayer.

Thus, at the turn of the decade, a division began to form within the congregation's inner circle. The board of directors was split between admirers of Moishe and detractors. The influential Religious Affairs Committee was split between supporters and critics of Moishe's religious and political visions. In the midst of the thirty or forty people who would show up regularly for Friday night and Saturday morning prayer services, a chasm was beginning to form.

Rhoda Fogel and Camille Vigeland had both come to Willamette around the same time, had both been converted by Moishe within the same year, and at the turn of the decade, were both on the board of directors of the synagogue. They also both served on the Religious Affairs Committee. Since her conversion, Rhoda had grown closer and closer to Moishe and Yohanna, developing a trusted friendship and similar religious and political ideals. However, Camille had had a personal falling out with both Moishe and Yohanna, and found herself alienated more and more by Moishe's religious leanings towards Reconstructionism, as well as his leftist politics. This caused a strain in the friendship between Rhoda and Camille. They both had had so much in common in their coming to Judaism—they had been raised in Christian homes, they had felt a special calling to Jewish tradition and heritage, and they had both been welcomed and converted by Moishe at around the same time. But now that they were both Jews, they were treading ever-divergent paths.

Josh Rosefsky and Charles Hoffman both came to Willamette around the same time and became good friends, as did their wives, Lynn and Jayme. Their children grew up together. Both couples were proudly involved with Temple Am Israel. Both Josh and Charles served on the board of directors, and both Josh and Charles served terms as synagogue president. Both Jayme and Lynn served on the Religious Affairs Committee, and helped run the Hebrew school for several years. But Charles and Jayme were close with Moishe and Yohanna and supported Moishe's religious vision and social activism. Not so for Josh and Lynn. The Rosefskys were never close with Moishe or Yohanna and were put off by nearly everything they ever did or said, from religion to politics.

Julie Horowitz and Jeff Bronner had both come to Willamette around the same time and had both gotten involved with the synagogue together, as friends and comrades in political activism. Both attended Friday and

Saturday morning services on a regular, weekly basis. By 1990, Julie was feeling more and more fulfilled by the congregation's move towards Reconstructionism. But Jeff disapproved. While Julie and Jeff shared similar politics, when it came to religious practice, they diverged. Even though Jeff Bronner had been raised with no religious training as a child, he steadily found himself more turned on to traditional Judaism, as opposed to the progressive, Reconstructionist brand that Julie so loved.

Rhoda and Camille, the Hoffmans and the Rosefskys, Julie and Jeff—devoted friends and devoted congregants, who slowly began to find themselves on opposite sides of a divide. Rhoda, the Hoffmans, and Julie were close with Moishe and supported his religious growth and social activism. Camille, the Rosefskys, and Jeff didn't get along with Moishe, to greater or lesser degrees, and they had their differences with his religious and political positions. Another member to join the ranks of those growing dissatisfied was Lenny Levitan.

In 1990, Lenny was the epitome of an involved synagogue member: he taught at the Hebrew school, served on the Religious Affairs Committee, and was an active member of the board. Although raised as an Orthodox Jew, he had compromised his religious upbringing since moving to Willamette. Being part of the Jewish community had been more important to him than maintaining certain religious observances. It was always somewhat of a sacrifice. But with Temple Am Israel being the only show in town, he felt he had no other choice.

Yet eventually, for Lenny, the compromise became too great. When Rabbi Moishe began rewriting certain prayers, Lenny felt it was just too much.

As Lenny explained:

Basically, Rabbi Kohner was taking Temple Am Israel—for a long time it was a very standard, Conservative minyan, and that really fit everybody's needs. He really—Rabbi Kohner, for a long time—kept the center . . . basically everybody to the left and everybody to the right really felt comfortable at Temple Am Israel. And he was slowly taking things off to the left. The main thing—now that I remember—was he decided to change the language of the Aleynu. He thought it was not politically correct enough. And, looking back on it, that probably was the number one event that really got us started. Because basically I was on the Religious Affairs Committee at the time. Jeff Bronner was, Irv Mendel was.

"How did Moishe want to change the Aleynu?" I asked.

He wanted . . . to reword it, which is basically the way they use it now at Temple Am Israel. . . . there's one line in particular in the Aleynu that . . . [he pulls a prayer book off the shelf in his living room and reads to me] let's see . . . 'That we don't take our inheritance with theirs, and that they bow down to emptiness and bow down to a god that does not save . . . ', which we say at Bayt Emett . . . and Rabbi Kohner just didn't—he changed—he basically went through the Aleynu line by line, crossed this out, replaced it with other stuff . . . we just felt that—you know, enough is enough. We had to draw the line . . . so the Aleynu was the one that, I think, really catapulted this group to form.

Although Lenny cited the changing of the Aleynu as the issue that pushed him over the edge in terms of loosening his undivided commitment to the synagogue, I suspected that there were other issues at play. After all, if Lenny was on both the board of directors as well as the Religious Affairs Committee, why couldn't he influence the congregation's decisions regarding things like prayers and style of worship? Why did he feel powerless in fighting what he considered to be a deterioration of traditional Jewish practice? If he didn't feel he was in a position to influence Moishe or the congregation, who did he think was? "Julie Horowitz," he declared.

She basically—I don't know how it is now—but she basically ran the shule.

"Really?"

One hundred percent. She ran the shule . . . It's the Jewish women. Temple Am Israel was always run by Jewish women. Powerful Jewish women.

"Can you name some?"

I think Leslie and Julie . . . Moishe Kohner and Yohanna . . .

"She was a big—?"

Oh, she pushed everybody around. She was unbelievable.

I was interested in his mention of "powerful Jewish women" running the *shule*, and so I asked him to elaborate. He spoke about "feminism."

Moishe's so left-wing. He's extremely on the left. Anything traditional—out the window. And he was pushing the shule all the way to left and basically, you know, had a very . . . feminist agenda.

"What would that be?"

Well, partly because his wife is such a, you know—Yohanna is a very extreme feminist. Which, I mean—none of us had any problems with that at all—it just basically, it took the shule from being a middle-of-the-road, welcoming place for everybody, to a very, very extreme left-wing agenda, and people didn't want to be part of it anymore.

"So what were the elements of that left-wing agenda?"

Going through the service and changing all the masculine terms to either feminine or non-gender specific . . . um . . . gay and lesbian rights, you know, that was really his thing—which none of us really had any problems with—but we didn't feel it was appropriate for the rabbi of the community to do that.

"And Yohanna's role?"

Everybody knew that she was—that she was Moishe's voice. It was obvious . . . she was pushing the whole left-wing agenda.

Like Lenny Levitan, most of those I interviewed who went on to eventually form the breakaway Bayt Emett also expressed their feelings about the changing of the Aleynu, and then some.

Irv Mendel, an older member of the congregation who served on both the board and the Religious Affairs Committee, expressed his initial grievances:

> The single most thing in my mind was arrogance and ignorance on the part of the leadership of Temple Am Israel . . . the fact that Kohner could rewrite the Aleynu, a prayer that is attributed to Joshua, that he had the arrogance to rewrite that is—it's just an indication of what was going on. And then they changed the liturgy to make it sexually neutral. Where, when one speaks of the creator of the universe he uses the word 'He', doesn't mean that it's a man, a masculine person. It's just a way of speaking. So they did a lot of crazy things. Which for a while, you know, were tolerable. But then it got to a point where it was just beyond the point of no return.

Ingrid Kessler came to Willamette in 1990. Before moving to town, she had been told that the synagogue was traditionally Conservative, so upon her arrival, she was greatly disappointed. Her first time at the synagogue happened to be on a Saturday when Yakov was leading a Jewish Renewal service in a back room. She was horrified that musical instruments were being played on *Shabbes*, even if only in the back room. So, with an invitation by Irv Mendel, who quickly saw her as a potential ally, Ingrid joined the Religious Affairs Committee in an attempt to counter what she believed was a detrimental diluting of Jewish tradition. As for the Aleynu controversy, she recalled:

> The Aleynu? Yeah, it's jokingly called 'The Aleynu of the Week'—do you know that joke? Yeah, around here people would call it 'The Aleynu of the Week' because it started getting changed a little while we were there but after that I started to hear it was often changing on a weekly basis. And that's when it got to a level of absurdity. . . . It started to get into a thing of like such a dissatisfaction with the Judaism, such an unwillingness to maybe look at it and see where the value is . . . and it turns into 'The Aleynu of the Week.' It was starting to get to be a farce . . . and very little education there. People didn't really even know what they were doing when they were changing it. And there didn't seem to be much interest in education. There was

more interest in changing it to be fitting right with the western value—so nothing was offensive, from a western point of view—without any interest in educating themselves on the Judaism before you do that.

Lynn Rosefsky expressed her dissatisfactions, which, like Lenny Levitan's, included—but were certainly not limited to—the changing of the Aleynu:

There was an increasingly dramatic and dynamic voice of some very liberated women which—everything got angry and hateful. . . . I mean, it was always very egalitarian, but then they started changing words . . . they finally changed the Aleynu and took out this very essential part. And so it got to the point where. . . . There were people that would say the old Aleynu over the new Aleynu, and it was very heavy—very heavy stuff to be going on in a place of worship. A lot of anger.

I asked her to elaborate on the "very liberal women" element:

There was a group of women—and Yohanna was very strong, a very strong part of that—and what we started learning was that Moishe was pretty ineffectual and couldn't make decisions that he could stand by. He was very easily swayed. And these—this was his wife, these were his wife's colleagues— and so . . . the Religious Affairs Committee became a jumble. There were people pushing Reconstructionism. Irv Mendel was the only man on the committee that was arguing for keeping things stable . . . and then I got on the board. I sort of found my way onto the board. And then from the board I found my way onto the Religious Affairs Committee. And what surprised people was that—you know, seventeen years before, when I had been with Yakov and Yoav, I had actually learned a lot. So I wasn't just sort of this harebrained person who was trying to create a reaction to everything. And so I actually had some stuff to offer. I had some knowledge of traditional Judaism . . . and so I became a combatant . . . and uh, it cost friendships, caused some real knock-down-drag-outs. Board meetings were incredibly ugly.

Josh Rosefsky, like Lenny Levitan, was extremely active in the congregation. He had served a term as president, and was on the board of directors. He also happened to be one of the largest financial supporters of the synagogue. And yet he, like Lenny Levitan, felt powerless in affecting the congregation. And also like Lenny, he saw Julie Horowitz at the center of things. As he recalled:

> You had some people who were in key roles at Temple Am Israel who came from very different backgrounds. You had Julie Horowitz who came from a very Reconstructionist family in New York, and she's very knowledgeable and very strong in her views. And she wanted a more—I guess, more Reconstructionist . . . trying out different things. Yakov had always wanted to bring more music in, and that's his love. . . . Rabbi Kohner was also going through changes. He was ordained Reform but he was looking into the Reconstructionist movement, and seeing a lot of things he liked.

Josh continued with the issue of the Aleynu:

> Around 1990 . . . for High Holidays one year, they announced that they were gonna change one of the prayers—the Aleynu. And we're gonna delete this sentence about being the chosen people . . . so I remember people grumbling about it, and I really didn't know much about it . . . so I just started reading on my own about the Aleynu and started learning about how important a prayer it is, and how profound and sublime a prayer it is. It's an incredible prayer, and here they wanted to take out things they didn't agree with . . . and it really—it really bugged me. So I wrote a letter to the board—a fairly strong letter—basically saying that it was wrong to do this and this was supposed to be a community that's open to accepting all points of view and—so there was a lot of controversy about it . . . it was that crack in the wall, that you could have patched up at that point, but it really just started pulling everything apart.

Bruce Wallin, who was a friend of Josh's, was also irritated by the changing of the Aleynu:

> What I saw at Temple Am Israel was a casting aside of this very tradition that I saw valuable. I found it arrogant and repugnant to tinker around with

prayers that were—depending on what prayer it was, it may have been a prayer that was a thousand years old or two thousand years old—to tinker with a prayer or a custom because it didn't seem politically correct in 1990 or 1995, it just seemed the height of intellectual arrogance.

Bruce's wife, Amanda, agreed:

That kind of tinkering with the prayers, tinkering with the language, tinkering with observance . . . did not make me feel comfortable. And I think ultimately what it got down to was a different way of approaching the so-called Holocaust from within—the secularization of Judaism— . . . we are losing more and more Jews to secularization than we lost to the Nazis— . . . so I think that Moishe Kohner . . . took the approach that in order to stop this secularization—this Holocaust—and the loss of Jews, we are going to make our synagogue and our Judaism as open and as inclusive as possible. 'Come on in! If you're a Jew by patrilineal descent, we'll change that! Come on in and just be a Jew. If your kids are from a mixed marriage, come on—bring 'em in, so what if you still have a Christmas tree in your house?! We don't care! Come in, you know . . . it's all okay. If you're a leftist—we're gonna bring in—we're gonna make Martin Luther King Day a haag, you know, we're gonna do whatever it takes to be all-inclusive.' . . . now, I don't agree with that.

Camille Vigeland served on both the board as well as the Religious Affairs Committee. She found the changing of prayers very uncomfortable. For instance, she was irritated by the changing of prayers to make them non-gender-specific, or politically sensitive:

Aside from the fact that they were changing gender stuff to make it neutral, they were also—they would . . . include stuff to be politically inclusive. You know, they included 'Take care of Israel AND ISHMAEL AND DRUZE'—oh, they were always adding about Druzes and this and that. . . . They would eliminate entire portions of the liturgy that were considered to be racist . . . you know, you couldn't dwell too much on being chosen people because somehow that was discriminating against other people. And they were very big on gender issues. So, you know, you could never say 'He'

for God. . . . *It seemed like the more Jewish I was getting, the less Jewish
they were getting. It was really bizarre. . . . It seemed to be more concerned
with political correctness than it did with traditional Judaism.*

Camille was also specifically angered by the changing of the Aleynu,
especially they way she perceived it took place:

*So these influential people, including Moishe, found what to me is some
superficial—what superficially would appear to be sexist or patriarchal or
discriminatory aspects of Judaism—offensive to their political sensibilities, or
whatever. And so they sought to change Judaism because they weren't fash-
ionable. And the last straw for me was when . . . um . . . the Aleynu was
changed. And it was changed by fiat. And I remember exactly when it happened. There was a prominent doctor in town . . . she died in childbirth
when she was forty. And there was a huge outpouring in the community and
lots and lots of Willamette doctors showed up to services on that Friday.
Well, the Aleynu was changed that week. And the excuse given to the
board, you know, the board said, 'What is going on? The Aleynu? You're
changing the Aleynu?'—it was apparently that one of the doctors commented to Yakov, who was then the cantor, that they were personally offended by
the phrase that goes, you know, 'give them false hope, but you haven't made
us like other people in the world, you've made us special and such.' Well,
this person took offense at it. And so Yakov and Moishe—so as not to offend
Christians who might possibly come to our service—changed the Aleynu and
completely dropped that line from it . . . when they changed the Aleynu, I
said I just can't deal with this. It's like we're embarrassed to be Jews. You
know, like I'm gonna go over to the Congregational Church and say, 'I'm
offended that you say Jesus Christ is the messiah, and if I might be there then
I want you to change your liturgy because you might offend me.'—Come
on! . . . it just struck me that they were ashamed to be Jews, . . . ashamed
to behave in a way that was consistent with traditional Judaism.*

Julie Horowitz, who supported the changes in the Aleynu, offered a
completely different version of what happened:

I kind of shlepped Moishe along this path further and further away from these traditional language things, and also tried to talk to him about some of the Hebrew. And so we started saying [recites prayer in Hebrew] . . . instead of saying 'Who has chosen us FROM all the peoples of the earth'— 'Who has chosen us AMONG or WITH all the peoples in the earth.' Honestly, every single primitive culture—almost—has its own name for itself or its own mythology in which THEY are the true human beings and everybody else is just sort of 'Other.' And it's primitive. It's not necessary at this point in human development. And in fact it's destructive to create these artificial barriers that don't further the cause of mutual understanding and respect. So, um, people were concerned about that. So some of that may be my fault. I think Moishe was there—he just needed to have it pointed out to him.

"What about the people who objected to the changing of the language, and the way it was done?"

They were religiously ignorant, which is why they were so threatened when something that they hadn't thought about was suddenly challenged. For ten years at the High Holidays we had been doing an Aleynu—you know, we put an Aleynu into our insert, a paperback additional service that we used— that was a Reform—a modern—Reform Aleynu. It didn't include the original language of the Aleynu—which was the Martyr's prayer! Which was said by people who were having their skin torn off or whatever, who had every reason to be angry. The Aleynu says we must declare the sovereignty of God, who [speaks the Hebrew] has not made us like the other people of the earth [more Hebrew], and hasn't shaped us like the other families of the earth, [more Hebrew] and who has not made our fate like theirs, and has not cast our lot among—you know, it was very clearly saying WE ARE DIF-FERENT. And if you're being killed by everybody, you feel that—we are different. We've got a very heavy load, but we will declare God's sovereign-ty. It was—it's the Martyr's hymn, and as such it has some historical integri-ty. But to get up and say that at the end of every Shabbat service . . . well, I had grown up in a Reconstructionist congregation where we didn't say it. Kaplan put other language in there . . . so Moishe already substituted a Reform version with more tolerant language . . . for ten years we'd been saying this Reform Aleynu that had different language in it. And for what-

ever reason, the Religious Affairs Committee decided to make mention of
that fact in the newsletter or something, before the High Holidays. Big mistake. We had already been doing it for ten years—Josh Rosefsky
FREAKED OUT that we were changing the holy prayers. I mean, Josh
Rosefsky didn't know bubkis about the holy prayers, at that point. But he
didn't want anything to change. I mean—so these people were conservative
politically and they were conservative religiously.

Yohanna Kohner had a spin on the Aleynu controversy that was similar to her friend Julie Horowitz's:

The Aleynu—for the most part the book remained the same. And they put
in an insert. I don't remember the year that they made the insert and put the
insert in the prayer book, it must have been around High Holidays, as usual.
I think it's good to sort of stay away from the concept of chosenness. Also,
the Aleynu is a private prayer said together. So if somebody says Aleynu and
asserts the concept of chosenness, that's fine. If somebody says Aleynu and
does not assert the concept of chosenness, that's fine, too. People can make
choices . . . but you know, people are used to saying things a certain way
and it's hard for them to change it. But I never thought the Aleynu was a big
issue . . . but that's what Bruce Wallin said in public—it was actually in the
papers—that Moishe had changed the liturgy and liturgy that had been recited for over two thousand years. He doesn't know the history of the Aleynu!
[Laughs] . . . That's why I'm saying to you—people were making statements
and talking about things that they didn't know nothing about. Nothing
about.

Zack Norman had grown up in an Orthodox congregation in Buenos
Aires. Like Yohanna, he had been raised with all the trappings of strict
religious Judaism. And Zack agreed with Yohanna that the changing of
the Aleynu was a welcome innovation:

Rewriting the Aleynu was, I think, good. It's hard to sing it, it doesn't fit the
meter or the rhythm much. But understanding the history of the Aleynu . .
. and seeing what the additions were, makes a lot of sense. You know, I
learned from Moishe and Yakov that—yes—Judaism is forever changing.

129

We are evolving. The word is—and it isn't. There are as many interpretations perhaps as there are people.

The division over the Aleynu seemed rather arbitrary, in terms of which people took which side. Lenny Levitan had been raised Orthodox, and was disturbed by the changing of the Aleynu. Yohanna and Zack had also been raised Orthodox, and yet they supported the changes. Camille Vigeland and Rhoda Fogel had both been converted by Moishe around the same time, and both were equally involved with the synagogue, and yet Camille was terribly troubled by the changing of the prayer, while Rhoda appreciated it. Neither Bruce nor Amanda nor Josh nor Lynn had had anywhere near the Jewish education or religious training that Julie Horowitz had received growing up as a child, and yet they were the ones taking a stand on behalf of "traditional Judaism" when the issue of changing the Aleynu arose.

It was indeed hard for me to discern whether or not the Aleynu controversy was actually a straightforward religious conflict over prayer, or rather, a smoke screen controversy hiding other, deeper rifts that had been long fermenting within the congregation. This was a challenge for me throughout my research: trying to understand when a controversial issue was to be understood at face value, or when was it to be recognized as an issue that was merely a front for more "hidden" troubles. For instance, I continually asked myself: was Lenny Levitan *really* so put off by the changing of a few sentences in a prayer, or was it the "powerful Jewish women" who "ran the *shule*" that really caused him greater discomfort? Did Josh and Lynn Rosefsky *really* feel a deep-seated theological and spiritual pang with the changing of the Aleynu, or was it simply a potential issue that they could rally around in order to vent their more mundane dissatisfactions, such as their personal differences with Moishe and their disapproval of his political and social activism? Bruce Wallin, Camille Vigeland, Irv Mendel—how much of their dissatisfaction was purely religious in nature, and how much of it actually stemmed from underlying personal, social, or political differences? Whatever the answer, it was clear that this handful of disgruntled congregants was reacting to something. They were reacting either to the growth of the congregation and the resulting loss of intimacy, or to Moishe's political activism, or to his criticism of Israel's oppression of Palestinians, or to his firm stance on gay rights, or to his gradual embrace of various Reconstructionist tenets, or to his insistence on gender neutrality within prayer, or to his changing of certain prayers such as the Aleynu, or perhaps to all of these combined. Either way, this group began to take form in a shared reaction to perceived transgressions. That was clear. But what wasn't clear was what form or manifestation their reaction would take.

They decided to become Orthodox Jews.

Lenny Levitan Picks Up the Phone

Jeff Bronner grew up in Los Angeles without religion. His family was Jewish, but strictly in the cultural sense. Echoes of Yiddish, remembrance of the Holocaust, socialist values, and a mild disdain for God—especially believers in God—were the elements that had composed his childhood Jewish identity. When he moved to Willamette in his early twenties, he became a political activist, fighting against nuclear power and environmental destruction. He befriended Julie Horowitz, and through her, developed a connection to Temple Am Israel. His connection, however, was largely social. He taught Hebrew school, and his banjo was a well-loved element of each year's Purim spiel. But by the late eighties, as a bachelor in his thirties, Jeff Bronner found himself wanting God.

> I started realizing I didn't know everything anymore, you know? You kind of run out of—you start realizing your limitations. And so I thought, well, gee, what should I do? . . . so I figured, well, maybe I should check into this Judaism stuff.

From attending synagogue on a purely social level, Jeff shifted his focus and began to seek a more spiritual connection. He took some classes on rabbinic philosophy from Rabbi Kohner but found them lacking. He also became disturbed by the lackadaisical feel of the weekly religious services. It seemed to Jeff that most people in attendance seemed more interested in gossiping about so-and-so than communing with God. He still continued to attend services regularly—since they were the only services available—but he also began trying to study cabala on occasion with Irv Mendel.

> And that's how I realized that Judaism had this whole—I knew that there was three thousand years of information . . . and I started to see the unity of all this primary work. Then really I could say I became a theist at that point. I could really understand how Hashem was one, and that there was a thing called—that I would call—Hashem. That was kind of surprising . . . I used to think, 'I'm never gonna catch onto this God stuff.' But when I saw how it all fit together, it made perfect sense . . . so then I started thinking: well, this is really fascinating. All this stuff—Hashem created this universe, and gave all this information over to the Jewish people. I wonder what it would be like to put a little of this into my life [laughs jovially].

At about the same time Jeff Bronner was feeling this internal need to connect with God, Josh Rosefsky heard from Lenny Levitan that there was something he might be interested in on Tuesday nights. Something Jewish. But not something at Temple Am Israel. What could possible be going in Willamette that was Jewish and didn't involve Temple Am Israel? Abe Shibel's Talmud class.

For decades, Abe Shibel, the physics professor who also happened to be an ordained Orthodox rabbi, had been offering weekly Talmud classes at his home. Usually he only got one or two participants, often students from the University. But Lenny Levitan started to show up. And then he brought along Josh Rosefsky. Josh had never even seen a page of Talmud in his life, but he was open to learning. And he liked getting away from the scene at Temple Am Israel. Soon, five or six more people were regularly attending, including Jeff Bronner.

Very few other people in the community knew who Abe Shibel was, but those who did, had a less than flattering opinion of him. Kevin Abrams, who helped run the congregation's finances, said,

> Abe Shibel . . . was not a member of Temple Am Israel and was this—I guess, Orthodox, I think—rabbi lurking in the background. I think he had met Moishe and was extremely antagonistic and negativistic about Moishe. But he was like this ghost figure that I never met, lurking in the woods.

As Zack Norman recalled:

That man . . . well, he always used to go to Portland for services, yes, Abe Shibel. Whom I didn't know, and what I had heard was disquieting to me. But I reserved my opinion, because I really didn't know. . . . I was disquieted because to be froom *is to be counted in a* minyan—*not to go to another city.*

John Meyers agreed with Zack:

Abe is an interesting character. He's been an important background person. Abe is the original 'Other Synagogue Man.' He'll always find something wrong with any community—some reason to not belong. . . . I personally think Abe Shibel is a fairly confused human being, who has a very strong fundamental, Orthodox background, but I don't respect at all his inability to really . . . be part of a community of some sort.

Arthur Edelmann, a professor of literature at the University, never liked him:

He never joined the Temple, by the way. Because the Temple wasn't religious enough for him. My own personal opinion? That he's full of shit. I mean, if you can't join the Temple—you join what's available. You don't have to eat from their kitchen, you don't have to do this—but I thought it's one of the functions of joining the Temple is you're—you become part of the community. He did not—at all. And he was an irascible guy in the first place. . . . He was one incredibly, amazingly uncompromising, difficult personality.

When Judith Malka heard that some members of the congregation were meeting regularly with Abe Shibel:

I was pretty horrified. Because Abe Shibel had been really insulting in his attitude towards the synagogue, and it was treyf *and all that . . . I thought he was rude, he had no respect for us, he had no respect for our practices.*

But those who were feeling unhappy with what was happening at Temple Am Israel needed an alternative. And Abe Shibel provided that alternative. Those who were dissatisfied with Rabbi Moishe or Temple Am Israel's drift towards Reconstructionism came to realize that they actually had somewhere else to go for a Jewish connection: the weekly class led by Abe Shibel. And this Abe Shibel was no liberal, loosey-goosey rabbi, but an Orthodox scholar of Talmud. This Abe Shibel was not out to rewrite prayers, or make God gender-neutral, or liberate Palestinians, or welcome homosexuals. This man was about traditional Judaism—or at least what Lenny, Josh, Jeff, and a few others considered traditional Judaism to be.

While not shirking their responsibilities over at the synagogue, this handful of men began gathering in Abe Shibel's living room every Tuesday night, and truly enjoying themselves.

As Josh Rosefsky recalled:

Abe Shibel . . . he was teaching a class. I don't know if you know his background? Well, he had studied at Yeshiva University—an ordained rabbi—I'm not sure what happened . . . but he decided he didn't want to be an active rabbi. He went to physics, went to Harvard—brilliant man. He once let slip that he studied privately with Soloveitchik for several years, and that's something that very few people did, on a private basis. . . . He wouldn't belong to Temple Am Israel, didn't go to any social activities there, had very few friends . . . and he started having a Talmud class every week. And that really was the basis for Bayt Emett. . . . I got involved during the last few years of it. . . . First of all, he's an incredibly brilliant man . . . and he had a very unique way of teaching Talmud to beginners, which really helps a lot . . . and at the Talmud class he would divert from Talmud and get into discussing the holidays, just before the holidays. And we spent several weeks just talking about the prayer service and what it's composed of. So we were just learning a lot and it was just exciting and it really wasn't even that social a group at that time . . . there really wasn't a strong identity to it. It was just something we liked to do.

While Josh was being stimulated by the education, Bruce Wallin—who also began attending the Talmud class, upon Josh's recommendation—found himself appreciative of Abe Shibel's politics, more than anything else. For Bruce, Temple Am Israel was just too liberal, too concerned with "political correctness." But the political climate of Abe Shibel's living room felt different. For instance, when controversy flared at the University over issues of multiculturalism and diversity within the school curriculum, Abe Shibel took a conservative position, arguing publicly against a proposed minority studies program. Bruce respected Abe's courage in standing up against what he perceived as the University's liberal narrow-mindedness:

> *Abe Shibel was a physics professor and he was a highly visible figure in the anti-multicultural movement at the University, which was, of course, a very unpopular position at Temple Am Israel . . . I mean, it would have been taken for granted across the board in Temple Am Israel membership that the multicultural movement is a highly laudable enterprise and nobody could criticize such a thing; it's benign and valuable and how could anyone be opposed to such a thing? But Abe Shibel is a very serious and principled person, and he led a nearly one-man battle against that movement at the University, and I really respected him for that. He's an adamant, vehement, vociferous man and he made a lot of people angry. He doesn't mince words, and so probably his personality had something to do—and that, it seemed like every issue that would come up, there was this Temple Am Israel liberal kind of view about politics and religion and social and academic issues on one side, and then there was those of us on the other side, to varying degrees. Not everybody's as right-wing as me for example, or Abe Shibel.*

So Bruce Wallin found a political ally, Josh Rosefsky found a teacher, Jeff Bronner found a spiritual guide, and Lenny Levitan found a fellow Orthodox Jew. A few other people began to attend, some more consistently than others, but soon around ten people were meeting regularly. Lynn Rosefsky occasionally accompanied her husband. Camille Vigeland sometimes came. So did Ingrid Kessler.

Usually Talmud would be the sole focus of the class. But now and then the topic of discussion would drift to other matters, such as shared dissatisfaction over Temple Am Israel. And Abe Shibel was quite comfortable critiquing that establishment, as well as Rabbi Kohner, neither of which had he ever held in any respect. As Mike Fish recalled:

Abe wouldn't have much to do with Kohner. Abe would once in a while dismiss him as an idiot [laughter].

As Josh Rosefsky put it:

Abe was real clear about describing why he never got involved in Temple Am Israel. . . . There was a lot of sort of dissonance between Temple Am Israel and what we were learning with Abe. And I think we, I think we never had a lot of respect for the direction that Temple Am Israel was going, and the leadership over at Temple Am Israel, so it was easy to scoff at what was going on there.

What bound this group, then, was a shared unhappiness with Temple Am Israel, a shared dislike of Moishe Kohner, and a growing desire to learn about a more traditional approach to Judaism. And it was hard for me to discern which impulse was more primary: the desire to rebel against Temple Am Israel, or the desire to explore Orthodox Judaism.

Sometimes after Talmud class, the group would go out to Bruce Wallin's restaurant and shmooze well past closing time. Discussions about Jewish identity abounded. Discussions about God, and prayer, and the future of Judaism. Discussions about Israel. Discussions about friendship and community. Discussions about what was going on at Temple Am Israel. For a while the group was limited to these Tuesday night Talmud/shmooze sessions. But when it was learned that an Orthodox rabbi from New York was coming to town for a visit, the group's goals became focused.

Rabbi Ravad, a short, white-bearded, ruddy-faced Orthodox rabbi from New York, travels the world urging Jewish communities to build *mikvahs*. A *mikvah* is a ritual bath that, according to *halakhik* law, is a necessary element of any Jewish community.

It was actually through Rabbi Moishe Kohner that Rabbi Ravad found his way to Willamette. Moishe had been at a conference of rabbis in New York where he was handed a video about *mikvahs*. He brought that video back to Willamette and many people were impressed by its contents.

They felt that a *mikvah* would be a great addition to the community. Someone called the number on the back of the video box and got Rabbi Ravad. That person was Lenny Levitan.

Lenny told Rabbi Ravad that a small group of people in Willamette, Oregon, were interested in building a *mikvah*. Rabbi Ravad said he would be out to Willamette in three days. Lenny was thrilled. But then Rabbi Ravad called back: in three days it would be Saturday—*Shabbes*. Was there an Orthodox *shule* in Willamette where Rabbi Ravad could pray? Lenny Levitan paused, and then assured the rabbi that he would not go without an Orthodox service. After hanging up the phone, he picked it right back up again. He called Josh, Jeff, Abe, Irv, Bruce, and as many other people as he could think of who might be interested in getting together for an Orthodox service on Saturday.

But where could they hold the service? There were the back rooms of the synagogue, which the Jewish Renewal folks used from time to time. But there was also the Oliff house. The Oliff house (named after Rabbi Oliff), was across the parking lot, and was the synagogue's administrative center. It had two offices, a small library, and a small kitchen. That would be perfect.

So Lenny picked up the phone and called up Rabbi Moishe Kohner: Would it be alright if they held a separate Orthodox service in the Oliff house that coming Saturday? "Of course," replied Moishe. "Why not? If you want to do something Jewish in Willamette, Temple Am Israel is the place."

So that Saturday, out in the Oliff house, a separate Orthodox service was held. There were about thirteen people. Ten men were there, to be sure. For Orthodox Jews, ten men—and only men—are the minimum required to compose a *minyan*, which must be present in order to conduct a full *Shabbes* service.

The service was a bit disjointed, but it took place. Lenny Levitan led the prayers and read from the Torah (Temple Am Israel had two Torahs, and Moishe let them use one). Jeff Bronner led a couple of songs. Abe Shibel even attended—his first time setting foot upon Temple Am Israel premises. It was an exciting morning. For most in attendance, such as the Rosefskys and the Wallins, it was the first full-fledged Orthodox service they had ever experienced. It felt enriching, invigorating. And the proximity to the rest of Temple Am Israel congregation only served to heighten the feeling of excitement. After all, there was everybody else out in the main sanctuary doing their usual liberal service with Moishe at the helm, but across the parking lot, back in this house, pure Orthodox Judaism was happening. It felt rebellious, it felt radical, it felt intimate. As Lenny Levitan recalled,

> *So we did an Orthodox minyan, and that was, in my eyes, that was the first—that was the beginning—that was the very essence of the beginning of Bayt Emett.*

Rabbi Ravad left town the next day, but the group realized what was possible. A potential had been actualized. Why not continue? And so they began holding separate Orthodox services once a month in the Oliff house. Abe Shibel suggested that they call their little group Bayt Emett—Hebrew for "House of Truth."

Naming themselves didn't mean they were no longer a part of the congregation. Not at all. They were all still committed members of Temple Am Israel. They still went to services in the main sanctuary throughout most of the month. They still served on the board. They still served on committees. They still paid their dues. But when that one Saturday morning came around once a month, they simply went their own way into the Oliff house. But maybe *simply* isn't the proper word. They went into the Oliff house, but it wasn't simply a situation of separate religious services. It was the first overt, physical manifestation of the schism.

Orthodoxy

Lenny and Ginger Levitan began to seriously practice Orthodox Judaism. Although Lenny had grown up Orthodox, soon after he and Ginger moved out to Willamette, he had slacked off. Ginger had never lived an Orthodox lifestyle, and besides, for a young couple off in Oregon, the rules and rituals Orthodox Judaism demands were easy to let slide. And it wasn't like there were many other Orthodox Jews to offer support or any of the sort of social milieu that Orthodoxy tends to require.

But now they were back into the swing of things with a kosher kitchen at home and the full observation of the Sabbath. Lenny helped Ginger learn how to deal with separate dishes and how to prepare kosher food. They stopped driving from sundown on Friday to sundown on Saturday. No use of electricity, either. Lenny put his *keepa* back on, as well as his *tseet-tseet*. Ginger began covering her head with a scarf and wearing long skirts. Prayers were recited upon waking, before and after every meal, and after various other activities throughout each day.

And they were not alone in this Orthodox immersion. Josh and Lynn Rosefsky joined them. So did Bruce and Amanda Wallin. And Jeff Bronner. And Irv Mendel. And Camille Vigeland. With the Levitans as a model, all these other people began trying to live more Orthodox lives. It was exciting: learning about the laws of *kashrut*, ceasing from all creative activity on the Sabbath, covering their heads, experiencing "real" Judaism.

For the Rosefskys, this immersion into Orthodoxy was quite sudden. Through talking with a friend back East, Josh heard about a conference being held in Ohio for small Jewish communities, sponsored by a group of Orthodox rabbis. With the encouragement of his Talmud class buddies, he decided to go and check it out.

So I figured I'll go. . . . to this conference. And it was real scary to do that, because I had never been in a real formal Orthodox environment . . . and I didn't really know that much about ritual and all these things. So I went to this conference and I was immediately accepted by everyone and just welcomed in very warmly. People were saying, 'Oh! We even have someone from Willamette, Oregon! Nobody knows where Willamette, Oregon is!' . . . you know, people were just . . . very, very warm. And to be in that setting where I was with these people for 48 hours, and it was like being immersed in this whole other world. And about halfway through it I suddenly got this memory of my grandfather—and his shule—and I was four or five years old, standing next to him in shule, and just all of a sudden I just felt like he's standing next to me now. And it was really kind of an overwhelming experience, thinking about that, and thinking that I was going to carry this on. And it was a real uplifting thing—to realize that. And it's carried me through, even to today, thinking that this is important and to carry it on . . . just thinking about my grandfather and carrying this on at least one more generation.

As his wife Lynn recalled:

So he ended up going to this small-communities conference, and I remember him calling . . . on Saturday night, and I was on pins and needles because at that point he kept saying, you know, 'Maybe we should look at Conservatism, you know, this Orthodoxy is crazy.' And I, of course—typically in taking it all on—said, 'No, we gotta do the whole thing. If we're kosher we gotta do this. I'm going to start covering my hair. We'll do the whole thing. . . . ' So he called me—it was like one o'clock in the morning . . . and he was just flying. He said, 'This is it.' I said, 'What do you mean? You mean we're really gonna do it?!' And he said, 'There's no way back.' And I was exhilarated. I could hardly sleep I was so excited.

When Josh came home, he called up his parents and told them that he and Lynn had decided to become Orthodox Jews.

They were really just very negative. They thought of religious Judaism as, you know, black hatters and payisses and Old World, and my mother . . . when we announced to her that we were gonna kasher our home—'Why are you going to do something so retro?' you know, 'What's the point?' So there was a lot of negativity around my entrance . . . into religion.

Despite the negative response of his folks, Josh found plenty of support among his new circle of friends in Willamette. And the Orthodox *Shabbes* services in the Oliff house were wonderful.

Most people didn't know much about Orthodoxy, but there's a sense of just liking the dignity and the, um, I don't know. . . . I liked the quietness, the privacy of it. It was a very dignified service, it was very straightforward. There wasn't a lot of hocus-pocus to it.

Amanda Wallin, who had grown up with an even less religious background than Josh, explained her reasons for becoming Orthodox:

I think as you approach middle age, you realize that—that you're mortal. That ultimately—it will be over. I think that is a horrifying thought in a very real, very primal sense . . . and so as you become closer to the end of life, as opposed to the beginning, I think that we look around and we need something to somehow quell that fear. That's one reason. Another reason is that many of us spent our twenties and some of our thirties . . . in such revolution against the societal norms and mores that we were brought up with . . . and so what we said is, you know, 'I don't want these rules and let's erase everything and find out what it is that we do need.' But . . . freedom is not license. Hedonism certainly is not pleasure . . . so . . . we need moral absolutes. I think we need moral absolutes.

Lilly Hayden came to Willamette while following the Grateful Dead. At age twenty-two she had already dabbled extensively in Native American spirituality as well as Tibetan Buddhism. She got a job teaching at the Temple Am Israel preschool at about the same time the Bayt Emett group was forming. She attended a service out in the Oliff house and was immediately turned on. The traditional service moved her and she immersed herself completely, claiming that it wasn't about anything other than connecting spiritually:

I really believe in the . . . it's just a matter of connectedness. You know, we're in this world and if we live a conscious life—and for me, that consciousness is epitomized in observing the Torah. Performing the mitzvote is really important, because if you are, then you are bringing yourself closer to Hashem . . . you are staying connected to that divine essence . . . the mitzvote—they were given by God in the Torah and . . . it's just goodness . . . I mean, it's all right on.

For Josh, there was a nostalgic element to his exploration of Orthodoxy. For Amanda, it had to do with coming to accept her own morality. For Lilly, Orthodoxy represented a compelling spiritual lifestyle. But for Irv Mendel, well, he joined along with the Orthodox group because he simply couldn't stand what was happening at Temple Am Israel, especially the move towards Reconstructionism:

Because that's a very destructive type of Jewish activity. I wouldn't even call it Judaism. It's a denial of Judaism . . . here is a document, a statement—which I photocopied—that the Reconstructionists put out. . . . Their prayer books delete references of Jewish chosenness . . . hope for reinstitution of the sacrifice . . . individual reward and punishment . . . bodily resurrection. . . . It is assumed that not every word of Scripture is factual or divinely ordained . . . that is not Judaism. Judaism is based upon chosenness, upon belief in a Moshiakh ben David, in reward and punishment, and the fact that every word of Scripture is divinely ordained. And once you deny that—you don't have Judaism anymore.

This move towards Orthodoxy by a handful of members caused a serious stir at Temple Am Israel. For decades the synagogue had been a liberal institution, and most people tended to belong for reasons other than God. They belonged because they wanted to be part of a Jewish social/cultural community, they wanted to send their kids to the Hebrew school, they enjoyed the traditions and the holidays. Few came for the spiritual connection. And suddenly, here was a group of people becoming Orthodox. And who was it? People like Lynn Rosefsky—onetime member of the old hippie commune on University Street! And Jeff Bronner—onetime leftist political radical. And Camille Vigeland, who had only converted to Judaism a couple of years earlier, under Moishe's liberal tutelage. And Bruce and Amanda Wallin, who didn't seem to know the first thing about Orthodox Judaism when they joined the synagogue. In fact, Bruce wasn't even Jewish until he too was accepted and converted by Moishe. And yet now the Wallins were boasting about how kosher their kitchen was.

The rest of the congregation watched the formation of this small Orthodox group with a mixture of amused curiosity and crude suspicion. And it was the latter that would eventually come to dominate.

One Small Battle in the Major Culture War

In 1993, Jack Wertheimer wrote a sober analysis of the state of contemporary Jewry within the United States. He titled his book *A People*

Divided. The title adequately summarizes his conclusion. Wertheimer describes the open hostility between Jews that began to reach a fevered pitch in the late 1980s as a result of the "Who is a Jew?" debate. Since that time, according to Wertheimer, a "great rift" has continued to grow and widen over a variety of issues—the very issues that broke apart Willamette's Jewish community: the role of women, acceptance of homosexuals, tolerance of intermarriage and patrilineal descent, and politics concerning the Arab-Israeli conflict.

Wertheimer speaks of "increasing levels of disunity and heightened polarization" (p.188) characterizing American Jewry; "shrill divisiveness, rather than pluralism, is the order of the day" (p.189). Wertheimer warns that "it is no longer possible—or wise—to dismiss religious polarization as peripheral to Jewish life. The divided world of Judaism imperils the unity of the Jewish people in America" (p.196).

Jewish author Rodger Kamenetz sums up the state of intra-Jewish conflict by pointing out that:

> The wars are mostly of words, but the passions are vigorous and often divide communities and families. There are Orthodox Jews who would never step in a Reform Jewish Temple, and Reform rabbis who denounce the Orthodox as narrow-minded bigots. . . . [V]ery often in Jewish life today the sparks are not from uplifted souls, but from the clash of iron-clad identities (1994:19).

The split of Willamette's Jewish community can best be understood as but one specific manifestation of a broader division that is characterizing the greater Jewish community, and perhaps American culture in general.

Robert Wuthnow (1988), in his analysis of the state of religion in America, describes a realignment within American religious conflict: rather than conflict existing between different religious denominations, Wuthnow argues that the conflict is now primarily *intra*religious, "the division . . . is one that *cuts across* denominational lines"(p.219; emphasis in original). Wuthnow describes two broad opposing camps in this newly emergent intrareligious conflict: "religious conservatives" and "religious liberals." According to Wuthnow, "this division . . . has emerged as one of the powerful symbolic barriers around which American religion has become restructured"(p.13).

In other words, it is not Catholics against Protestants, but rather, (conservative) Catholics divided against other (liberal) Catholics, or (conservative) Protestants against other (liberal) Protestants. And it holds true that for the Jewish community the main sources of conflict are not to be found from relations with Gentiles, but from internal strife.

James Davison Hunter (1991) took Wuthnow's analysis even further, declaring that a "culture war" is pervading American society in general. Hunter notes Jewish "interreligious hostility" specifically, but situates it within this broader socio-religio-cultural division characterizing the whole of contemporary American society.

According to Hunter, there is an ever-increasing division, an ever-growing cultural conflict, between two generalized groups of Americans: those with an "impulse toward orthodoxy" versus those with an "impulse toward progressivism" (p.43). Those with orthodox tendencies are characterized by a commitment to an "external, definable, and transcendent reality," while the progressive-leaning folks tend to "resymbolize historic faiths according to the prevailing assumptions of contemporary life" (p.44). What separates these two groups, then, are opposing world views, or "competing systems of moral understanding" (p.42).

This division permeates nearly all American denominations. A given cultural issue arises, and the two camps find themselves in opposition. For example, in recent decades, the role of women is but one distinct issue that has stirred internal conflict among American Catholics and Protestants as well as Jews.

The schism of Willamette's Jewish community fits neatly within this "culture war" paradigm. On the one side: those with tendencies towards orthodoxy, who would go on to form the conservative Bayt Emett. This group is characterized by its desire to "get back to tradition," and is decidedly suspicious of moral sentiments or religious guidelines that seemed to be driven by contemporary social morality—what they would often dismiss as "politically correct" notions of the nineties. What is important for these Orthodox-oriented Jews is submitting to God-revealed moral guidelines that were presumably established thousands of years ago, which thus gives them an unalterable, intrinsic moral authority. So, for example, if traditional Judaism has clear guidelines concerning the role of women, those guidelines are to be upheld and respected, regardless of contemporary cultural standards or an individual's personal sentiments.

On the other side: those with tendencies toward progressivism, who would compose the liberal Reconstructionist camp dominant within Temple Am Israel. This group is characterized by its desire to be innovative and exploratory in its approach to Judaism and is decidedly suspicious of any attempt to cling to, or defend, perceivedly oppressive or outdated elements of traditional Judaism. What is important to them is adhering to a Judaism that is in accordance with their current social-cultural-moral beliefs. So, for example, if traditional Judaism has clear guidelines concerning the role of women, and those guidelines run counter to their contemporary, feminist-inspired notions of gender equality, then Judaism needs to be mended, fixed, reconstructed.

I asked Rabbi Sapperstein of Bayt Emett to discuss the difference between his congregation's orthodox approach to Judaism, and the liberal approach of the Jews of Temple Am Israel.

In the simplest theological terms, the difference is whether a fifteen-second event in history happened or not, right? If God gave the Torah on Mt. Sinai, then Judaism is one thing. If he didn't, then it could be something else. It could be anything else. But it's not that. So, it all boils down—it essentially all boils down to that one fifteen-second event in history. And a few other principles that go along with that. The eternity of Torah, the eternity of the relationship between God and the Jewish people, the veracity of Torah—that what we have today is the same document, and that includes the oral law. So there's maybe four or five or six principles that, within Orthodoxy, are fundamental. And if . . . and basically where the non-Orthodox drew the line two hundred years ago, beginning two hundred years ago, when they were—invented themselves. So, again, there's a number—it's a very difficult question, because I don't know what to focus on . . . the eternity of . . . . the permanence of the relationship between God and Israel. It says in the Torah that that will never change . . . again, the most fundamental—the event at Har Sinai. If God revealed himself to three million people standing around the mountain and said this is your Torah, and gave it to them, and everybody witnessed it, then Judaism is recorded and the Torah must be true. If that didn't happen, if Judaism was a creation of the wisdom of

Moishe and later prophets or some combination with the Bible being—the humasch being an edited work—as the Biblical critics call it, then it's . . . well, it's a man—there's no authority behind the religion. So it can be—it's malleable, it can be whatever you need it to be. And that is exactly the state—I'm not even saying that critically—I'm saying that's a stated understanding from non-Orthodoxy . . . and on the micro level in Willamette, my take on it is that people's feeling is that the difference between one and the other community, is the authenticity of the traditional Jewish sources.

To hear someone speak from the progressive position, I talked to Julie Horowitz. She was one of the primary movers and shakers in the drive to make Temple Am Israel more of a Reconstructionist congregation. According to Julie (echoing her mentor, Rabbi Mordechai Kaplan), Judaism exists for the Jewish people—not the other way around. Contemporary Jews need not blindly follow a rigidified form of Judaism established thousands of years ago, but should shape Judaism to fit their needs and values as they live in the here and now. Unlike Rabbi Sapperstein's understanding, which views the precepts of Judaism as essentially God-given and unalterable, Reconstructionism views the precepts of Judaism as the outgrowth of Jewish civilization and, as such, open to restructuring as that civilization evolves. As Julie explained:

Judaism is an evolving religious civilization. . . . The Judaism of 19th-century Europe was not the Judaism of the Torah or the Talmud or the Renaissance. . . . It has evolved in every age. And the Judaism that flourished in Spain under freedom was extremely progressive. Maimonides was advanced—was more progressive than Rabbi Sapperstein in his world view. He knuckled under to the pressure of other people of his time, generally Jews from outside of Spain . . . so whenever Judaism has existed in a state of freedom, it has grown by leaps and bounds. And even when we were existing under tremendous duress at different periods, we had always—like a sponge—sucked up elements of the culture around us. There was huge Babylonian influence on Judaism. Enormous Greek and Roman influence on Judaism, and to some extent, Christian influence, although less because of the incredible negativity of the Christian world . . . Egyptian influence in Judaism, my goodness. Lots and lots of what came into the culture after the

Exodus was from Egypt, including Moses himself. And Midianite influence.
It's Jethro who teaches Moses how to organize the society, and . . . so my
answer is that we're simply continuing the organic process of Judaism evolv-
ing and that Judaism has gone through lots of flips and flops. The mehitzah
and the seclusion of women was a Muslim influence that came in later in the
Middle Ages. Um . . . and there's more to learn. Maybe the world—it ain't
over 'til it's over, but if we ossify and rigidify and don't turn over the soil, we
will rot and die. And . . . and that would be a terrible thing.

These two approaches, these two world views of morality and understandings of Judaism, came into conflict. The result was schism. It is
impossible to compromise or reconcile the understanding of a Judaism
based on eternal truth given by God at one point in history with the
understanding of a Judaism based on evolving/relative truth stemming
from the experienced, ever-changing lives of the Jews of a given time and
place.

And the division of Willamette's Jewish community—this impossibil-
ity of compromise—was not an isolated incident. It was clearly one case
of a broader, general division characterizing the American Jewish community at large, and perhaps general American society, as well.

Chapter   Six

THE SCHISM

Mutiny?—By and large, most members of Temple Am Israel loved and supported Rabbi Moishe Kohner. A handful did not. Most members of Temple Am Israel were liberally dovish when it came to the Arab-Israeli conflict. A handful were not. Most members of Temple Am Israel supported Moishe on his social activism around the issues of Palestinian and gay rights. A handful did not. Most members of Temple Am Israel were interested in learning more about Reconstructionist Judaism. A handful were not. Most members of Temple Am Israel accepted various changes to the liturgy, changes that stressed more gender equality as well as less ethnocentrism. A handful did not. This handful tended to be the ones becoming Orthodox.

Thus, when the members of this small Talmud study group led by Abe Shibel began holding *weekly* separate Saturday morning services out in the Oliff house, there was clearly much more that divided them from the rest of the congregation than mere religious propensities.

Some people were wary of their motives, suspecting that their new religious path was much more about rebelling against Temple Am Israel, or expressing shared enmity towards Rabbi Moishe, or the gathering together of like-minded political conservatives, and much less about finding a traditionally spiritual connection to God.

However, for the first few months, things went relatively smoothly. Most people didn't object to these newly-Orthodox members of the synagogue going out to the Oliff house for their own *Shabbes* service.

But then the small group decided that they wanted more. They were now meeting every Saturday on a weekly basis—not just once a month— and they started to feel stifled back in the Oliff house. The space they were using was rather cramped. They decided that they wanted to be inside the actual synagogue. Not, of course, in the main sanctuary, but at least in a back room. After all, why should they be excluded from using their own synagogue? Why should they be stuck out on the other side of the parking lot? They were members of Temple Am Israel just as much as anyone else. Indeed, they were some of the most prominent members. So they put in a request to the board that they be allowed to use a back room of the synagogue for their weekly Orthodox services. The board approved their request.

Every Saturday, then, two simultaneous services were held. The Orthodox service in a back room of the Temple, and the more liberal service in the main sanctuary. Camille Vigeland described a typical Saturday morning at that time, and the differences between the two services:

> Okay, in the main sanctuary . . . there might be drumming, singing, there was always electrically amplified sound . . . and they were using this increasingly impoverished liturgy, you know, always tampering with it . . . and people dressed pretty casual—I mean—slobbily. . . . There was not much Torah learning going on . . . and then there'd be a sermon but it very, very, very frequently had nothing to do with the week's parsha. You know, it could be whatever demonstration was going on . . . whatever is the local cause celebre . . . Okay, in the back room . . . you've got separation of sexes . . . a service that's virtually entirely in Hebrew—the front services were virtually entirely in English—the back was almost entirely in Hebrew. There's no singing. There's no electricity.

The fact that there were now two simultaneous Saturday morning services being held at Temple Am Israel did not necessarily mean schism. It did not mean a division was imminent, or even necessary. Separate groups from within the congregation had gone and done their own thing from time to time. There were the Jewish Renewal folks, who had held separate services on occasion for years, and there had never been a problem. Hadn't the policy of Temple Am Israel always been one of accepting diversity and accommodating a variety of Jewish denominational styles?

But things started to fall apart.

The differences between the two groups became more and more pronounced. And the growing rift became clear on the various boards and committees. On the synagogue board of directors, half were people who studied Talmud with Abe Shibel, took part in the monthly Orthodox services in the back room, and found themselves becoming more and more traditional in their religious orientation. The other half of the board of directors was composed of those who were suspicious of Abe Shibel, were protective and supportive of Moishe, and were becoming more and more Reconstructionist in their religious orientation.

According to John Meyers:

> *The board was totally split. Meetings were shouting matches, and that is probably where the actual split happened—within the board and the people that were running the community from the board level. . . . Personalities and tensions rose and became sort of central . . . and it also focused on Moishe's personality. This was a growing group of people that didn't like Moishe.*

Although everyone had known each other for years, some even intimately, friendships and casual acquaintances suddenly gave way to suspicious, tenuous connections and fragile tolerance. A communal situation similar to what social anthropologist Victor Turner has dubbed the "social drama" began to unfold. According to Turner (1974:15), a social drama exists where "conflicting groups and personages attempt to assert their own and deplete their opponents' paradigms." In other words, an "us versus them" structure began taking hold of the community.

And then, amidst all this growing tension, Rabbi Moishe's contract came up for renewal. The board of directors had to decide whether or not to recommend granting Moishe another three-year contract. However, this decision was compounded when some members of the board felt that it was time to give Moishe a lifetime contract. They felt that since Moishe had been in Willamette for over fifteen years and had led the congregation's growth so successfully, it was time he was granted full tenure.

Most members of Temple Am Israel supported giving Moishe a lifetime contract. But some of his detractors (primarily those in the Orthodox camp) felt that a lifetime contract was not warranted, insisting that not everyone was equally happy with his job performance. The board—divided between supporters and detractors of Moishe—was unable to agree on a contract recommendation. So they decided to open the debate up to the entire congregation and find out just how much support there was out there for Moishe.

A Rabbi Review Committee was formed to assess the community's feelings regarding Moishe's contract. Josh Rosefsky was on the committee, as was his longtime friend, Charles Hoffman. They were now in different circles in terms of their religiosity—and their relationship with Moishe—but they still felt that they would be able to work well together on this project.

The committee drafted a call for written opinions and mailed it to every member of the synagogue. Nearly a third of the congregation responded. The committee received about 100 letters. According to their final report:

> Seventy-one respondents favored granting the Rabbi an extended contract. Ten listed pros and cons with some indicating a limited term appointment. Fourteen recommended that the Rabbi's contract either not be renewed, or, if renewed, that the Rabbi not be granted a continuing contract.

Based on their findings, the Rabbi Review Committee decided to recommend offering Moishe a lifetime contract. But Josh Rosefsky objected. As Charles Hoffman recalled:

> Josh felt very strongly that we should get rid of Moishe. . . . Now, Josh Rosefsky was on the committee, and he refused to subscribe to the recommendations . . . but we did a fairly exhaustive survey . . . we received 99 letters . . . anyway, it was overwhelming support for Moishe . . . and it really got bitter. It got bitter because it became very personal. And it was personal towards Moishe. And, you know, with all the warts and blemishes of a person like Moishe, he did not deserve the sort of personal attack that he got. And I really think that was the foundation of the schism. I think that had—because I can remember arguments here in the living room where we would have—the members of the committee, you know—these were not people that walked into this discussion with a predetermined bias about how this study should come out. They were willing to say, 'Let's look at the data and give the congregation a report that reflects the view of the congregation.' And every time—Josh—every time something would come up, Josh would try and put something negative about Moishe into the report. And there were

six or eight people sitting in the room, and we'd say, 'The data doesn't sup-
port what you're saying!' And, you know, it became very personal. And I
think that that was the foundation of Bayt Emett. It had much less to do with
religious practice, and whole lot to do with how people felt about Moishe.

Charles and Josh argued, and there was certainly more to their dispute
than merely a contract. They were old friends suddenly at odds over
everything from politics to kosher food to Moishe Kohner. And this last
point of contention was the sorest. Charles considered Moishe a dear,
warm friend who had served the community with heart and vision. Josh
considered Moishe a misguided liberal who had steered the community
down a slippery slope of disrespect for Jewish tradition. Feelings of betrayal and enmity marred their discussions, which often erupted into hostile
arguments.

The rest of the committee was also entangled in the debate. But they
sought to put their emotions on hold and simply study the results of the
survey. Given their interpretation of the responses, it was eventually
decided that while they should acknowledge that some leading members
of the community had various problems with Moishe, he should still be
offered his lifetime contract. The Rabbi Review Committee submitted
this recommendation to the board, which voted (narrowly) to accept it.

The Orthodox members, those who had been against granting Moishe
a renewed contract, were furious with this decision. Lynn Rosefsky—who
was on the board at the time—felt snubbed. She called up Irv Mendel,
and they both decided that the recommendations of the committee were
simply unacceptable. They felt that Rabbi Kohner didn't deserve such a
generous contract.

Lynn and Irv decided to hold a "special meeting" in the synagogue that
next week, when Moishe—conveniently—would be out of town. The
purpose of the meeting would be for "all those people" who had opposed
his contract renewal to get together and express their feelings.

As Lynn explained:

We had petitions that were circulating to undo the findings of the Rabbi
Review Committee. Because we felt that it was basically a total bamboozle.
It had been pushed through that Moishe get a lifetime contract. And we

assembled people—I spent nights and nights calling all these members who never showed up, these older people, 'Could you come to our meeting? Could you sign our petition? This is what we're trying to do . . . if people want Moishe to stay, that's fine. But let's really get counted—let's get an accurate count. Let's not have this pushed through . . . '

Under Lynn's leadership, the Orthodox group mobilized, and a week after the board had decided to grant Moishe his lifetime contract, a special meeting was held in the main sanctuary of the synagogue, chaired by Lynn Rosefsky, Josh Rosefsky, and Irv Mendel. However, those in attendance weren't limited to the Orthodox camp. Others had heard about this meeting, and showed up, too. The atmosphere was tense.

As Lynn recalled:

Oh man, people were furious! People were screaming at us—our friends! Charles Hoffman got up and screamed at Josh and I: 'How DARE you do this! Josh, you were on the Rabbi Review Committee, what right do you have to go out of the process?!' . . . There must have been 75 to 100 people. And the personal assaults were intense. I mean—the personal assaults. I had one gal say to me, . . . 'How can you call yourself Orthodox when you serve meat on a cheese pizza at your business!'—I mean, really calling into question—I had several people say, you know, 'How can you own a non-kosher deli and here you're trying to push Orthodoxy!' And we looked at them and said, 'You have no right to criticize us. We're not trying to push Orthodoxy. We're not trying to make this community Orthodox. We just want to be included. We don't want to basically be told that our rights don't count.' And we were being told that.

One member who was supportive of Moishe, and went to the meeting, was Rhoda Fogel. She recalled:

All three of them had been very vocally against Moishe for years. They called a meeting in the sanctuary of the Temple. It was sort of a 'palace coup' type meeting. They called up some of their friends and supporters— they had a petition all drawn up that was basically a 'get rid of Moishe' petition. Of course, I wasn't called about this. But I got wind of it, and since I was head of the Religious Affairs Committee at the time, I went. And one of their major objections was that Moishe had become a Reconstructionist, and in their eyes, that . . . is like being an atheist . . . and it was very bitter. It was very painful. A lot of people signed it . . . some of them were people that I had not seen in a long time. Others were people that were very good friends of mine, and I was astonished when they signed it. . . . They had made specifically targeted phone calls . . . and it wasn't something that was published in the newsletter. It was done on the sly. Otherwise, a lot of people would have turned out in support of Moishe. So I thought that was kind of a dirty deal.

So did Charles Hoffman. Like Rhoda, he too got wind of the special meeting, and showed up. He was furious:

It was after the Rabbi Review Report came out—that's why I was so furious about what was going on. You know, the congregation had expressed its views, had spoken, and the board had taken an action, and then this rump group starts coming in—after the fact—and starts—they lost. They had clearly lost. . . . I remember being there at the meeting. . . . Lynn and Josh were behind it. . . . I showed up. I was there. I don't know if I was invited or not. There were probably maybe twenty people. . . . It was people that weren't particularly great fans of Moishe . . . and I was angry about it. I was really angry. Because they had had an opportunity to speak, and they did speak—they wrote letters to the Rabbi Review Committee, and the Rabbi Review Committee did a very highly professional report . . . it was a quality job. And what they were after was Moishe's hide.

"So did you speak at this meeting?" I asked.

Oh, yeah. I said basically that. I said that this is—this is after the fact. That everybody had an opportunity to put in their two cents—and I remember Josh responding back to me—in tones just as harsh as my tone—that he had tried to get one sentence in this report and had had a very difficult time doing that. And that was true. That was true. But it was because the other members of the committee weren't sure it should be included in the report. And some modified form of the criticism was in there, but it wasn't—it wasn't the sort of criticism that it was so damaging that it would have cost Moishe his job. And, you know, the whole process was enormously painful for Moishe. And I think that that's what was very difficult for me . . . I think based on what he contributed to the community and what he built in the community, he should not have been treated with the level of disrespect and hostility that was directed towards him.

Laura Diamond recalled the animosity this special meeting generated throughout the community:

There was a meeting that the Rosefskys organized. . . . Lynn was on the board— . . . she was on the board of Temple Am Israel—but she was cre-ating a meeting outside of the process. In other words, . . . in most healthy organizations and you're a board member, you bring that issue to the board, in a closed session, and then it becomes more public. Well, Lynn and Josh went outside of that process . . . and I think it was perceived as almost like— what do you call it when sailors go against the captain? A mutiny. Because there's a level of trust when you have been asked to be on the board of a syn-agogue. That you have an allegiance. And they kind of went out of that process and it created a lot of contention.

Indeed, Josh recognized the contention this special meeting stirred up. While at the time he had felt that it had been a necessary action—that those who had their criticisms of Moishe's job performance had a right to air them publicly—he later conceded that the meeting may have caused more harm than good. He recalled the story:

There was a desire to give Rabbi Kohner a lifelong contract. And a lot of people opposed it. And it was fairly bitterly fought in the committee. There was widespread support for him. We got over a hundred letters in support of him. Most of the people said, 'He was there for me when I needed him' . . . . but this was sort of railroaded through—'Let's get this done with, we don't want any controversy to come out of this, let's get this done real quickly . . . . ' So it was rammed through. And uh—I made a strategic mistake. Which was—it was already sort of a done deal, and they were gonna ratify it at a general meeting—and someone from the Bayt Emett group who was oppos-

ing Rabbi Kohner, said, you know, we should have a big meeting and let the community know where we stand. And I said, yeah, let's do it. And we got together, we set it up, we made phone calls, sent out letters, and we got about sixty-five people at this meeting. And it was—it was something that should have been done six months before, when the Rabbi Review Committee was meeting. That would have sent them a message. It was really too late to do anything. And it just raised a lot of negativity and bad feelings . . . it was seen as being sort of disloyal to the community—that this was already going through, why bring this up now? It also put Lynn and I in a negative—as sort of in this role as being the opposition . . . and it really wasn't the right thing to do. It was more for a show than for effect, than accomplishing anything. I was very naive about it . . . anyway, that was a real strong—it put us in the role as being people who were sort of out to destroy things . . . and we probably were, to some extent.

Rumors and the Like

It was still one big community, but hardly one big happy family. The rifts were political, personal, as well as religious. Disgusted with the renewal of Moishe's contract, Lynn Rosefsky quit the board, midway through her appointed term. The Orthodox camp became more resolute in their practices and more distinct in their separation from the rest of the congregation. Many members of the rest of the community became increasingly suspicious of them, viewing them as a group of disgruntled Moishe-haters, out to destroy the unity of Willamette's only Jewish congregation. As a result, the Orthodox group felt themselves ostracized by their own community—made to feel unwelcome in the synagogue that they had worked in and supported for decades.

Anger rose, on both sides. And suddenly, this anger and suspicion gave way to actual manifestations of ill will.

Kevin Abrams had been a member of the community since the mid-seventies. A liberal, both politically and religiously, he supported Temple Am Israel's move towards Reconstructionism, he welcomed the changing of prayers to make them non-gender specific and less ethnocentric, and he joined Moishe—as a friend and fellow activist—in the fight against the Oregon Citizens Alliance. Kevin felt passionate about issues of egalitarianism and gay rights, and he was one who was very suspicious of this small, newly-formed Orthodox group.

Many members of Bayt Emett had been his close friends since the days when he first moved to Willamette. He knew Lynn from the days at the house on University Street, he had participated in Camille Vigeland's conversion process and, as a financial advisor, he had helped Bruce Wallin establish his restaurant. But now things had changed. These people had changed. Kevin viewed their new Orthodox lifestyle with worry and dread. "What had happened?" he wondered. "How could these people swallow the conservative, rigid traditions of Orthodox Judaism?"

Kevin had always harbored a visceral distrust of devout religiosity. And this visceral distrust was extended to the Bayt Emett group. To Kevin, they represented much more than simply "getting back to tradition." He suddenly saw them as fundamentalists and he felt that it was no mere coincidence that while the rest of the world seemed to be getting more dangerously conservative—Israelis were shooting Palestinian children and the Oregon Citizens Alliance was persecuting homosexuals—fundamentalism was suddenly popping up in Temple Am Israel. For Kevin, old friends had suddenly become The Enemy.

He disclosed to me that, as tensions mounted, he contributed to the anger germinating throughout the community by actually spreading false rumors. As he explained:

> Again, this has to be—this part MUST be confidential. It was very painful for me . . . that all this Orthodox stuff was going on when the OCA was revving up its guns against homosexuality, and pushing its agenda. And I'm very concerned about homophobia, sexism. And racism. And classism . . . and the OCA was so awful and hideous and ugly and so powerfully affecting my world, my circle of friends, and possibly me—because I'm Jewish and who knows if Jews aren't next—what's next on the agenda. I took their destructiveness very seriously . . . and the OCA seemed to be a reflection of a growing right-wing movement in the country—it wasn't some bizarre abnormality in origin. It seemed to be a reflection of what was going on in the country and around the world. But when it gets down to your own city and your own block, and your friends—then it's no longer the abstraction.

It's very personal. I felt personally concerned about this. And I couldn't extricate what was going on in the OCA and what the Bayt Emett group was doing. And I saw the Bayt Emett and their need for—their move towards conservatism, Orthodoxy, fanaticism—I knew Irv Mendel was fanatic, and I thought Abe Shibel was fanatic—as an extension of the OCA. But the OCA is outside my house. But the Bayt Emett group was inside my house. And I got crazy. I became very irrational and I said some things that I regret. . . . I had heard a couple of offhand rumors, or distorted rumors, about the Rosefskys' denigration of their workers—the lesbians that worked for them—a lot of lesbians were working for them. And I heard that the Rosefskys were supporting the OCA—and it seemed impossible and ridiculous—but in my craziness I just got enormously angry with them. These had been very good friends of mine. People I really loved, and thought of as brother and sister. And instead of going to them with 'Where are you in all of this?' . . . I decided that they were the enemy. And I even mentioned it to a few people. I don't think a lot of people. But I'm ashamed that I would have done something like that. But I think eventually Lynn heard about that. She hasn't spoken to me. . . . so I let my emotion get carried away. And I was part of the enmity . . . there wasn't good will on my part. I've never apologized. I've never talked to the Rosefskys about my suggesting that they were OCA supporters.

Kevin's deliberate rumor—that the Rosefskys were supporting the Oregon Citizens Alliance and denigrating their lesbian employees—kicked up direct animosity towards Lynn and Josh, and by extension, the entire Bayt Emett group. And the members of that group who heard the rumors were quite stunned. Why were they suddenly being slandered as antihomosexual, OCA supporters?

At about the same time that false rumors such as Kevin's were igniting hostility throughout the community, an article coincidentally appeared in a right-wing Jewish newspaper in New York, the *Jewish Press*. The *Jewish Press* was notorious in Willamette for being rabidly antigay and openly supporting the antigay movement in Oregon. For instance, in the thick of the gay rights debate the *Jewish Press* had run an editorial supporting the Oregon Citizens Alliance and their drive to legally block civil rights for homosexual Americans. The editorial declared, in part:

A statewide referendum . . . in Oregon is attracting considerable national attention. This measure . . . would prohibit so-called gay rights legislation and government (taxpayer) funding of homosexual political groups and activities. It would also forbid the teaching in public schools of homosexual behavior, including gay same-sex "marriage," as being normal. . . .

The JEWISH PRESS, which has long stood for traditional Torah values, hopes that Ballot Measure 9 decisively passes, and urges its readers and friends in Oregon to vote for it. . . .

. . . we affirm that homosexual behavior is condemned and prohibited by our sacred Torah as being sinful and immoral.

. . . Gays and lesbians are no more valid a minority group than are adulterers, people who commit incest, alcoholics and drug addicts. For gay radicals, incidentally, to say that, supposedly because they are born that way, they therefore cannot control or stop their abnormal behavior is absurd! We all have free will.

. . . we urge voters in Oregon to give a resounding victory to Ballot Measure 9.

This editorial, in and of itself, had little to do with Temple Am Israel and the Bayt Emett group directly. However, a subsequent article did. Soon after the above editorial was published, another article on Oregon appeared in the *Jewish Press*. This article was about Willamette, and Temple Am Israel, specifically. And the article was written by the father of one of the members of the Bayt Emett group.

The article "reported" upon a tiny, newly-formed Orthodox group in Willamette, Oregon, struggling against the debauchery of its parent congregation, Temple Am Israel. The article began:

In Willamette, Oregon, a city of some 117,000 people, a small group of dedicated Jews have broken away from a Conservative Jewish congregation, a congregation that has degenerated to such an extent that it now welcomes gays and lesbians into its midst. Disgusted with paganism that parades as "progressive Judaism," intellectually honest Jews in Willamette have formed the Bayt Emett.

If Kevin Abrams' rumors had stirred up the suspicions of the community that the Bayt Emett group was possibly antigay, this article only solid-ified them. Here was a national Jewish newspaper, well known for its bla-tant homophobia, attacking Temple Am Israel for welcoming gays and lesbians, in addition to practicing "paganism." The article decisively served to give unfortunate credence to Kevin Abrams' slander that the Bayt Emett group was indeed antihomosexual.

Whether anyone in the Bayt Emett group supported the article and sanctioned its publication or not, it served to deepen the communal divi-sion and fan the flames of hostility that were flickering with increasing frequency.

And then came the episode involving Rhoda Fogel's husband. Under the tutelage of Rabbi Moishe Kohner, Rhoda had converted to Judaism in the early eighties. Through the years she remained a supporter and dedi-cated friend of Moishe's, and as a member of the Religious Affairs Committee, she worked hard to enact certain Reconstructionist prac-tices, such as ensuring that prayers remain gender-neutral. Rhoda's hus-band, John Cohen, also considered himself a liberal, Reconstructionist-leaning Jew. He, too, was a supporter and friend of Moishe's. But he was also interested in learning Talmud.

Although he had little in common with the likes of Lenny Levitan or Bruce Wallin, John began attending Abe Shibel's weekly Talmud class. He didn't go to socialize or learn more about how to practice Orthodox Judaism. He simply wanted to study Talmud.

So John, an extremely soft-spoken man, attended Abe Shibel's class regularly for several months, keeping to himself and quietly soaking in the words and wisdom of the rabbinic texts.

Then one night the subject of women came up. According to John, horrible things were said. As his wife, Rhoda, told me:

My husband, John, used to go to that group, with Abe Shibel, for Talmud class. Most of the people that were in that group eventually became core founders of Bayt Emett. My husband John used to go to that group because he likes to learn Talmud. . . . One time, he was there, in the midst of all this turmoil, and the subject of what was going on at the Temple came up. And one of the individuals said that 'any woman who wants equality in Judaism deserves to be raped.' At which point John said, 'I object.' Abe Shibel, how-

ever, did not object. Everyone there sided with Shibel. John argued with them. He was the only one! Finally he got up and walked out. You know, [sigh] . . . he loves me. He has respect for women as equals. He wasn't gonna learn Talmud with people with that kind of attitude. You know, Yohanna and I have both been raped in the past. This was very threatening for us—that this was the prevalent attitude among the people who were founding Bayt Emett.

What Rhoda claimed that her husband had heard that night at the Talmud class spread rapidly throughout the community. There were already suspicions that the Orthodox group was antigay—now they were allegedly advocating the rape of women! As Yohanna Kohner recalled:

Rhoda's husband communicated some of this to me. There were members of the congregation who were very antiwomen. All along. And apparently there was one moment when there was a class with Rabbi Shibel and one of the men said, you know, 'a woman who seeks equality deserves to be raped,' or something like that. Well, nobody tried to shut him up. Nobody tried to correct that statement. And it sent a few of us—once we heard that and we knew who said it, and there was this affiliation of Orthodoxy there—that sent us flying. . . . I was raped by an Israeli policeman at the age of 16 . . . . so when this man said that horrible thing about women who seek equality deserve to be raped. . . . I flipped. And I wasn't the only one.

Several women, led by Rhoda Fogel, drafted a letter to the president of Temple Am Israel. One paragraph read:

The environment that this conflict has created makes it difficult for people to present their disagreements, and feel that they will be heard and responded to in a constructive manner. There has been personal harassment in an effort to intimidate people who have spoken out in support of our Rabbi. Rabbi Kohner has been referred to as an ignoramus who knows nothing of the Halacha: " . . . he has nurtured, at Temple Am Israel, every perversity and deviancy that can be found in this town." Also, at Rabbi Shibel's weekly Talmud classes, which are attended by some members of the Bayt Emett group, derogatory comments about our Rabbi, women, and homosexuals were openly made, comments like the above one about our Rabbi, and comments to the effect that: women who want equal rights "deserved to be raped", and that these "women are shitting on men."

The letter, which called for the severing of ties with members of Bayt Emett, ended with the following declaration: "We who tolerate a social climate that permits discrimination actually help perpetuate oppression."

The community was in an uproar over the story. Could such vileness actually be uttered by this Orthodox group? Could Josh, Lenny, Bruce, and the others actually express such misogynistic sentiments? Abe Shibel had such a bad reputation that many who heard the rumors were inclined to believe the worst.

The members of the Talmud study group adamantly denied that any such comments were ever made. They vehemently insisted that the story was a falsification, an ugly rumor, a tactical lie purposely spread with the intention of rousing up more anti-Orthodox sentiment. Like the trumped-up rumors that the Rosefskys were aligned with the Oregon Citizens Alliance, they felt that this was yet another ugly rumor meant to stir up more suspicion and rancor in an attempt to malign them and their move towards Orthodoxy.

Josh Rosefsky recalled:

There was a lot of discussion about the role of women in the synagogue, the role of women in Jewish life. There was never any derogatory things said about women . . . we never found out who said this, or who came away from the class saying, 'They were saying derogatory things about women.' And really the only thing we came up with, which was—I don't know how strong a possibility this was—but that . . . John Cohen . . . he was hard of hearing. And it was thought maybe he heard something wrong and brought it back to his wife and this rumor spread. That's all we can figure out . . . but that did a lot. I mean, that rumor spread all through Temple Am Israel.

Did John Cohen simply misunderstand an offhanded remark? Or did the members of Abe Shibel's Talmud class actually make such horrible remarks during a discussion on the role of women—so horrible that John Cohen, after trying to argue against the remarks, got up and left and reported immediately to his wife and friends the open misogyny of the newly-forming Bayt Emett? I have no idea what the "truth" is, but I know that the incident was monumental. Many members of the community became vociferous in their disgust with the new Orthodox group, and in turn, members of the new Orthodox group became incensed—and deeply hurt—that such notions would be believed and given credence regarding their feelings about women.

In the midst of this growing tension, Shira Deener decided to throw a Hanukkah party open to the entire congregation. She was witnessing this hostile disintegration of the community and found it disconcerting. She wanted everyone to get together and celebrate the festivity of Hanukkah.

The Levitans were invited, along with everyone else, but Lenny decided not to go. His wife Ginger went. She didn't have such a good time, to say the least.

Lenny told me the story:

This was really the event that really, I think, created the big split for us. Um, there was a Hanukkah party at Shira Deener's house . . . Shira and Tom— very nice people. And Ginger—I didn't go. First of all, it was Christmas Eve. It was December 25th or something. . . . I said, 'This does not feel good to me.' First of all, you know, basically—why are they having a Hanukkah party on Christmas Eve? I mean, a bunch of Jews having a Christmas party? So I didn't go. But Ginger went. . . . so basically Rhoda Fogel and Miriam Shimmel attacked my wife—STRONGLY—about Bayt Emett. They said that there's no way that Temple Am Israel—that they're ever going to allow Temple Am Israel to have an Orthodox minyan with a mehitzah at Temple Am Israel. And basically Ginger came home crying. In tears . . . just totally in tears . . . she told me what happened and I couldn't believe it. . . . Basically, you know, Rhoda and Miriam were saying 'Orthodox Jews treat women like . . . like blacks were treated in the South, like slaves.' Just all the stereotypical garbage.

Jeff Bronner was at the party. He recalled:

Ginger Levitan was there and somebody just like—just started taking her on—started saying, 'How can you be in this minyan that degrades women?'

And just went on and on, like attacking her, and other people were, too, like really very severely . . . and they went on and on. For some reason Ginger didn't leave. She just stayed there and took this for a long time, until she was really hurt.

So Ginger had been at Shira Deener's Hanukkah party, and had been confronted by several women who wanted to discuss Orthodox Judaism and its treatment of women. For Ginger, it wasn't a discussion, but an attack. These women were criticizing her for becoming more Orthodox, and for willingly being affiliated with Bayt Emett. Wasn't she aware of the vicious comments regarding women that were spoken at Abe Shibel's Talmud class? Did she believe that women seeking equality should be raped? Didn't she know that in Orthodox Judaism women were treated like second-class citizens? How could she as woman support such things? Some people at the party came to Ginger's defense. Others joined in along with Rhoda and Miriam. The Hanukkah party erupted into a heated debate over Judaism and the treatment of women.

The topic would ultimately be the severing razor that cut the community in two.

And Then the Firestorm

According to Charles Hoffman:

At one point the people in the Bayt Emett group decided that they couldn't abide by the liberalism in the regular service. They wanted to have services in the back of the synagogue . . . and people were saying, 'Well, okay, we're willing to tolerate this.' And then they decided that that wasn't traditional enough, and they had to put up a mehitzah. And then the firestorm.

The communal division had grown steadily, as had the enmity, and things finally came to a head over the issue of the *mehitzah*. Every single person that I interviewed characterized the *mehitzah* issue—or the treatment of women that it symbolized—as the ultimate straw that broke the camel's back. The battle over the *mehitzah* was it.

165

A *mehitzah* is a physical divider or barrier that is customarily placed between men and women during Orthodox services. Since the Bayt Emett group wanted to go all the way with their Orthodox observance, they erected a *mehitzah*—a small wooden, fence-like wall about four feet high—down the middle of the back room. And when it was realized by more and more people (primarily a group of feminist-conscious women), that the Orthodox services in the back room of Temple Am Israel involved the use of a *mehitzah*, the contention became such that it was ultimately unresolvable.

Adam Lowy recalled:

Evidently they put up a mehitzah, *and what I heard was that when that information was spread around—I'm sure it went like wildfire—I think some of the people in the feminist subgroup were very angry about that and didn't think that should be happening in their temple.*

According to John Meyers:

I think the issue that actually caused the split was the separation of men and women—the mehitzah. *The Orthodox group wanted women separated and wanted a division. And a very significant membership said, 'That is morally repugnant to me. I could not belong to a synagogue—we cannot allow a division of men and women in prayer in our synagogue.' And I think that's the issue that actually sent one group packing.*

According to Julie Horowitz:

I think Moishe didn't realize that they had a mehitzah, *or I think he didn't realize the implications. Once he got home and spoke to his wife, I think he realized the implications. And some of the other women in the community were very, very angry. I think the* mehitzah *was THE linchpin from the point of view of our community ejecting that group. Um, and they ejecting themselves. Because it was a very key symbol.*

According to Camille Vigeland, who took part in the Orthodox services in the back room:

The ultrafeminists at Temple Am Israel became very alarmed—including the rabbi's wife—that there was a mehitzah *anywhere on Temple Am Israel property.*

"Even if it was only in a back room?" I asked.

That's right. They saw it as an offense to God and to all, you know, politically correct Jews and it couldn't be allowed.

Lynn Rosefsky, like Camille, saw the whole controversy stemming from the actions of overly-sensitive women. As she explained:

Well, mostly it was just very, very high-minded feminists—I'm sorry for the titles. I don't like doing that. It is a dismissive thing to do. But they were going for the jugular. . . . These women basically had come through horribly abusive relationships with men. And they didn't like ANYTHING that smacked of patriarchy . . . so these gals—one, oh she's—unbelievable depths of hostility—apparently had been abused . . . but anyway, so these women—it became sort of a blood-fest.

As David Decker recalled:

Yeah, the mehitzah *did become the major breaking point . . . I know the majority of the congregation was willing to take a live and let live attitude, . . . but there was definitely a core group who felt that the* mehitzah—*anywhere on synagogue premises—was a violation of what Temple Am Israel was supposed to represent . . . because it implied an implicit recognition by the Temple, or by the congregation—of which they were a part—of the separation of men and women. They felt that since the constitution and the bylaws of the synagogue recognized the equal participation of men and women,. . . it was a violation of both the spirit and the law of the synagogue—and they shouldn't be allowed. . . . It got very heated.*

According to Joanna Edelstein:

There was a group of feminists—I guess you could label them that way—

who were very offended by the fact that we had a mehitzah *in the back room, and they could not walk into the synagogue and feel comfortable. The doors were closed, nobody could see it—but they couldn't walk into the synagogue and feel comfortable. They couldn't worship when they knew that this horrible, degrading discrimination was going on in the back room . . . now, what bothered me was . . . the women who were participating in the back room were participating completely voluntarily. This was nothing that we felt we were being discriminated against, or degrading, or whatever. And what they were basically saying was—that they were denying us our right to worship the way we wanted in the name of not discriminating against us, when in fact, I thought they were. So there was a lot of anger about that . . . I think that's a lot of what led to the split.*

Mike Fish recalled:

It was really a fight with a group of principally women . . . finally this group of people became so unhappy and so incensed, one person actually said that they felt physically ill each time they walked into Temple Am Israel and knew that the Bayt Emett group was davening in the back room.

For a handful of members of Temple Am Israel, the mehitzah was simply unacceptable. It was an abomination, an evil. It represented a form of sexist discrimination that ran completely counter to the well-established liberal ideals of the congregation.

A small group formed, largely made up of women, in opposition to the Orthodox group, based on the fact that the latter was non-egalitarian and used a mehitzah. They became known as the "anti-mehitzah" group.

This small anti-mehitzah group, led primarily by Rhoda Fogel and Yohanna Kohner, felt that allowing for a diversity of Jewish practices under the roof of Temple Am Israel was one thing, but allowing antiegalitarian practices was quite another. To this small anti-mehitzah group, the ideals of gender equality were more important than the ideals of tolerance. To tolerate gender inequality was simply beyond the pale of Temple Am Israel's policy of welcoming diversity.

Over the years Temple Am Israel had developed a strict policy of male/female egalitarianism. Prayers had been rewritten so as not to be exclusively male in nature. References to God were always couched in gender-neutral terms. Both men and women were allowed full and equal participation in the services. Both men and women were allowed to read from the Torah. Both men and women could wear the same religious garb, such as *keepote* and *talliseem*. And to this small group of women, the use of a *mehitzah* to separate men from women negated all that Temple Am Israel stood for.

As Yohanna explained:

This synagogue was always democratic. This synagogue never had inequality. So all of a sudden, what you're doing by having a mehitzah *is inviting inequality into equality. And I know that I have to be a tolerant human being, but . . . I will not tolerate intolerance . . . and you could see that was the beginning of everything . . . the issue of sitting apart polarized the whole community. The issue of* mehitzah.

Rachel Kantor, one of Yohanna's allies, explained:

We were not able to tolerate intolerance, is what it really came down to. It was very difficult to tolerate something in which women were not accepted on one side—that there was a place actually in the synagogue space that we could not be. That was really the deal. It was that the men were counted and the women weren't. It was running against everything that Temple Am Israel stood for. My friend, Rose, went one time. She didn't know, and she went in the back, where the Bayt Emett service was. And she sat on the men's side—not knowing. She was feeling so good, she said, and then someone came over and told her that she was on the wrong side. She went on the other side, she sat down, and she just started crying. It was just—it is like the back of the bus kind of thing.

Rhoda Fogel—whose husband John had recently quit the Talmud class in response to statements he had heard advocating the rape of women— was adamantly opposed to the *mehitzah*. Even though it was in a back room, Rhoda felt it shouldn't be allowed anywhere within Temple Am Israel. She explained:

What was really going on was that they put up a mehitzah. Which is something that Moishe had been opposed to. And they did it anyhow. It was kind of a direct challenge to his authority as the rabbi. And they refused to count women in the minyan. And, you know, Moishe and Yohanna were very strong on egalitarianism . . . and there were a lot of arguments over the whole mehitzah issue—many. My husband, John, finally resigned over that issue because he said he would not—he wrote a letter to the board saying he would not be a member of an organization that's gonna discriminate on the basis of gender.

It is important to realize that along with the *mehitzah*—the physical barrier between men and women—there exist many other issues of gender regulation in an Orthodox service. Not only must men and women sit separately, but women's voices must not be heard during prayers and songs, women must not wear the same holy garb as men (*keepote* and *talliseem*), women are barred from publicly reading the Torah (the highest honor of the *Shabbes* service), women are not allowed to lead any prayers, and finally, women do not count in the making up of a *minyan*. A *minyan* is a group of ten men—and only men—necessary in order to hold a full *Shabbes* service. Israeli scholar Susan Sered (1992: 15) succinctly sums up the gender imbalance of traditional Judaism:

> Traditional Judaism addresses the deity in the masculine gender, teaches that God's message was conveyed primarily through men (Abraham, Moses), bestows the privilege of leadership (rabbinate and priesthood) upon men, has traditionally excluded women from such central areas of religious expression as study and vocal participation in the synagogue, places prohibitions upon menstruating and postpartum women, and discriminates against women in matters of inheritance. Men write the prayers and make the laws . . .
>
> . . . Women are systematically barred from access to Jewish knowledge. In the Talmud, it is written that it is preferable to burn the Torah than teach it to a woman . . .

Thus, for many, the *mehitzah* was merely the tip of the patriarchal iceberg.

Hugh Leon was one of the few men that joined the anti-*mehitzah* group. As he explained:

Moishe and Yakov and Julie [Hugh's wife] had worked very hard over the whole issue of women's equality and gender-neutral language. Julie was radical about the need for women to be seen as equal . . . so a mehitzah—*although Orthodox people say, 'Oh, it's really sweet and nice because the women get to pray in their own fashion'—is too much of a political statement for Julie and for many other people. And it isn't just the* mehitzah. *The* mehitzah *also declared that women are not only not to be seen and heard, but they cannot be counted for the* minyan. *That is a political position. Maybe not being seen and praying by themselves isn't a political thing, but not being counted as part of the Jewish community really is unacceptable.*

Charles Hoffman was another man who supported the anti-*mehitzah* group:

A number of women felt very, very strongly that the mehitzah *was just evil, and that Temple Am Israel should not tolerate having the* mehitzah *in the four walls of the synagogue. And I tended to agree with them. It just struck me that the congregation . . . I saw it as a community issue. That is, the community decides the values that govern the religious practice. And consequently, if the congregation . . . were to make a decision that gender equality was of value for the congregation, then we shouldn't have the* mehitzah, *. . . and I tried to convince Moishe that this was not a rabbinic issue, it was not a religious issue—it was a community issue.*

Despite growing objections, the Bayt Emett group continued to use the *mehitzah* during prayer services in the back room. So every Saturday morning at Temple Am Israel, in the main sanctuary was the egalitarian service with rewritten prayers, non-gender-specific liturgy, men and women wearing the same holy garb, conducting the same practices throughout the service, and sitting together. In the back room was the Orthodox service, with only men leading traditional (non-revised) prayers, only men wearing certain holy garb, only men conducting various practices, and men and women sitting separately—divided by a *mehitzah*.

And the situation could not continue. The anti-*mehitzah* group became more and more vociferous. Either the *mehitzah* had to go, or the Orthodox group would have to leave. It didn't matter that the Orthodox service was in a back room, it didn't matter that the members of Bayt Emett were some of the most involved and dedicated members of the congregation, it didn't matter that Temple Am Israel had always prided itself on being a congregation open to diversity, it didn't matter that Rabbi Moishe had initially given them the permission to use the back room on Saturday mornings. They had erected a *mehitzah*, and to these women, the *mehitzah*—and all the restrictions against women that went with it—ran counter to everything Temple Am Israel stood for.

The members of the Orthodox group were shocked and angered by the demands of these women. Hadn't Temple Am Israel welcomed all kinds of Jewish practices? Wasn't it Rabbi Kohner's stated policy that "if you want to do something Jewish, Temple Am Israel's the place?" Wasn't the Bayt Emett group Jewish? Indeed, if anyone was violating traditional Judaism, it was the liberals in the synagogue! How dare the Orthodox group be told that their form of worship—*traditional Judaism*, no less—was unacceptable! How dare they be told that they couldn't worship in their own synagogue—the synagogue they had helped run and helped finance for decades. Josh Rosefsky had been president of the congregation. His wife had served on the board of directors. They were two of the most generous financial donors. Lenny Levitan had faithfully taught at the Hebrew school and served on multiple committees. Camille Vigeland was on the board. Irv Mendel was on the board. Jeff Bronner was on the Religious Affairs Committee. This was just as much their synagogue as anyone else's! How dare this contingent of feminists demand their eviction!

Mehitzah: The Ultimate Showdown

To be sure, not everyone wanted the Orthodox group to be kicked out. Not everyone had a problem with their use of a *mehitzah*.

For instance, although Jayme Hoffman certainly had her share of grievances with the Orthodox camp, including her personal falling-out with the Rosefskys after their "oust-Moishe" meeting, she still felt that they should be allowed to pray in the back room. The *mehitzah* didn't bother her:

You know, let 'em be. . . . They want to do it?—Because that had been the beauty of the synagogue, You want to do this? Fine. You want to do that? Fine. So it didn't really bother me.

Jocelyn Herzberg, a member of the board, considers herself a feminist. She teaches women's studies at the local university, and always loved Temple Am Israel's insistence upon gender equality and openness to gays and lesbians. And she also believed that the Orthodox group had every right to use a back room to pray as they saw fit, regardless of the gender inequality involved. As she explained:

If they wanted to have a mehitzah, *fine. Let them have it. I mean, I just didn't see what the big deal was. Let 'em do it. You don't have to go. So they share our space? Big deal! I mean, it did not offend my feminist principles in the least. I don't want to do it, but I—this is what Orthodox Jews do, so if you don't like it, don't be an Orthodox Jew! . . . This is a community with not all that many Jews, one building—let's share. I mean, what's the big deal? As long as they weren't forcing me to do it, I was satisfied.*

According to Julie Schoenberg, who was on the board:

I did not mind at all. I just kept saying to people, 'We're all Jews, you guys, let's try to get along. If we cannot get along as Jews, how do we expect to have peace in the Middle East, peace on our planet? We have to start here at home' . . . I feel we have to be tolerant of our differences as Jews, or we're never going to go anywhere.

Zack Norman had grown up in an Orthodox synagogue in Buenos Aires, but over the years at Temple Am Israel, he came to embrace Moishe's vision of Reconstructionism. He was proud of the congregation's insistence upon gender equality, and still, he saw nothing wrong with a voluntary Orthodox service being held in the back room. Zack disagreed with the anti-*mehitzah* group. As he explained:

> *The quarrel over the* mehitzah, *to me, is stupid. Because if the men and women who go to such a service are happy with it, good luck to them. I respect it, you know. Nobody's twisting their arms and forcing them to go. They've got a choice. So those in our—'our' meaning the usual Temple Am Israel congregation—who were very vociferous, very loud-voiced in object-ing to the* mehitzah, *started seeing it as a transgression against women, against humanity. I think this is ridiculous. This is silly. It's somebody else's horse they're flogging. Leave it alone.*

According to John Meyers:

> *There was no reason on earth why the Orthodox group couldn't have their service in the back room while Moishe and Yakov's could be run up in the main congregation . . . if people want to have a service in another room with a division between men and women, I would say that's fine . . . it's not what I want to do, but it doesn't bother me at all that they want to do that.*

But the anti-*mehitzah* group, whether they represented the feelings of the majority of the rest of the synagogue or not, continued in their drive to expel the Bayt Emett group. Leading the ranks were Rhoda Fogel, chair of the Religious Affairs Committee, and Yohanna Kohner, Moishe's wife.

Moishe found himself caught between trying to placate this anti-*mehitzah* group, which consisted of some of his most consistent supporters (not to mention his wife), and trying to be fair to the Orthodox group. Even though those in the Orthodox group had been some of his most derogatory detractors, he still felt that they had a right to use the syna-gogue space. He may have had his personal differences with them, but his policy of inclusivity had always been one of his most prominent guiding principles and he felt it would be hypocritical to allow everyone else the ability to pray as they saw fit and not extend this acceptance to the mem-bers of his congregation that had embraced Orthodoxy.

Weeks passed with Rabbi Moishe walking on a thin tightrope of com-munity placation. The members of Bayt Emett had little respect for him (they didn't care for his politics on Israel, his social activism, his push towards Reconstructionism, his rewriting of nearly every prayer in order to foster gender neutrality, and so on), and thus, even though he was allowing them to remain in the back room, this did little to improve his relationship with the members of that camp. Yet by allowing them to stay, he was increasingly alienating his group of core supporters.

He was receiving constant pressure from both sides and his footing became less and less sure.

Yohanna, Rhoda, and the rest of the anti-*mehitzah* crowd kept reminding him of the Orthodox group's sexist restrictions on women, their potential hatred of homosexuals, and perhaps most damaging of all, their lack of respect for Moishe. They continually reminded Moishe that those in Bayt Emett had never liked him and had even tried to oust him. They reminded Moishe that many in the Orthodox camp didn't even consider him their rabbi anymore, but flocked around Abe Shibel, a man whose major claim to fame in the community was his refusal to join Temple Am Israel.

Hugh Leon was among those who constantly told Moishe that his toleration of the Orthodox camp in the back room was both spiritually and personally mistaken.

As Hugh explained:

The core people of Bayt Emett did not accept Moishe as their rabbi, or as a rabbi, a man to be respected. And that's a very key issue. Apart from ritual . . . they did not accept him as their rabbi. They had so much disrespect for him. And that's not acceptable. You can be critical of the rabbi . . . but you can't say, 'I negate you as our spiritual leader, or as a spiritual leader.' They negated Moishe's intelligence and competence . . . the negativity around Moishe was so extreme, that he was negated as a spiritual leader.

According to David Decker:

I think Moishe was attempting to be accommodating—but at the same time, it was evident, to me at least, that he felt personally affronted. This was partly because many of them refused to recognize him as a rabbi.

Moishe was consistently bombarded by the anti-*mehitzah* group's litany: the Bayt Emett group was antiwomen, probably antigay, and blatantly unreceptive to Moishe's authority as rabbi of the synagogue, and hence, they should be ejected.

While Moishe's ear was being rigorously tugged by his immediate circle, from the other side, he received just the opposite messages. The Orthodox members argued that they weren't sexist, but simply traditional. They weren't oppressing women; the women *chose* to pray there of their own volition. They insisted that they weren't antigay, but that such rumors had been spread with the sole intent of maligning them. They may have had their personal differences with Moishe, but Temple Am Israel was still their synagogue, and they had every right to pray upon its premises as they saw fit. How is it possible, they asked, that the congregation can welcome Evangelical Christians within its walls to sing gospel music, Native Americans within its walls to lead healing circles, and every form of Jewish New Age experimentation, but not traditional Orthodox Judaism?

Danny Lamdan explained:

> *The people at Temple Am Israel were always talking about honoring diversity, but the tension was it always seemed to be honoring diversity—except for traditional Judaism!*

If Moishe kicked out the Orthodox group, he would be kicking out some of the most important, well-learned, and financially supportive members of the congregation, as well as violating his own principle of communal inclusivity.

However, if he allowed them to stay, he would be alienating many of his core supporters, including his wife. Those people who had backed him all these years in his social activism on behalf of gay rights and Palestinian rights, who had helped him along the path of making the congregation egalitarian in terms of gender, who had eagerly welcomed his exploration of Reconstructionism—they were the members he risked alienating if he allowed Bayt Emett to stay.

According to Roger Diamond:

Moishe got into a situation where he was being pressed by his circle of advi-
sors to not allow this repugnant behavior to exist within the confines of
Temple Am Israel, because Temple Am Israel had clear directives . . . that
were in conflict with those practices. Both sides became increasingly militant
and increasingly less willing to work their issues out. And it developed very
rapidly into—on both sides, I think—a desire to end the relationship that
existed at that point. It got nasty, and personal affronts were thrown by all
parties. Moishe got nasty, Moishe's supporters got even nastier, the people
who led Bayt Emett got nasty, and all of them were both privately and open-
ly confrontative and affrontive.

As Moishe struggled, so too did the community. Things escalated. The
two camps became more adamant and active in asserting their positions.

In the eyes of the Orthodox camp, the *mehitzah* was merely one more
aspect of Orthodox Judaism to be respected, another element of traditional Jewish practice to be defended. They viewed those that were
against its use as extremist feminists, knee-jerk liberals, and, ultimately,
desecrators of Judaism. They considered the criticism of the *mehitzah* as
just one more aspect of a Reconstructionist onslaught intent on destroying every last vestige of traditional Judaism.

In the anti-*mehitzah* group's eyes, the *mehitzah* meant institutional
oppression of women. They viewed those who supported its use as sexist
pigs, potential rapists, and just another manifestation of religious fundamentalism's ugly resurgence throughout the world.

It was thus the "Desecrators of Traditional Judaism" versus the "Sexist
Male Chauvinists." The FemiNazis against the Rapists.

As Josh Binder put it:

The closest analogy that comes to mind is bulls pawing the ground and feint-
ing at each other.

Surely there was so much that the two camps disagreed about, from
Israeli politics, to publicly supporting gay rights, to gender equality within practice and prayer, to personal feelings about Moishe, and so on. And
yet it was the *mehitzah* issue around which both camps formally rallied.
The fight over the *mehitzah* became the ultimate showdown.

As Bruce Wallin recalled:

This mehitzah *became a symbolic fixation for the most leftist types at Temple Am Israel. And somebody wrote a petition and circulated a petition to forbid us to* daven *in that fashion. Now, it was a ludicrous situation. Everybody who went to the Bayt Emett service, except for Abe Shibel, was a member of Temple Am Israel. And for what it's worth, about half the people who went were women who are highly articulate, educated, serious people, professional women and mothers, who do—and in my humble opinion—ought to be able to choose how they* daven. *But then there was another group of people, the Temple Am Israel people, who thought that wasn't relevant that these people chose to* daven *in this way, that it shouldn't be allowed because it was inherently oppressive.*

As the Rosefskys had done in their unsuccessful attempt to boycott Moishe's contract renewal, the anti-*mehitzah* group drew up a petition to have the Bayt Emett group evicted from the synagogue. The petition read, in part:

We support the principle of egalitarianism at Temple Am Israel, including the full participation of men and women in the minyan and other aspects of Jewish life; and we are opposed to any religious services at Temple Am Israel that exclude members on the basis of gender or sexual orientation . . .

. . . and we are opposed to *mehitzah* barriers that segregate women from men in our synagogue . . .

. . . and we oppose the use of our Torah scrolls in any services that deny access to some of the Jewish people [i.e., women] . . .

. . . and we oppose the use of Temple Am Israel, which is a *public* facility of the Jewish community, for any religious services that enforce sexual discrimination.

The petition catalyzed both camps. As Josh Rosefsky explained:

They passed this petition around . . . which basically said that because we're against women, we don't stand for equal rights and we don't stand for human rights, we shouldn't be allowed at Temple Am Israel . . . that we

*should be thrown out, . . . and it was a very catalyzing force. It immediately
made us a group. It gave us an identity. It gave us a focus—our survival
was at stake. What were we gonna do if we got thrown out of Temple Am
Israel? . . . All of a sudden . . . we were the outlaws of the Jewish community.*

Kevin Abrams was one of twenty-five people who signed the petition
seeking the Orthodox group's eviction. As he explained:

*Rhoda Fogel created a petition declaring that we will not have—that any
organization that wants a* mehitzah *cannot be a part of Temple Am Israel,
or affiliated with Temple Am Israel. I signed it. I think twenty-seven people
signed it. Which wasn't a lot. Trish [Kevin's wife] did not sign it. Trish was
trying to be a peace-maker. I said, 'Fuck it . . . I'm gonna say what I think:
that is disgusting, those people are disgusting.' I was not nice. In retrospect,
I played in to part of the enmity . . . there wasn't goodwill on my part.*

The debate flared throughout committees, board meetings, and informal gatherings. During the height of the controversy, many people wrote
letters to the board of directors expressing their opinions.

I have selected two letters, one from John Cohen and one from Sally
Fish, which I think best capture the position of each camp.

John Cohen wanted the Bayt Emett group evicted. He wrote the following letter explaining his position:

Quite suddenly, behaviors that most of us have opposed all our adult lives
are welcomed into our synagogue. It is as if the civil rights struggle, the
women's movement, and 200 years of social legislation had never
occurred. Truly amazing. We will not allow discrimination in the work-
place or in political life, but at Temple Am Israel it's OK.

We heard [during the previous night's community meeting] many elo-
quent justifications of "tradition" and "thousands of years of Jewish history." As if history were not a catalog of horrors. . . . I am sure you know that
women, slaves, and cattle are a single grouping for many purposes of
Orthodox Judaism. Perhaps you have also heard that "God does not hear
the prayers of men and women who pray together" (in the words of our

Bayt Emett's spiritual leader). Very few of us would buy into pernicious notions like these, but under the rubric of religious tolerance, they are now acceptable at Temple Am Israel.

. . . During the recent past we have seen right-wing organizations take over churches, political parties, and community organizations throughout this country. These groups draw their energy from religious fundamentalism. This is why I am so fearful for Temple Am Israel's future. For the first time since the founding of our congregation, Temple Am Israel has a mehitzah . . .

I have a feeling that we have just seen the introduction of a double standard, in more ways than one. Behaviors that are forbidden in the Sanctuary are OK in the back room. . . . [W]hile the dehumanization of women and homosexuals may be despicable in the Sanctuary, it is legitimate religious expression elsewhere in the building. Am I the only one who feels as if he has entered Wonderland? This would be exciting if it weren't so frightening. I am not especially concerned about the women who choose to sit behind the mehitzah. That is their right. We always have with us those who cannot see that "sitting at the back of the bus" involves a loss of human dignity. To me the great surprise is that so many others at Temple Am Israel are willing to turn a blind eye to it.

I sincerely hope that the so-called Bayt Emett, which isn't very "emett-full" ["truthful"] except in its dehumanization of women, will find a way to pursue its religious goals outside of Temple Am Israel . . .

In defense of the Bayt Emett group, Sally Fish wrote a letter urging the congregation to accept their Orthodox practices in the back room:

It sounds as if we have been polarized into two warring factions. One side wishes to conform their religious observance to traditional practices; the other, to alter religious practice to conform to the lifestyle and principles they have chosen. Is there no room here for a middle ground?

Temple Am Israel strives to serve the spectrum of Jewish observance. Great effort has been made to accommodate even those families for whom religious practice is limited to dropping off their children at the door. The disenfranchised, the gay or lesbian congregant, the single parent, the Jew who has chosen mixed marriage—are all invited to participate in a religious life of their own interpretation. Why is this courtesy not extended to the Jew who wishes to explore a traditional approach?

. . . Some Jews believe that circumcision isn't necessary for a Jewish identity; for some, the realities of life mean they must shop or work on Shabbat; some believe it is not necessary to marry another Jew; some believe that marriage itself is unnecessary. All of us have chosen to observe those practices which are meaningful to our lives, while at the same time ignoring others. The traditional Orthodox group takes one approach, the regular service takes another.

I have not yet attended the Bayt Emett, but I've talked to women and men who have found the experience meaningful. There are many distractions at the regular service. It can be uncomfortable to sit beside our gender counterparts. The wording changes that promote an egalitarian approach can be distracting, and for some those changes take away from an understanding of the prayers.

Some women don't feel an aliya [*aleeyah*] the highlight of their spiritual life. Women who choose to attend the traditional minyan appreciate the mehitzah because it gives them a sense of privacy in their prayers, similar to the feeling one has when wrapped inside the tallit [*tallis*]. Some women like the mehitzah because it relieves them of the need to relate to men during prayer . . .

If the issue is the worry that women are excluded, I submit that any time we define ourselves, we risk excluding someone else. Hadassah is a women's Zionist organization. If you don't agree with its goals, you won't want to belong. The Al-Anon meeting held at Temple Am Israel is meant only for those overcoming substance abuse. . . . [T]he Jewish Renewal service seek to reach an underserved group. . . . Congregants have been free to attend these gatherings, and Temple Am Israel has tolerated and encouraged this diversity. Diversity now demands that we tolerate a traditional approach as well.

Those women who participate in the Bayt Emett service have not felt oppressed by the rules of observance. They are mature and thoughtful women who deserve the respect of the larger community, despite their having taken an unpopular stand.

Not all Jewish women desire the egalitarian path chosen by Temple Am Israel . . .

Honor Diversity within our own traditions.

Amidst this mounting tension, Rabbi Moishe was finally swayed. He ultimately came to agree with his wife and her friends who composed the anti-*mehitzah* group that the Bayt Emett group, because of its use of a *mehitzah*, which violated the Temple's policy of gender equality, would have to leave.

Moishe signed the petition calling for their eviction.

Lenny Levitan was crushed. As he recalled:

They put a petition together saying basically that because of the practices—the mehitzah—*racist, sexist practices of the* minyan, *that it was our duty to make sure this cannot happen in our* shule.

"How did that make you feel?" I asked.

Oh, mad. Really mad . . . and they were very, very aggressive . . . and Rabbi Kohner signed it. He put his name on it.

"How did that make you feel?" I asked.

Felt like shit. Felt I was betrayed . . . we always felt that his wife, Yohanna, really ran him—ran the show. . . . She's a very powerful lady. Extremely powerful. And she was one of the people that helped design this petition . . . so I called Moishe up and I said, 'How dare you. This is unbelievable. How could you do this?' And he basically said he agrees with everything the petition says. So it was a big stink in the community. A big split. People were taking sides . . . especially the fact that the Rabbi came out so strongly against us. And we basically—actually, that was the thing that really galvanized Bayt Emett—was this petition.

The *mehitzah* controversy was it. Moishe had signed the petition. The Bayt Emett group, if they insisted on using that *mehitzah*, would have to leave.

A Big Symbol of Gender Regulation

While there had been so much that divided the two camps once they were at the point of schism, it was the battle over the *mehitzah* that ultimately proved to be *the* divisive controversy. Moishe's politics concerning the rights of Palestinians had caused division, liberal changes in the liturgy had stirred up many, greater acceptance of intermarried couples had put some people at odds, and the issue of homosexuality was an underlying source of friction. But it was the *mehitzah* controversy that ultimately split the congregation in two.

And the *mehitzah*'s power to divide stretches beyond the cozy confines of Willamette. As Norma Baumel Joseph (1992:120) maintains, the particular issue of the *mehitzah* "has become the hallmark of the divisions that exist among American Jewry." Judith Plaskow (1990:190) agrees, noting that the separation of the sexes by a *mehitzah* is a "highly contentious issue, which has split many a U.S. congregation."

Why the *mehitzah*?

Most likely, it is its *symbolic, gendered nature*. The *mehitzah* is a symbol: a tangible, mundane thing in and of itself, yet imbued with spiritual, cultural, and moral meaning. Symbols are often at the center of irreconcilable religious differences. But there's more to it than that. Not only is the *mehitzah* a symbol, it is a symbol that concerns *gender*. This doubly powerful aspect of the *mehitzah*, its *symbolic nature*, and its *embodiment of meanings of gender*, can best account for its decisive role in the schism of Willamette's Jewish community.

Since Emile Durkheim's (1915) classic study of the origins of religiosity, scholars have been exploring the ultimate importance of symbols in religious life (Geertz, 1966; Turner, 1967; Ricoeur, 1972; Bynum, Harrell, and Richman, 1986), especially within religious conflict. Susan Sered (1997:3) argues that "religious conflicts tend to be, by definition, conflicts over symbols (symbols are, after all, the currency of religion)."

Fred Kniss (1996:8) confirms that "ideas and symbols play a role in most religious conflicts." Kniss characterizes religious symbols as "cultural resources" and suggests that "since concrete cultural resources are not likely to be divisible, they are more likely to result in intense, all-or-nothing battles ending in schism than compromise" (p.12). As support for this insight, Kniss looks at Mennonite history, in which he found that struggles involving concrete cultural resources were nearly three times as likely to end in schism as those overly-abstract resources. The significance of the *mehitzah* (a concrete symbol) in the schism of Temple Am Israel, offers further support to Kniss' argument.

And the power of symbols within religious life is substantially strengthened when gender enters the picture. Gender—the socially constructed understanding of what it means to be "male" or "female"—is at the heart of religious life. As Mary Jo Neitz and Marion Goldman (1995:6) persuasively argue, religious identity "is inextricably tied to understandings of gender and sexuality." Indeed, gender is "central to the meaningful interpretation of contemporary American religious organizations and markets" (p.271).

Religious life hinges on implicit and explicit understandings of gender. According to Caroline Walker Bynum, "It is no longer possible to study religious practice or religious symbols without taking gender—that is, the cultural experience of being male or female—into account. And we are just beginning to understand how complex the relationship between religion and gender is" (1986:1).

Howard Eilberg-Schwartz (1994:5), drawing upon such feminist scholarship, rightly declares that "gender is not just another subject that intersects with religion, but is central to the work that religion accomplishes and the way in which it goes about it."

In short, religious life is largely about making sense of existence. Religious life tends to focus on major questions of *being*: Why are we here? What is one's proper place in life? In one's family? In one's community? In the cosmos? In God's kingdom? Presumably, religion addresses these questions of existence, of being. And since gender is an integral and central aspect of existence, religious issues or symbols that address gender cut to the very core of our being.

The *mehitzah* is just such a symbol—a symbol of what I call "gender regulation." Gender regulation is the process by which a community (in this case, religious) attempts to define, institute, and justify "masculine" and "feminine" behavior and roles for its members (Zuckerman, 1997).

Whenever gender regulation is challenged—especially within patriarchal religious traditions—the result tends to be one of contention and conflict. Some examples include controversy over women's roles within Catholicism (Manning, 1997; Ranke-Heinemann, 1988; Iadarola, 1985; Wallace, 1993), Mormonism, Episcopalianism (Prelinger et al., 1992), American fundamentalism (Balmer, 1994; Brown, 1994), Eastern Orthodoxy, New Religious Movements (Aidala, 1985; Jacobs, 1989, 1991), Spiritualist groups (Haywood, 1983), and the Protestant ministry (Lehman, 1985).

Judaism is a patriarchal religious tradition (Plaskow, 1990; Wegner, 1988), and many recent studies of American Jewry have highlighted gender regulation as a major component of Jewish religious identity (Cantor, 1995; Adler, 1973; Heschel, 1983; Grossman and Haut, 1992; Fishman, 1993; Cohen, 1980; Shepherd, 1993; Frankiel, 1990; Kaufman, 1991; Greenberg, 1981; Davidman, 1988, 1991; Biale, 1984; Sered, 1992; Schneider, 1984; Heilman, 1973). As Rachel Biale (1995:ix) writes, "[w]omen's communal roles, women's spirituality, gender relations . . . and feminist theology are among the most vital issues for discussion in contemporary Jewish life."

Again, the *mehitzah*'s power to divide was rooted in its symbolic nature, and the additional fact that what it symbolizes concerns meanings of gender. And while the *mehitzah* is so salient in contemporary Jewish life, a similar controversy exists within contemporary Christian life concerning female ordination. Mark Chaves (1997:6) has stressed the extent to which gender-conscious debate over female ordination in Christian circles is essentially symbolic at roo. "A denomination's policy allowing (or prohibiting) women's ordination is better understood as a symbolic display of support for gender equality (or of resistance to gender equality) than as a policy either motivated by or intended to regulate the everyday reality of women inside the organization" (p.6).

Susan Sered's recent study of feminist challenges to patriarchal authority within Israeli society offers a relevant paradigm for understanding symbolic gender regulation and religious conflict. According to Sered, there are two ontologically different sets of issues at play within patriarchal religious systems: "women," which designates "female people who have varying degrees of agency within specific social situations," and then "Woman," which designates "a symbolic construct composed of allegory, metaphor, fantasy and (at least in male-dominated religions) men's psychological projections." According to Sered, when someone or something challenges a religious system's assumptions of "Woman" the result is often religious conflict, because "'Woman' as a symbol is often associated with some of the deepest and most compelling theological and mythological structures in the religious tradition" (Sered, 1997:1-2).

The case of Willamette's Jewish community lends support to Sered's insight, for the battle over gender regulation was more than just a community disagreeing over random policies or principles. It was a situation in which members within a religious system disagreed over central structures and meanings within that system: structures and meanings of gender, especially concerning the role of women.

The symbolic weight of the *mehitzah* controversy, and the gender regulation that it entailed, were clearly evident when those involved discussed the matter.

As Julie Horowitz explained:

Temple Am Israel was progressively becoming more and more egalitarian in the language about God, in the language about the Jewish people, and all that stuff. And so this was a real shocker that there was a mehitzah in this building, in this house, which had always been dedicated to these values. And it was seen as offensive—some women would even use the word abominable. It was an abomination. The women who were most offended by it— two women in particular—had lived in extremely Orthodox communities and so they knew, in their experience, what went along with that—the next step became violence against women. I mean, it was not stretching the point for them. It was an obvious progression from one level of male superiority . . . to another. And they'd both experienced it. And they were perhaps the most vocal . . . the mehitzah is a social control mechanism—apropos social control, this whole thing is really, really ancient. And from a Marxist analysis, it's all about men owning the means of production, controlling women's bodies, controlling women's power. And it's really ugly to me. Because I also hold the view that before the patriarchy we actually had a sane society. And then there was this wave of migration of people who had iron, and who practiced unbelievable atrocities called war, who destroyed a worldwide, maybe million-year-old—or I don't know how-many-year-old—ten thousand-year-old matriarchal, pacifistic, agrarian society, where women had been hon-

ored, where God had been honored but in a female form, the earth had been seen as a mother that brought forth life, women were held in reverence because life came forth from them, they were held in awe . . . and so I have a deep rage at the patriarchy in general, and what the mehitzah represents to me is the control of women, the silencing of women . . . so the patriarchy is the source of all evil—that's a given. And the mehitzah is a symbol of the patriarchy, a symbol of keeping women suppressed. . . . Um, I do know educated women who choose to pray behind the mehitzah, and if it weren't for the politics of it, I might be interested in it myself. But with the rest of it, with the not being counted in the minyan, with the need to be silent, with the not being allowed to touch the Torah, with the idea that my menstrual blood is dirty, unclean, an evil—with all those pieces of it, there's no way I can . . . and I resented it terribly when men that I knew in other contexts, who were very, very liberal and wonderful—we were great friends and we agreed on so many things and they were very progressive in their lives—and then they'd go daven there. I couldn't believe that they would do that, that they didn't understand the implications of sitting in the front of the bus . . . so it's a big symbol for me.

For Yohanna Kohner, who led the fight against its usage on Temple Am Israel property, the *mehitzah* was much more than just a small wooden fence. As she explained:

We [the anti-mehitzah group] brought up this issue about how can you allow for Jews to say that women who seek equality deserve to be raped— and then you come to the congregation and you want a mehitzah?! I mean, what kind of attitude do you stand for? Are you going to rape us here? What is it you are promoting? You want to promote the rape of your daughter? And so it went from the mehitzah to rape! And Rhoda and myself and a few people—our conversation was not mehitzah. Our conversation was, 'You with your penis and your rigid authority, you want to do us in! One more time, like the others! You're not here in the congregation because you want a Jewish life. You're here to impose your male chauvinist power in the last bastion that is resisting you!'

Kevin Abrams agreed with Yohanna, viewing the *mehitzah* as institutionalized oppression with violent implications:

When you ask me what I think about the mehitzah, *lingering underneath is that—systems perpetuate certain propensities. And a system that perpetuates divisiveness and power against women, and rigidity . . . then it perpetuates violence. By the very nature of its system . . . it boils down to violence and eventually rape. It perpetuates 'I am better than you . . . I am superior and have the right to inflict my ideas on you . . . make you obey.' And in male/female relations, that can engender violence and eventually rape. This is extreme, but that's some of my core philosophical and emotional views of fundamentalism.*

Rhoda Fogel, Yohanna's close friend and co-leader of the anti-*mehitzah* group, explained her feelings:

The purpose of the mehitzah *is to divide people. To exclude a group of people. And that's what it does . . . it's apartheid. It's the back of the bus. You know, women don't count in the* minyan. *And your voice is despicable, and you're not a full human being.*

According to Shira Deener:

There are many things about Orthodoxy, but the whole attitude toward women is the major, major factor for me. And so the mehitzah, *it represents—I'm not interested in the separation—I see it as a status—the men are more powerful than the women and it's a way to maintain that.*

As Jocelyn Herzberg recalled:

I guess I probably asked somebody, 'Well, what is the point of the mehitzah? *Why do they have it?' And somebody said—and I'm not sure if this is true—that so men can really concentrate on the praying and they don't have this constant distraction of the women . . . well, I don't like that. I mean, why should—women aren't distracting. Women can pray just as hard as men if they want to pray. It just kind of implies that women are, you*

*know, sexual and they might just—they can't focus enough to really con-
centrate as hard as the men, and they better keep them separate. . . . I don't
want to live in a world where that's the idea, that women are lesser than
men.*

Yakov Tish, for years, had led periodic Jewish Renewal services in the
back room. However, those services had never created any communal rift.
Yakov believed that it was the Orthodox camp's use of the *mehitzah*, and
all the gendered meanings it symbolized, that was the reason their separate services caused division:

*Some of the principles of framework of Temple Am Israel were being direct-
ly confronted—such as egalitarianism. That was a bottom-line commitment
for Temple Am Israel. That women were—are fully participating in everything . . . when you have a* mehitzah *and the women can't be shaliakh
tzibbur, that's already a different status within the congregation, at least as
understood from a liberal perspective . . . that was very threatening to people, . . . to have a throwback right in their face, was very painful and threatening, to many people.*

According to Arthur Edelmann:

*The mehitzah became this symbolic—it IS a symbolic division in space—it
became kind of a point of reference, 'Oh, you can't do that'—'And why
can't you do that?'—'Well, because it's an affront to women.' But the
women who are praying that way—they made that choice . . . these women
had made that choice. But there was a group—and largely a group of women
. . . who could not abide by that. That this was an affront to them. And
some of them to the point of describing it—and I think in an absurdly—more
than an absurdly—a disgusting manner—as symbolic rape.*

The gendered symbolic associations of those who opposed the *mehitzah*
were quite powerful, and deeply negative. For them, the *mehitzah* con-
jured up feelings of patriarchal oppression, male superiority, violence
against women—indeed, some went so far as to associate the *mehitzah*
with literal rape.

However, as is the case with symbols, the mehitzah held dramatically different associations for others in the community. Members of the Orthodox camp found comfort in the mehitzah. For them, it represented a connection with tradition, a useful tool for quelling unwanted sexual arousal, and a positive recognition and reinforcement of the "natural" differences between men and women.

According to Amanda Wallin:

I don't need to sit next to my husband during shule, you know? I sit next to him plenty. And as a Jew I think that we all need to go before God alone. So there are lots of practical reasons to have a mehitzah because as women, we're primary care-givers for the kids and we're up and back and up and back and we don't have the same requirements of us in Judaism as men do. I think that it's naive to think that people are not attracted sexually to other people . . . in that, if you're worshipping together it could have an effect on your ability to concentrate, you know,—that's kind of stretching it. There are lots of reasons. And the most important reason is that's what the Torah says, and I feel comfortable with it. So the fact that men and women worship separately is kind of a nonissue to me . . . the notion that there is something inherently oppressive or discriminatory about dividing men and women is a foolish notion, in my opinion.

According to Irv Mendel:

Now that I've experienced the mehitzah, I can see how it works. I do see its value. There's a lot of misperception among the general public, which has leaked over into the Jewish community, about men and women—their roles in creation. And I think that one of the problems is that women are trying to be men and men are trying to be women. And whenever they do that, they don't succeed very well . . . and this relates to the mehitzah. Men have different lifestyles, different drives, different emotions than women do. And I think the mehitzah helps to preserve that, to permit the men to gain a higher level of religiosity, of spiritual achievement, with the mehitzah. And I think that—although I've never discussed this with women—I suspect that might be true for them, too.

According to Danny Lamdan:

I would think of the mehitzah *in terms of—there's no doubt about the fact—no matter how liberal-minded you are, that the presence of women is—can be—and I don't mean distracting in a necessarily negative way— but there is a different feeling if I'm sitting next to a woman, or I'm sitting with women, versus being separated from them. And when you're talking about prayer and you're supposed to be communicating with Hashem, like if a woman came in that, you know, you were sexually attracted to or something, you know, that kind of thing. These are subtle things that do have an effect. You can deny it, but there's no doubt about the fact that I'm gonna feel or think differently if a woman sits next to me or not, or being alone.*

According to Laura Diamond:

I think it serves a valuable purpose. I think that men and women are differ- ent. I just kind of like my own space, so I don't want anyone being around me. . . . I find the mehitzah *to be, on a personal level, fairly liberating.*

like women who
find veiling to
be liberating

According to Jeremy Erdely:

I'm not going to be the knee-jerk feminist and say, 'Mehitzah!'—you know—'it's bullshit!' Because I realize from my knowledge that when men and women are together, the hormones and the passion flows. And if one truly is there to attempt to commune with the eternal, then anything that one can do to keep that experience pure and keep that channel clear, is fine.

According to Joanna Edelstein:

I remember about the mehitzah—*the gender role differences in Orthodox Judaism was something I didn't used to understand, and it sort of bothered me, viewing it from the outside. But as I learned more about it, it made per- fect sense. And it was basically based in reality. Males and females are dif- ferent, and have different needs. . . . I just couldn't believe at how upset— how they could be so offended—they didn't understand. We were not feeling bad as women, . . . we chose to be there. My husband doesn't go. So I didn't go because I was just following my husband. I go by myself. . . . I just felt they didn't get it . . . for liberals, they were being incredibly close-minded.*

For Lilly Hayden, the *mehitzah* is helpful in separating the essential differences between men and women:

It has to do with different realms . . . men and women have different spiritual energy. . . . I think that it's more powerful for men to channel masculine energy and women to channel feminine energy. I don't know why. Maybe it's a cultural thing? But actually—no. I think it's MORE of a cultural thing for us as Americans to think that people, you know, men and women together can do anything . . . I don't think that's true. I mean, I'm a purist, in that sense. I really, really am. I think that there are fundamental differences between men and women . . . so the mehitzah is like—it separates the energies and makes each one of them more powerful . . . that's why I think the mehitzah is important.

For Camille Vigeland, the *mehitzah* means reconnecting with God's ultimate plan for men and women. As she explained:

You just have to—you have to believe, just deep in your heart, that God's in control of the universe, that the laws have a reason . . . that if you keep the laws, the Jewish people will continue forever . . . so is it more important to me that . . . for three hours once a week I sit on the other side of the mehitzah—is that more important to me than assuring the continuity of the Jewish people? I don't think so.

For members of the Orthodox camp, the *mehitzah* was a symbol of tradition, as well as an appropriate reinforcement of the "essential" differences between the sexes. For members of the anti-*mehitzah* group, it was a symbol of oppression, as well as a reinforcement of patriarchal, sexist oppression of women. These two symbolic meanings clashed. In the words of James Davison Hunter (1991:131), "the mere existence of one represented a certain desecration of the other."

Compromise was not possible.

For the Orthodox camp, tradition was more important than respecting gender equality. For the anti-*mehitzah* group, gender equality was more important than respecting tradition. "Tradition" and "Gender Equality" were the supreme symbolic values that cut to the core of each group's understanding of what it means to be a Jew, and the *mehitzah* was the symbol that became imbued with those conflicting values.

The *mehitzah*, as a symbol, embodied two opposing visions of Jewish identity, and above all else, two opposing forms of gender regulation. It thus became *the* tangible "thing" around which the community could battle and ultimately divide.

It is important to remember that this battle among a bunch of Jews in Willamette, Oregon, arguing over a *mehitzah*, though seemingly unique, is actually embedded within a general debate that has enmeshed American religion and society since the advent of modern feminism. It is without question that *the cultural significance of feminism was a salient social factor informing this schismatic battle.*

As Mark Chaves (1997:46) has noted, modern "second wave" feminism has "left untouched virtually no organizational field, including religion." Jack Wertheimer (1993:19) has discussed the impact of feminism on American religious life, and succinctly concludes that feminism has

> challenged all American religious groups by raising profound questions about both gender roles and sexual mores. Few organized religious groups have been able to ignore the feminist agenda. In both churches and synagogues, women have demanded inclusion as religious celebrants and congregational leaders, as well as revisions of liturgy to reflect their experiences and rites of passage. These challenges to tradition have polarized churches in the last quarter of the century, dividing religious conservatives and religious liberals. Each of the Jewish religious movements has reacted, with the most liberal and the most conservative responding with the greatest alacrity.

To adequately analyze the impact feminism has had on American culture, American religiosity, and Jewish life, would take several volumes, at least. Suffice it to say that many of the ideological particulars of this case of religious schism were clearly manifestations of a general sociocultural framework that feminism has had a significant role in shaping.

Chapter Seven

THEN THERE WERE TWO

They Part Ways—The Bayt Emett group left. Some say they were kicked out. Others say that they left of their own volition.

According to Mike Fish of Bayt Emett:

I felt kicked out. I felt that there was something that could have been done—there could have been a stable equilibrium, remaining in the back . . . but I felt pushed out. I felt pushed out.

But according to Hugh Leon, of Temple Am Israel:

It's very clear that they left Temple Am Israel, and it's very clear to me that they felt that they were kicked out—that there was enough emotional animosity aimed at them that they felt extruded. That they couldn't have a mehitzah . . . they felt, to them, was being kicked out. That was a set-up. I think it's kind of like the adolescent who feels kicked out of the nest as they emancipate.

Either way, be it a situation of harsh eviction or rebellious flight, where there had only been one Jewish congregation in Willamette for decades, now there were two.

The members of the Bayt Emett group resigned from their positions on the various boards and committees of Temple Am Israel, they took their children out of the Hebrew school, they had their names removed from the mailing list. They withdrew their financial support. Now their energy was focused on creating a new congregation.

At first the Orthodox group met in various members' homes, celebrating *Shabbes* in the living room of the Levitans or the Rosefskys or the Wallins. But within a couple of months, financial support arrived. Josh Rosefsky had made an important contact at that small-communities meeting he had attended back in Ohio. Through this contact, an

Orthodox organization in New York agreed to provide the Bayt Emett group with three full years worth of funding in order to rent a building and hire a rabbi.

They immediately rented a space. There was a vacated computer store on the corner of a strip mall that suited them perfectly. And it was directly across the street from Temple Am Israel. They claimed that they didn't choose that spot so as to antagonize or compete with Temple Am Israel. Rather, it was simply the perfect location—equidistant from everyone's home, and, since the members of Bayt Emett would be walking to *shule* every Saturday, that was important.

Soon they hired a rabbi. Fresh from a yeshiva in Jerusalem, married with four kids, decidedly Orthodox, Rabbi Sapperstein came to Willamette to lead his very first congregation.

Feelings throughout the community, after the division, were tense. Those in Bayt Emett felt rejected and therefore resentful. They saw themselves as the victims of knee-jerk liberalism run amok. Thus, while they were excited about their new synagogue and their new rabbi, they still suffered from a lingering bad taste over all the rumors and conflicts that had led up to the schism.

Those remaining at Temple Am Israel felt abandoned, and they were angry that some of the most learned and financially supportive members of Temple Am Israel had "jumped ship." They accused the members of Bayt Emett of deserting them, of putting their own petty needs above the needs of the community. Some people were wary of their newly-found Orthodox ways, suspicious of anything that reeked of fundamentalism. And some suspected that their embracing of Orthodoxy wasn't even genuine; they felt that the members of Bayt Emett had simply used "religion" as a guise to express other grievances. As Susie Kohner explained:

> Bayt Emett—the whole thing was in reaction to the political stuff, both the Middle East and feminism—egalitarian prayer, the changes in the prayer based on wanting to be more egalitarian, and the talk about gay and lesbian stuff—it seemed to me that the people were trying to make a political statement more than a religious statement.

According to Laura Diamond, an unfortunate level of animosity continues to divide the two congregations:

The breaking away now is such that there is a real level of discomfort. There are people at Bayt Emett, for example, who will not set foot in Temple Am Israel . . . there are people at Temple Am Israel . . . who will not set foot in Bayt Emett . . . and that is really unhealthy.

And the fact that they are right across the street from one another keeps the oppositional dynamic alive and well. Kevin Abrams of Temple Am Israel was quite disgruntled about Bayt Emett's decision to relocate right across the street:

I have become enjoyably intolerant of Bayt Emett and what they stand for and what they are doing. And I have no desire to be an integrator . . . I am very upset that they are a half a block away . . . if I never have to deal with those people and their issues, that's fine with me.

Julia Wallace, who has taught at the Temple Am Israel Hebrew school for years, was blunt about her lingering feelings towards Bayt Emett:

There was a lot of anger. There were a lot of feelings. But in the end, I think that we have peace in the house—because we now have two houses. I won't go so far—because I'm a prejudice person—I won't go so far as to say I bless them to do what they are doing. I'd like them to fall through a hole in the earth, frankly. I have no good feelings about those people or what they do. In fact, I think I'm put on this planet to resist fundamentalism in all of its many forms. . . . I have absolutely no interest in, or respect for, fundamentalist religion of any kind. I think it's really dangerous, destructive, backward . . . and its time has come and should be gone. Obviously it's not gone—it's back with a vengeance . . . so I won't say I bless them to do what they're doing . . . I'm incredibly furious that they're in our lap.

Lynn Rosefsky, whom many considered to be the leader of the Orthodox group, told me that life in Willamette is simply not the same for her anymore ever since the split:

There's probably still a half-dozen people that still won't even look at me if they know I'm around. And mostly they are those women that we talked about—they just can't accept—I'm sure they feel that I destroyed everything they stood for.

Yohanna Kohner expressed her feelings in the aftermath of the schism:

The Rosefskys and people like that—all of a sudden, they're making a very serious commitment to Jewish life. But they couldn't do it in a loving way. They had to bust and blast at somebody, and Moishe was their football. They had to justify themselves and their activities AS OPPOSED to somebody else. They didn't know enough of Jewish history to realize that you can deviate and go your own way without the breakdown of the community.

Charles Hoffman's biggest regret is the loss of friendship he experienced as a result of the schism. Many people who had come to Willamette in the seventies, who had formed a community and raised their children together, had been put at odds against one another in the midst of the communal tension. Charles' differences with Josh Rosefsky were never resolved. They became estranged, as did their wives. The two couples had always shared major holidays together, and Passover was always the best loved. But as the Rosefskys became more Orthodox, and the community began to divide, those shared holiday gatherings stopped. Today, they celebrate Passover separately. In fact, they no longer socialize at all, for any reason. They only see each other if they happen to bump into each other in the grocery store. And those encounters are generally stilted and stiff. Even their children stopped playing together. As Charles lamented:

I don't think we will ever have the sort of trust that we had before this happened.

According to Pete Ruskin:

The friendships, and the personal relationships, and the expectations were never really healed.

According to Dick Strickstein:

One thing I'm upset about is that I don't see those people anymore. That's the biggest thing I miss. Because these were people that were friends and all of a sudden it's Shabbat or High Holidays and—a lot of times that's the only time we see our friends who are Jewish . . . and now they're at their service and we're at ours. . . . We don't cross paths. . . . From that standpoint, I feel that that part is tough.

According to Mike Fish:

It upset people and it made people into other people's enemies . . . it's really curious—there's some people that were easy to make up with when the separation was all done. But there are other people who, it seems—they seem totally unapproachable.

According to Roger Diamond:

I was disappointed in the breakup . . . disappointed that I really do feel that there could have been room for minyaneem *of virtually any practice in a community that truly embraced diversity. And that a* mehitzah *should be no more repugnant to a lesbian couple than a lesbian couple should be repugnant to an Orthodox Jew. The fact of the matter is that they are both repugnant to each other, but there—that doesn't mean that the community can't tolerate that level of diversity. They may not be able to worship in the same room together. But we ought to be able to tolerate them as a community. It's disappointing.*

John Meyers was also upset over the split:

I thought it was a horrible thing. I thought it really was terrible. I thought it was a slap in the face to Moishe . . . it indulged the worst nature we have as Jews of wanting the "Other" synagogue, you know. Rather than putting our marbles in one strong unit, the tendency to divide and become weak was inherent in our past, and I felt that we were falling to that temptation. I felt that we weren't strong enough to maintain two communities. I really thought it was a mistake. But the formation of Bayt Emett did a lot of things that were really positive. One is, it got all of the complainers out—and that was a big relief. I mean, it really gave a place for all the complainers to go and complain somewhere else.

The informant who expressed the clearest feelings of regret over the schism—viewing it as a sad conclusion to conflicts that could have been handled in a more loving, respectful fashion—was Yakov Tish. He saw the breakup of Willamette's Jewish community as a tragedy that should have been avoided.

Yakov had been one of the early pillars of Willamette's Jewish community. Since his days running the Jewish commune on University Street, Yakov had been a mainstay. He had become a well-loved cantor over the years, he had been ordained as a Jewish Renewal rabbi, and he had worked alongside Moishe since the latter's arrival.

Where had Yakov Tish been during the whole communal struggle? Aside from serving the congregation as cantor and studying more and more within the Jewish Renewal tradition, what had he done while the community was falling apart at the seams?

Interestingly enough, hardly anyone mentioned Yakov during their interviews. They would talk about the Rosefskys, Yohanna, Moishe, Rhoda Fogel, the Levitans, Abe Shibel, the Wallins, and others. But never Yakov. The general consensus was that Yakov had laid low during the struggle. He had kept to himself, neither coming out strongly in support of the Orthodox camp, nor clearly favoring the anti-*mehitzah* group. In fact, several people expressed resentment towards Yakov for not taking sides, for not actively supporting their given position. But most people simply acknowledged that Yakov wasn't the type to get involved in conflict and they understood (albeit reluctantly) his ambivalence.

And of all those I spoke with, it was Yakov who expressed the greatest amount of sadness over the schism. For Yakov, the Jewish community should have stayed united. To him, the split represented the inability of Jews to get along and work through their differences.

As Yakov explained:

People were not really responsible on the level that it really required about communicating with each other in a respectful way. People indulged in a lot of behaviors that were shameful, quite frankly. A lot of l'shon horah. And in a sense I don't want to be speaking l'shon horah against the community, but quite honestly, it was very painful to hear—from all sides—there was a general lack of spiritual awareness to the weight of words . . . there was really a lack of kavode. . . . I definitely saw the community—many people without the ability to navigate in a way that was respectful to others . . . I think that people started relating to each other as symbols, rather than people. I think that it got to that level of depersonalizing and hardening and starting to be Bearers of Truth, rather than human beings with humility.

"Symbols of what?" I asked.

Of the right way to be political, of the right way to be Jewish. I think that in some way, all the accusations that traditional Judaism will hurl at liberal Judaism, was definitely a part of it. And I think the fears on the part of liberals of the symbol of something like a mehitzah coming into the shule, was just too loaded with power of what that could lead to, in terms of diminishing human rights for women in the community. That it couldn't be a process on a level where everybody could see that we're all searching spiritually for something, and this is the material we're all working with. It fragmented to where those explorations became challenges, threats to each other, rather than seen as multiple expressions of a unity. I think that was it—that if respectful communication had been maintained, we would have all stayed humanized to the level that we could have embraced the unity and worked our way through the challenges of spiritual exploration. Once that kavode came to a low level . . . the line lowered to that level where people could really hurt each other with words and mock . . . then people became just positions against positions . . . it was very tragic. Very painful. I had really hoped that we could have been a community in which we would have had the broadest form possible, the broadest spectrum of possible expression for the sake of exploring what that means as a bigger organism. And it was very painful that people were not committed to that at all . . . and we took a step backward in terms of taking the moment that we were given as an opportunity to do some very profound tikkun, of working through the relationship of Orthodoxy and liberal Judaism.

Yakov had seen the communal problems as an opportunity to bridge the gap between liberal and conservative Jews, a gap that seems to be growing day by day. He didn't want the Jews of Willamette to fall victim to this ugly breech. He wanted them to work through it, to show the rest of the world's Jews that progressive and Orthodox approaches to Judaism can be mutually tolerated. However, Yakov's hopes weren't realized. The Jews of Willamette did fall into opposing camps of progressive and Orthodox, camps that were unable to see past their differences. As Yakov explained:

I felt very committed to keeping the community together. And it was very, very painful to see. I mean . . . I had a terrible sense of loss around the opportunity to do such an incredibly important tikkun. *You know, spending time in Israel and seeing the division between secular and* harraydeem, *and seeing the vileness of those relationships, over and over again, and how that's just breaking the house of Israel. I mean—that's just horrible. So I felt like we had a chance here, without people shooting guns at us—I mean, really, to live in a society where you are free, you don't have that kind of pressure as Jews for survival, like Israelis do . . . we couldn't even do it on a low level. So it was a very big disappointment. It was a very big disappointment for me.*

"Is there a lesson here for other communities?" I asked.

Well, I think we learn from our mistakes, and I think a lot of mistakes were made . . . and there are a lot of things to learn. On the side of liberal Judaism, I think there's a need to be open to people who have a need to explore Orthodoxy, and to not be so judgmental, to not deny them that exploration . . . not to be so threatened by that exploration. And I think that Orthodoxy needs to understand that liberal Judaism is as principled, and has as much integrity and as much divine guidance and imperative as their understanding of Judaism, and needs to relate from that sense of openness to respecting other expressions of Judaism. In future opportunities for common work, those are lessons that I personally hope I'll be paying attention to—to not indulge in petty judgment . . . and I hope that I'll be conscious enough to demand the mutuality of kavode, *to not—as many liberal Jews tend to disempower themselves in relationship to what's called 'Torah-true' Judaism—it's not Torah-truer than liberal Judaism. And I think that Orthodoxy needs to understand that they're partners in creating the Jewish peoplehood . . . so those are lessons.*

Despite the definite uneasiness and feelings of failure that permeated the community after the schism, many people ultimately expressed relief over the split. Many people said they viewed it as a "good thing" after all, as something that "needed to happen." And while virtually everyone acknowledged that the split had been an "ugly" experience, rife with enmity, ill will, rumors, slander, and feelings of betrayal, most of my informants felt that it was perhaps a positive growth for the community in the end. They felt that Temple Am Israel had simply become too small to satisfy everyone's needs, and that it was good now that there was an alternative for those seeking a more traditional approach to Judaism.

David Decker's feelings were similar to those held by most of my informants regarding the aftermath of the schism:

I think the model we would have loved to have seen is that somehow we would have got some model where Jews of all different persuasions could continue to meet together as the community, while separating for the separate minyaneem . . . but in retrospect, I guess it's just unrealistic to expect that to sustain itself for very long. I think it's been much healthier having Bayt Emett under their own roof. I think relations are far better now, than when we were trying to accommodate everybody.

A Departure, a Death—a Curse?

While many people experienced their share of grief during the communal strife, it is without question that the person who suffered the most was Rabbi Moishe Kohner. When the schism occurred, Moishe was devastated. The tension leading up to the split had wracked Moishe's soul, and its ultimate conclusion had devastated his heart. He had struggled, perhaps more than anyone, in trying to keep peace, while at the same time, stand up for the principles he believed in. He had wavered between wanting his synagogue to be a place of tolerance and diversity, while at the same time, maintaining a commitment to egalitarianism and progressive ideals. The latter had proven to be of greater value for him. But the result—the breaking-up of the synagogue—was something that cut Moishe to his core. He had pacified his supporters but lost an integral segment of the congregation.

He was a man who had always prided himself on his love of creating community. And suddenly he was presiding over a community's rupture. He had spent nearly twenty years of his life caring for the Jews of Willamette, nurturing that community, and now he was at the center of its controversial division.

While many blamed the Bayt Emett camp for embracing Orthodoxy and insisting on a *mehitzah*, and while many others blamed the anti-*mehitzah* group for their knee-jerk feminism and lack of tolerance, Moishe blamed himself. And he wondered how it came to happen that certain people he had been close with over the years had somehow turned against him.

As his wife, Yohanna, explained:

Moishe developed himself as a rabbi who harmonizes, and who serves everybody and brings everybody, and nourishes everybody's individual style, but still develops community. The schism . . . had a bad effect on him—in the sense of betrayal. Camille Vigeland and Bruce Wallin were his students and his converts. The old man, Irv, was his student. Irv knew very little when he came to this congregation. Moishe backed him up for years . . . Camille was his student. She was his convert. He married her . . . he named all her babies.

Soon after the split, Moishe became seriously depressed. Exhaustion caught up with him. It had been several years of turmoil, from his ongoing battles with Lynn Rosefsky, to the flak he had constantly received over his stances on Israel, feminism, and gay rights, to the formal attempt to have him ousted, to the eventual split. His spirit was diminished. He felt tired, sad, and worn out.

According to Judith Malka:

One day, Yohanna said to me, 'You know, they're gonna kill Moishe. And that's when they're going to be happy.' She said, 'They are killing Moishe. They are absolutely killing him' . . . she felt this was absolutely destroying Moishe's health . . . I mean, I came around the corner one day and I saw him and I was stunned. He looked like—he looked like a destroyed person. I was stunned. I had never seen him look so horrible. This was in the middle of the worst of it . . . it was killing—clearly breaking his health. Really breaking his health down.

According to John Meyers:

He definitely felt horrified by the Bayt Emett break. He definitely felt these people had said, 'We don't have faith in you. You're not our spiritual leader.' That was definitely a slight to him.

According to Rhoda Fogel:

It broke his heart.

Two months after the schism, Moishe announced he was leaving. He had served Willamette's Jewish community for nearly twenty years, and it was time to move on. Even though he had been granted a lifetime contract a year earlier, in the wake of the split, he simply didn't feel good about remaining. Feelings were too sour in the community, and his own sense of personal failure didn't abate. It would be best for the community, and for himself, if he said goodbye.

He was offered a position at a wealthy Reform congregation in East Hampton, New York. After a tearful going-away party, the Kohners left Willamette.

Some people at Temple Am Israel were quietly relieved that Moishe had decided to move on. Though they may have personally liked him, they did view his politics as unnecessarily controversial, and his handling of the Bayt Emett faction improper.

Many others, however, were crushed that he left.

Most people at Temple Am Israel stated forthrightly that he had been the only reason that they were involved in Willamette's Jewish community. He had been the sole reason they had join the synagogue to begin with and the ongoing light that had kept them involved. Many people spoke of his personality—his warmth, openness, and perpetual dedication—as the single greatest factor in the community's successful growth since the seventies. They were sad to see him leave and viewed his departure as one of the greatest tragedies to follow the schism.

But not the greatest tragedy.

Eighteen days after leaving Willamette, Moishe suffered a heart attack. He recovered, but nine months later, a second heart attack killed him. He was playing tennis with a friend, one of the members of his new congregation, the sun was shining overhead, and all was well. He was fifty-one.

It was Julie Horowitz who called me to tell me the sad news. Her voice sounded fragile and shaken, and I hung up the phone feeling the same way. Though for the previous year I had been playing the investigative role of "sociologist," and had viewed Moishe mostly as a "character" in the community drama, his sudden death was personally and deeply felt. He was no longer the most important informant of my study, the one I was going to interview last—he was a gentle, loving man I had had the honor of knowing who had died too soon.

When I interviewed his wife, Yohanna Kohner, in her new home in Portland, the subject of his death brought tears to both our eyes. She shared some memorable particulars of his passing:

So after the funeral we got out and there was the hearse and then there was the limousine . . . our family went into this big limousine that had like twelve or thirteen people in there. It was a big one. And when we came back home, the driver, who is a black fellow in his sixties—a very distinguished man— opened the doors. And I gave forty dollars to Dalia [her daughter] and I said, 'I want you to give it to the driver.' Because I was walking away. And she went, and I didn't even make it to the front steps—he was right behind me. He said, 'Mrs. Kohner, I don't want your money.' And I said, 'You're the chauffeur and it's only right that you get something out of this.' And he said, 'No, you don't understand. I own the limousine.' And he said, 'Your husband and I were in the hospital at the same time . . . and we went to cardiac rehabilitation together.' And he said, 'Your husband was very kind to me. So I don't want your money.' [tears] . . . I have thousands of stories like that. Because everywhere I go, they just pop out, you know. And he used to go—wherever he went he had a way of making an impact and befriending people and helping people in a very quiet, unassuming way . . . I had to empty out his office . . . there was like seventy boxes . . . I couldn't deal with, so I hired somebody to bring a truck. And these two people came, two huge guys from South Hampton . . . and they had a truck, and for sixty-five dollars they were gonna transport it. And they came to the door and they had these dollies, you know . . . and they did that in like ten minutes—they had all these boxes stacked up. And I had my sixty-five dollars ready, plus the tip, and they looked at me and they said, 'No, we're not going to take this money.' And I said, 'Well, the Temple is not going to pay you'. I said, 'I am the one who asked that it be taken in the truck and I need to pay you because they're not going to give you the money.' And the guy said, 'Rabbi Kohner used to come to all our meetings—NAACP meetings in South Hampton. And tell me, what house in East Hampton has Martin's picture in the living room?' Moishe had a huge picture of Martin Luther King in his study, and when we moved to East Hampton, I put it in the living room because his study didn't have enough wall space . . . so anyway, these big tall guys, they just wouldn't take the money. And they just said, 'Anytime you need anything we'll just help you.' When I came to work . . . . this woman came up to me and she said . . . 'Your husband performed a wedding for my son about ten years ago.' She said, 'I want to tell you. He made a big difference in my son's life, . . . ' she said, 'he really made a big difference.' And I think that's the bottom line. You know, the bottom line is that—I mean, your thesis and your book is about congregational and religious sectarianism, but behind all of that there are human beings.

The congregation of Temple Am Israel was shattered upon the news of Moishe's death. The Hoffmans, Julie Horowitz and Hugh Leon, Rhoda Fogel and John Cohen, and several others, flew back East to be with Yohanna. In Willamette, over 1,000 people attended a somber memorial service. The audience was filled with a diverse array of people—nearly all tearful—who had known Moishe in one capacity or another: from ecumenical councils to human rights councils, from gay rights groups to the NAACP, from softball league to the Interreligious Committee for Peace in the Middle East.

His closest friend in Willamette, Ibrahim Hamide, a Palestinian, spoke for many when he said:

He was a 'peacenik'—a man of peace with a big heart, a big smile, and a contagious laugh. There was no hatred, no animosity in his heart for anything.

Unfortunately, amidst the pain of his untimely death, the hard feelings between the two camps were rekindled. Many felt that his heart attack was clearly a result of the stress of the schism. Some even went so far as to hurl blame directly at Bayt Emett. As Janie Strickstein recalled:

It was very bitter. It was very bitter . . . when Moishe left and had that heart attack, I mean the bitterness was so bad . . . I had been to a discussion one time . . . where somebody actually stood up and said that the other people—the Bayt Emett people—were the cause of Moishe's heart attack. Because they had caused so much bitterness.

According to Judith Malka:

He just wore out . . . and then the arguments at the end—the arguments were horrible . . . did anybody tell you about a rabbinic curse? Oh, this is so weird. Apparently Abe Shibel put a rabbinic curse on Moishe . . . Abe Shibel actually put a rabbinic curse on Moishe. There's something where— well, you can imagine —actually, these were talked about after Amir killed Rabin . . . there had been rabbis who stood in front of Rabin's house prior to the shooting, who had actually put a curse on him . . . after Moishe's death, I said, 'Oh, they're talking about the same thing.'

Aftermath

Soon after the split, and Moishe's death, Temple Am Israel underwent significant structural changes. Yakov, who had served the congregation as cantor, and had been a pseudo-rabbi to the Jewish Renewal folks over the years, was elected as the congregation's new head rabbi. After Yakov became the new rabbi, the congregation decided to finally fulfill what Moishe had been pushing for during the previous several years: official reaffiliation with a new denomination, Reconstructionism. Temple Am Israel became the ninety-first congregation in the country to join this dynamic, progressive denomination of Judaism founded by Rabbi Mordechai Kaplan, which stresses egalitarian principles, support for gays and lesbians, and a liberal approach to the interpretation of Jewish law.

Thus, where there had been one Conservative synagogue for decades, now that mainline, middle-of-the-road synagogue was divided in two—one segment had become Orthodox, the other Reconstructionist. A division of extremes: right-wing and left-wing, traditional and experimental, patriarchal and egalitarian. And the fact that they sat right across the street from each other only served to strengthen and reinforce their differences. Bayt Emett's congregational identity was solidified and its new Orthodox purpose perpetually affirmed when it looked across the street at the destructive liberalism it had successfully left behind, just as Temple Am Israel's congregational identity was simultaneously reinforced and its new Reconstructionist purpose perpetually affirmed when it looked across the street at the threatening traditionalism it had successfully resisted. Each was able to make sense of itself, and justify itself, in the face of the other.

There was so much that divided these two congregations, aside from the street that physically separated them. They embraced different styles of worship, they recited differently-worded prayers, they held different politics regarding Israel and gay rights, and they practiced different approaches to the regulation of gender.

Those who made up Bayt Emett, who had been so disgruntled by Rabbi Moishe Kohner's pro-Palestinian stance, now had a solidly right-wing leader, Rabbi Sapperstein.

Rabbi Sapperstein explained his politics regarding Israel:

Rabbi Kohner put up a Palestinian flag next to an Israeli flag, . . . he had Palestinians speak publicly at shule, . . . he lobbied against the U.S. loan guarantees for Israel's ability to absorb immigrants, and in general came out with a very pro-Palestinian position. . . . If you liked those things that he

209

did—if one liked what he was doing—then he would call him ahead of his time . . . if you didn't like the things he did, then what he did was ill-informed and divisive . . . my personal beliefs are that—clearly—that God chose to give Israel to the Jews . . . so theologically, philosophically, religiously—that the Arabs have their historic claims to the land are irrelevant. I don't care what their claims are . . . because I'm Jewish. My claims are Jewish, my history is Jewish, and more than that, I believe that reality is Jewish. Well, I shouldn't say that. Judaism defines the reality between God and the people. God gave the Jews the land and it boils down to that.

Whereas the members of Bayt Emett had been angered over Rabbi Moishe Kohner's peace activism, they now have a rabbi with a decidedly right-wing, God-Is-On-Our-Side position towards Israel. Rabbi Sapperstein also holds a much harsher, less tolerant view of homosexuals, compared to Rabbi Moishe Kohner's liberal position. As Rabbi Sapperstein explained:

Somebody asked me if I would give a homosexual an aleeyah. Well, why not? I give Sabbath violators aleeyahs, I give pig-eaters aleeyahs—like, what's the difference, right? If a guy was a murderer, you know, a gangster who shot people for a living, so okay, maybe I wouldn't give him an aleeyah . . . if a person was an activist, promoting something that the Torah calls a prohibition, and he's out—you know, he forms a Shop-lifters United Group—that person I could not give an aleeyah to . . . if the fellow who came in was very active, overtly politically promoting homosexuality and homosexual rights, is on TV and is a promoter, and he comes in and wants to give an aleeyah—that I have a little more difficulty with.

So, in addition to a solidly right-wing position regarding Israel, and an attitude that views homosexuality as a transgression somewhere on a continuum between pig-eater and murderer, Rabbi Sapperstein staunchly upholds the division that Orthodox Judaism advocates between men and women. At Bayt Emett, no woman can publicly read from the Torah or lead prayers. A woman's place is behind the *mehitzah*.

Rabbi Sapperstein explained his position regarding women and egalitarian Judaism:

I meet people all the time who are so burdened with misconceptions of Judaism. . . . They believe traditional Judaism . . . that we suppress women . . . that Orthodox women are, you know, second-class women, suppressed, not equal to men—right? But find me a Reform or Conservative woman whose education in Judaism is close to that of an Orthodox woman. Non-Orthodox women are Jewishly illiterate, largely. And if the Reform movement makes, you know, a dozen women into rabbis every year and that's 'equality,'—millions of reform women are illiterate, right? That's not equality. That's suppression.

"Why use the *mehitzah?*" I asked.

Men and women have been separated in religious practices going back to the times of the Temple, the Second Temple . . . the fact is that the synagogue, throughout history, was simply never a place where women historically went to . . . Judaism acknowledges that just like there are physical differences between men and women—and there is almost unanimous—now—understanding that there are psychological differences between men and women . . . and essentially differences in every area of personality. So too there are spiritual differences between men and women. And rather than try and squeeze men to be like women and squeeze women to be like men, Judaism acknowledges the differences and is constructed differently for men and women.

There is no question that things are different for men and women over at Bayt Emett. Difference based on gender is embedded into the structure of synagogue life: men conduct every aspect of the prayer service, from chanting the prayers to reading from the Torah, while women sit behind the *mehitzah.* But in addition to the structural differences of the worship services, there is a blatant numerical difference in terms of attendance. At any given religious ceremony, especially the weekly *Shabbes* services, men outnumber women by at least five or six to one. The majority of women who are "members" of Bayt Emett simply do not attend services. They stay at home and clean, cook, or tend to the children. Or attend services at Temple Am Israel. Three of the couples that I interviewed were divided over their choice of congregation. Mike Fish goes to Bayt Emett, but his wife goes to Temple Am Israel. Josh Binder goes to Bayt Emett, but his wife goes to Temple Am Israel. Laura Diamond goes to Bayt Emett, but her husband goes to Temple Am Israel. And it is the matter of gender equality that divides these couples.

Ingrid Kessler's case highlights the persistent significance of gender in the division between the two congregations. Ingrid had initially dropped out of Temple Am Israel because it was too liberal. She then tried Bayt Emett, but it was too conservative. And the treatment of women was central to her rejection of the latter:

> What the problem I think is—is that I see women not having the same respect as men, because I don't think they're as necessary as men. Then again, although Judaism says Judaism is a whole thing in your life and the home is very important and the woman is very important to the home— that's true. But the synagogue is sort of the center of learning, and the center of prayer. And when the women are not necessary there because they don't play a role, suddenly they just seemed devalued. And their opinions don't matter as much. And as people they don't seem to matter as much. And I see sometimes some women in Bayt Emett having a certain input in their style that I think could be very healthy for Bayt Emett—and they're ignored. . . . I'm thinking of one woman . . . that if she was a man I think she'd be a very main person in Bayt Emett—absolutely top, in there everywhere, always mentioned, always gone to for an opinion . . . but I think because she's a woman she just—even though she lives a real Torah life— she's kind of pushed a little to the side . . . and her style of prayer and input does not affect Bayt Emett very much—because she's a woman. And I don't think that's healthy . . . and then Bayt Emett started this women's class— and then the bizarre thing was that the women's class is on the same night as the Talmud class. So the women cannot go to the Talmud class if they want to go to the women's class, and that, to me, is instantly setting up a split.

Sometimes complete outsiders' perceptions can be insightful. To conclude this description of Willamette's recently divided Jewish community, I would like to offer two outsiders' views, those of Edik Akhmetshin and Brandi Baker.

One day, while I was in the midst of my study, a fellow graduate student from the University, Edik Akhmetshin, came to my office. Edik is from Kazan, Tatarstan. He had been in the United States for two years. Although his family was ethnically Muslim, he had been raised with virtually no religious training. He approached me because he wanted to go to a synagogue. He said he was "shopping around" for a religion. He had been to a few churches but wanted to give Judaism a shot. So, while still conducting my participant observation, I brought Edik along with me to Temple Am Israel that very next Saturday. It was a typical *Shabbes*: singing, casual dress, women and men equally involved, and so on. As we were leaving, I decided to take Edik across the street, to let him see the Orthodox service at Bayt Emett. Their *Shabbes* service was still well underway, and Edik and I came in and observed for about a half an hour. When we left, as we were walking back to my car, I was curious about Edik's impressions. What did he think of his first time among Jewish congregations? Which synagogue did he like better, Temple Am Israel or Bayt Emett? Nodding his head in the direction of Bayt Emett, he earnestly replied, "They are closer to God, I think."

Also while conducting my research, I was teaching a course on the sociology of religion. As a requirement for the class, my students were assigned the task of doing fieldwork at a religious service. They were expected to spend at least two hours observing the congregational activities and then write a paper on the experience.

Brandi Baker, twenty years old, a member of a sorority, with bright blonde hair and bright blue eyes, was one of my students. Brandi was from an Episcopalian and Catholic background but wasn't religious herself, and she didn't consider herself a feminist. Brandi asked me if she could go to a "Jewish church" to do her field observation. Brandi had never been inside a synagogue before, knew very little about Judaism, and thought it would be an educational experience.

I gave her directions to Temple Am Israel, but she accidentally walked into—and attended a *Shabbes* service at—Bayt Emett. In part of her paper, Brandi Baker wrote:

Although it was a warm and positive atmosphere, I was extremely shocked and disturbed by the blatant display of gender inequality. The placement of the physical barrier between the men and women was not something I have ever encountered before. Anna explained to me that men were not allowed to look at women during the celebration because they are considered to be very visual creatures and the sight of women would cloud their heads with inappropriate and unnecessary thoughts. Yet, the same rule and assumption did not apply to women. This discrepancy showed me the ignorance that I think their rules are based on. I question how it was ever determined that men and not women are visually oriented? To a greater extent, I question the notion that women's minds would not conjure up the same "inappropriate" ideas that men are supposedly thinking of? I find this dangerous belief to completely undermine a woman's sexuality and to ignore that women, too, are attracted to physical characteristics. This rule represents the idea that men and women are not sexual equals and that women have less significant sex drives. The fact that men are not allowed to look at women during worship also discredits that women have anything more to offer than just sex appeal. This rule indirectly makes the statement that women are primarily valued for their physical attractiveness and are not appreciated for their intelligence or personalities. Also, my other grievance was that the table in the front of the room where all of the activity centered around was on the side of the men, so the women could hardly, if at all, see what was going on. I can't see discrimination being more obvious.

Along the same lines, orthodox Jewish Synagogues follow the practice of restricting the Torah readings to only men. As mentioned earlier, it is an honor to be selected to read from the challenging Torah in worship, yet this privilege is not extended to women. Needless to say, women are also not allowed to become rabbis. This, too, is an obvious example of sex discrimination being practiced in their religion. It is a blatant statement that either women are incapable of performing the duty, or that they are not worthy of the honor. This infuriated me as a woman, for I felt these as personal attacks to my legitimacy as a human being.

For Edik Akhmetshin, Temple Am Israel was a nice place to visit. It was easygoing, colorful, and interesting. But it did little to stir his religious soul. Bayt Emett, on the other hand, struck a deeper chord. Though only observing their *Shabbes* service for about a half an hour, Edik had immediately felt a sense of tradition there, a resonating seriousness and truer worship of God.

For Brandi Baker, Bayt Emett's traditional style and seriousness were neither impressive nor inspiring. She walked away from that congregation feeling not as though it was closer to God, but rather, closer to a dangerous sexism that felt like a personal attack to her "legitimacy as a human being."

Was Bayt Emett a congregation closer to God, a congregation closer to what Judaism is supposed to be, or was it a bastion of patriarchal oppression and rigid routine cloaked under the self-serving garment of "tradition"? Was Temple Am Israel a congregation full of vital Jewish dynamism, a thriving congregation responsibly in tune with the growing needs and wishes of its members, or was it a stew of watered-down, ill-informed, misguided Judaism protected behind the self-serving shield of "innovation"?

The answers to these questions will be different, depending on which Jews of Willamette you care to ask. The religious, social, and philosophical understandings of what Judaism should be, and what Jewish identity is all about, are markedly different for the recently divided Jews of Willamette, who now congregate every Saturday morning on opposite sides of the street.

THE SOCIOLOGY
OF RELIGIOUS SCHISM

Sociological Theory and Religious Schism—This story of Willamette's Jewish community offers some significant insights, and raises some important questions, concerning the sociological study of religious schism in general.

To begin with, this ethnography represents the first in-depth case study of a religious schism on the congregational (micro) level. With the exception of an article written by E. Burke Rochford (1989) about a split within a community of Hare Krishnas in Los Angeles, all previous sociological studies have looked at schism on the denominational (meso) or global (macro) levels. The need to pay closer attention to religiosity on the micro level is clear. As sociologist of religion Meredith McGuire has suggested, "Rather than focusing on denominations and other umbrella religious organizations as the unit of analysis, we should try to understand the religious units to which believers are actually committed" (1997:99).

Certainly, the social dynamics of religious schism on the micro level are qualitatively different then those on the meso or macro level. For example, as this study has revealed, *individual personality dynamics are much more significant in schisms on the congregational level.* Who knows how things might have turned out if Lynn Rosefsky had had a warm, friendly relationship with Moishe Kohner, or if Abe Shibel had been a well-loved member of the community, or if Kevin Abrams had never spread a rumor? There is no question that the idiosyncratic personalities and unique relationships of the individuals of this community greatly colored, shaped, and determined this case of religious schism. Ultimately, sociologists of religion much resist treating religious schism as a monolithic phenomenon and recognize that the social dynamics at play are qualitatively different given the level (micro, meso, or macro) at which a given schism occurs.

But, theoretically speaking, there's more.

A prominent goal of mine while conducting this study was to uncover what had caused the split and, more specifically, what had caused some people to join Bayt Emett while others remained faithful to Temple Am Israel. Of course, the overt issues of contention were clear: the Arab-Israeli conflict, gender regulation, acceptance of gay and lesbians, and various Jewish matters such as the wording of important prayers. But, as a sociologist, I wanted to get underneath the overt issues and expose the underlying social sources of this case of religious schism. As I had confidently explained to my former boss, Eric Kline, while sitting in his used bookstore in L.A., sociological theory teaches us that religious schism is never just about overt religious or ideological differences, but rather, given religious or ideological differences are usually the outgrowth of preexisting, underlying social divisions.

In carrying out my study, I was ever cognizant of this well-established sociological premise that the source of religious schism, the cause of religious division, is never "just" religious or ideological in nature. Rather, there is inevitably something else at play—something social. As John Wilson (1971:1) states, the sociologist "sees schisms as the expression of social differences rather than the doctrinal and liturgical disputes they ostensibly represent." Or as Gus Tubeville (1949:30) notes, "religion may be used as a theater in which to act out conflicts arising from other issues."

Therefore, although I knew the Jews of Willamette disagreed about such ideological matters as the Arab-Israeli conflict or the wording of the Aleynu, I wanted to uncover more—I wanted to see if these ideological positions could actually be attributed to preexisting, latent social determinants. Hence, my ultimate question: *Was this case of religious schism actually the result of preexisting social differences?*

Before revealing what I found, it is necessary to quickly review the theoretical literature that had informed my inquiry.

Niebuhr and Others

As was mentioned earlier, the seminal sociological explanation of religious division comes from the work of H. Richard Niebuhr (1929). In a nutshell, Niebuhr asserted that religious division is seldom just a matter of opinion. Rather, "social forces" tend to be the underlying, determining sources of religious differences. Two divergent camps may disagree over an ostensibly religious matter, but the actual formation of those camps can usually be attributed to nonreligious, preexisting social divisions, such as differences in class, education, or race.

Subsequent studies have drawn from, and supported, Niebuhr's basic theoretical premise that preexisting social division is the determining source of religious division.

For example, Liston Pope's (1942) classic investigation of mills and churches in Gaston County, North Carolina. Like Niebuhr, Pope wasn't explaining schism directly, but rather, the plethora of different churches in Gaston County and their congregational composition. Pope found that socioeconomic factors greatly determined which churches congregants chose to belong to; religious divergence was thus clearly determined by preexisting class divergence. In short, the poor went to their churches, and the rich went to theirs.

Gus Tubeville (1949), in his study of a Methodist denominational rift known as the Pine Grove schism, found that religious division was also the direct result of preexisting socioeconomic division. He uncovered that a longstanding conflict between the wealthy, established families and the less wealthy, immigrant families directly determined the outcome of the schism. As in Pope's case, the rich went one way, the poor went another.

Robert Doherty (1967), in explaining the Quaker Orthodox-Hicksite denominational schism, found that class was again a predetermining factor of the division; in short, "wealthy persons became Orthodox while the less well-to-do joined the Hicksites" (p.44). Like Pope's and Tubeville's similar findings, Doherty's study concluded that the split "was clearly conditioned by socioeconomic pressures" (p.50).

Vrga and Fahey (1970), in their study of division within the Serbian Orthodox Church of North America, found that class wasn't the determining factor in setting the stage for division. But their findings still conformed to Niebuhr's general premise in that they were able to show how the split was actually "a reflection of antagonisms of nonreligious origin" (p.46). The two opposing camps embraced remarkably similar religious beliefs and ritual observances, but what clearly divided them were latent social factors such as recentness of immigration to the United States, the age of immigrants at the time of immigration, educational attainment, occupational experience, and political affiliation.

Although Stark and Bainbridge (1985) did not conduct any studies themselves, they have put forth some plausible explanations concerning the sociological nature of religious schism. They argue that schisms are likely to occur as a result of stratification or inequality within religious organizations. They go beyond mere economic matters (Niebuhr's emphasis), and suggest that stratification or inequality can be in terms of prestige or power. They assert that

> [w]hen people have very unequal levels of rewards, relationships between them are awkward and often embarrassing. The privileged fear envy. The disadvantaged risk a blow to self-esteem by close contact with the privileged. Where there is substantial inequality in a network, subnetworks will tend to separate as people pursue relationships with others who are similarly situated (p.103).

In short, inequality in a stratified organization creates an impetus for similarly-situated members to form cliques, which eventually sets the stage for faction formation, cleavage, and schism. Stark and Bainbridge's suggestion that preexisting social ties based on status inequality can be a determining source of religious schism conforms with Niebuhr's original premise in that the cause of religious division is located in the social realm, as opposed to the religious or ideological.

Shin and Park's (1988) study confirmed Stark and Bainbridge's theory. In examining forty-two Korean-American churches, Shin and Park found that internal power struggles between church factions—factions "formed on the basis of various 'social ties'" (p.243)—were the strongest predictors of schismatic division. Rochford's (1989) study of a schism within the Los Angeles Hare Krishna community also confirmed Stark and Bainbridge's model. Rochford found that the schism was the result of "social forces," namely, "long-standing cleavages" (p.163) and "preexisting interest groups" (p.166). By showing how religious schism can be the direct result of preexisting social division within religious organizations,

Shin and Park and Rochford have added further credibility to the general sociological model.

Liebman, Sutton, and Wuthnow's (1988) research on Protestant denominations in the United States indicates that vulnerability to schism is directly related to the size of a given religious organization. In sum, "the larger the denomination, the greater the tendency to schism" (p.351). Again, it is a social factor (the size of the denomination) that is looked to for explanatory purposes.

And finally, Ammerman's (1990) study of the denominational schism within the Southern Baptist convention. Ammerman found support for a "culture war" between liberal and conservative factions, expressed in divergent opinions largely over issues concerning private morality. And although Ammerman does emphasize matters of opinion in explaining the division, she also shows how the schism was clearly a reflection of pre-existing social divisions. Income was a strong predictor of which congregants would join the more conservative (poorer) or liberal (wealthier) camps; other predictors included differences in education, and occupational status of family of origin. These latter factors indicate continued support for Niebuhr's original premise that social factors such as congregants' class, occupation, or education can strongly determine their religious choice in a schismatic situation.

The sociological insight—that religious schisms are determined by social, nonreligious factors—is clearly merited, as the above research indicates. However, it may have its limits. In other words, while religious schism may very well often be the outcome of preexisting social factors, this may not always be the case.

No Preexisting Social Determinants

Much to my surprise, the schism of Willamette's Jewish community seemed to stand out as an exception to the traditional sociological paradigm. This was a shock to me, because from the outset, I had been quite confident that I would find some clear social difference between the two camps. But I was wrong. This was a case of religious schism that did not conform to the traditionally held sociological model; *the schism was not predetermined by latent social differences or preexisting social ties.*

As I had first explained to my former boss, Eric Kline, when I initially set out to study Willamette's Jewish community, I was confident that the sociological perspective would bear fruit. "Sure," I told myself, "this schism may *appear* to be solely about issues of religion, but certainly there is *something else* at play, some underlying social division."

I had some hunches. Based on my knowledge of the literature, I had a suspicion that class may have had an influence in predicting who would join which camp. I also suspected that perhaps the religiosity of people's parents may have contributed to the makeup of each group. As it turned out, neither suspicion proved correct. Much to my sociological dismay, every time I went searching for some such underlying social division, I came up with nothing. Existing sociological research could not help me explain away this religious schism as the mere manifestation of nonreligious factors.

The two opposing camps did not represent different national, racial, or ethnic groups. Nearly all were white Jews, all coming from essentially the same parts of the country, with nearly the same proportion of converts in each group. As mentioned above, class differences did not predetermine who would join which side. There was an equal amount of wealthy individuals in each camp, and no discernible differences in age, occupational status, or educational attainment. Of the latter, Wade Clark Roof (1994:52) has noted that education is the strongest predictor for people's religious attitudes and values, and that "more than anything else, education contributed to the deepening division between liberals and conservatives within religious communities. . . . " Not so with Willamette's Jewish community. Again, there was little difference between either camp in terms of educational attainment. Roughly 85% of those who were in Temple Am Israel's progressive camp had attained at least a bachelor's degree. The same was true for roughly 80% of the membership of Bayt Emett.

Internal stratification or preconceived status inequality, in terms of power and prestige, were not significant. Each camp had its share of powerful and prestigious members within the community. This judgment was based on the fact that each camp had a nearly equal share of members on various influential boards, and each camp had its share of past presidents and/or vice presidents of the Temple. For instance, approximately 45% of those in the progressive Temple Am Israel camp had served on the board of directors and/or the Religious Affairs Committee, as had approximately 45% of those who went on to join Bayt Emett.

Nor did the division appear to be the direct outgrowth of friendship bonds, social cliques or networks. Longtime friendships were actually split apart, for instance, the Hoffmans and the Rosefskys, Julie Horowitz and Jeff Bronner, and Julie Schoenberg and the Levitans.

The Hoffmans and Rosefskys had been best friends since the late seventies. They had regularly spent the Jewish holidays together, and their same-aged children had also been best friends. However, as the community divided, so too did their relationship. The Hoffmans remained leaders of Temple Am Israel, while the Rosefskys became leaders of Bayt Emett.

Julie Horowitz and Jeff Bronner had also been close friends. They had been political allies since the seventies, musical partners, and they had joined Temple Am Israel at about the same time, supporting each other over the ensuing decade. However, their relationship was broken as Julie pushed Reconstructionism and Jeff sought out Orthodoxy.

Another clear example illustrating the fact that preexisting social bonds did not predict into which camp individuals would fall, is the case of Julie Schoenberg. Julie stayed at Temple Am Israel, even though *all* her closest friends went to Bayt Emett. Julie had been especially close with Lenny and Ginger Levitan. However, when the division occurred, she stayed at Temple Am Israel. She had no social attachments with anyone there, but she simply couldn't sit beside a *mehitzah*. As Julie explained:

The majority of my friends were in Bayt Emett . . . . I did think about joining . . . I wanted to still daven with my friends, because that's who I sat with at Temple for ten years—eleven years—and all of a sudden now they're gone. And I'm sitting alone. So I definitely considered joining . . . and I just—the mehitzah—just not being counted as part of the minyan . . . so I decided to stay at the Temple . . . it took a lot of courage, because I felt like I would lose all my friends. That was the thing I was most concerned about. Because I wanted to keep—my friends are more important to me than my religion. But then I had to be true to myself as far as my Judaism .

. . the issue of equality is so strong within me. I cannot forsake that.

Julie wasn't the only one whose ideology proved stronger than her social bonds in determining which congregation she would join. David Decker was a "prime candidate" for Bayt Emett. He was dissatisfied with the liberal evolution of Temple Am Israel, he had few social bonds among the membership there, and he was a regular member of Abe Shibel's Talmud study group. But when the split occurred, though he had social ties with the Levitans, Rosefskys, and Irv Mendel, he simply couldn't be part of a congregation with such traditional/patriarchal gender regulation. Like Julie, he stayed at Temple Am Israel.

Other sociological factors were equally unhelpful in determining who would join which camp. As I mentioned above, I had my hunches that the way people had been raised might have affected their religious proclivity during the schism. That is, perhaps those who had been raised in Orthodox homes were more likely to join Bayt Emett, or maybe those who had been raised Christian were more likely to stay in the liberal camp. As it turned out, these hunches proved incorrect. Childhood religiosity did not determine who would join which side; each side had an equal share of members who had been raised Orthodox, Reform, Conservative, secular, or non-Jewish.

Nor were there any differences in terms of marital status, occupation of parents, or political affiliation. Nor was gender salient; each camp had an equal number of male and female supporters. True, the congregants were divided over issues of gender, but not *by* gender, per se.

Some attributed the split to the sheer growth of the congregation, but the fact that the synagogue population grew still tells us nothing about why some people went into one camp, and why some people went into the other.

In sum, *here was a schismatic situation marked by social homogeneity*, that is, the two divided groups did not differ in terms of race, ethnicity, age, class, sex, education, occupation, occupation of parents, religiosity of family when growing up, geographical place of origin, political affiliation, or marital status. (See Appendices 1 and 2.)

Since demographics or preexisting social networks such as cliques or friendship ties had no casual influence in determining which people would join which camp, it seemed to be a truly "ideological" battle, as opposed to the outgrowth of some underlying "social" factors. The traditional sociological paradigm was thus not applicable in explaining this case of religious schism.

Based on this conclusion, I threw up my theoretical hands and called Eric Kline in Los Angeles.

"You were right," I declared. "This actually was a purely ideological split. The two camps just disagreed over various religious and political issues and there were no clear social determinants dictating who would join which camp. The Orthodox camp did not differ demographically from the liberal camp, and it wasn't simply a case of preexisting social ties or friendships!"

Eric appreciated the call.

But others weren't so satisfied with my findings. My mentor, Dr. Benton Johnson, the chair of my dissertation, was sure I had overlooked something. He simply couldn't believe that there wasn't *something* social at play. He sat me down one afternoon, and over herbal tea, spoke to me in tones much more stern that his jovial disposition usually allowed. "I'm sure you'll find something, Zuckerman," he asserted. "There must have been something that determined why some people went into one camp, and others into the other camp. Keep looking, Zuckerman. You'll find it."

And I did find something, after all. There was a possible social factor, totally independent of the various religious and ideological issues that were debated, that may have had some significance in determining who would join which camp. It was a social factor that has been overlooked by previous sociological studies of religious schism: the members' preexisting relationship to their religious leader.

Relationship to Moishe

Upon closer scrutiny, I realized that several of the prominent members of Bayt Emett were people who had had a poor or negative personal relationship with Rabbi Kohner before the schism. And conversely, those who remained firmly in the liberal, anti-*mehitzah* camp of Temple Am Israel were people who had had a strong, positive relationship with Rabbi

Kohner prior to the schism.

The two most important members of Bayt Emett were Lynn and Josh Rosefsky. They were core founders and major players in the break away from Temple Am Israel. And from almost the first day Moishe had been hired back in the mid-1970s, Lynn didn't get along with him. And perhaps as a result of being Lynn's husband, Josh never established much of a rapport with Moishe, either.

Mike Fish of Bayt Emett had had a personal falling out with Moishe prior to the split. As Mike had explained, a psychologically unstable woman at his work began stalking him, causing great distress to him and his family. This woman, who wasn't Jewish, attempted to join the synagogue. Mike explained the situation to Moishe and asked him not to accommodate her. But Moishe welcomed this woman into the congregation in spite of Mike's pleas. Mike was disappointed by Moishe's actions, and their relationship was significantly soured thereafter.

As for the members of the liberal camp that remained loyal to Temple Am Israel, nearly *all* had good, positive, friendly relationships with Moishe. Rhoda Fogel and her husband John Cohen, Charles and Jayme Hoffman, Julie Horowitz and her husband Hugh Leon, Rachel Kantor, Zack Norman, John Meyers, and many others within Temple Am Israel were clear friends of Moishe's prior to the schism. Though there were many members of Temple Am Israel who may have disagreed with Moishe on certain political issues over the years, or may not have been extremely close with him, all those who stayed at Temple Am Israel were people who had a relatively positive relationship with him. They liked him as a person, and as a friend. And furthermore, no one who had a decidedly negative, bad relationship with Moishe stayed at Temple Am Israel following the schism.

The important theoretical point here is that there may be a subtle but salient causal link between people's relationship with Moishe and their later religious commitment. And since sociology's insight is that religious schism is often the result of nonreligious factors, this causal connection between people's relationship with Moishe and their subsequent religious choice during the schism fits the sociological paradigm.

I can't help but think of the blow-out between Charles Hoffman and Josh Rosefsky. They were best friends who had been close for over a decade. They were virtually the same age. Both had similar experiences in the sixties. Both became successful professionals in Willamette. They lived in the same neighborhood. Their wives were close, as were their children. They celebrated holidays together. And yet, in the midst of the schism, their friendship collapsed. Josh became an Orthodox Jew, while Charles supported Temple Am Israel's turn towards Reconstructionism. But their friendship did not strain as the result of mere religious differ- .ences. Things fell apart for Josh and Charles when they were serving on the Rabbi Review Committee, debating over Moishe's contract. Charles wanted to give Moishe a lifetime contract, Josh didn't. Thus, theirs was not a falling out over overtly religious matters. Theirs was a falling-out over Moishe. I can see the two of them, both nearly the same height, and with nearly the same receding hairlines, arguing in Charles' living room. At the heart of their differences was not religion, but their relationship with Moishe. As Charles had recalled:

> . . . [I]t really got bitter. It got bitter because it became very personal. And it was personal towards Moishe. And, you know, with all the warts and blemishes of a person like Moishe, he did not deserve the sort of personal attack that he got. And I really think that was the foundation of the schism . . . it became very personal. And I think that that was the foundation of Bayt Emett. It had much less to do with religious practice, and whole lot to do with how people felt about Moishe.

My mentor, Dr. Benton Johnson, was pleased with my observation concerning some members' preexisting personal relationship with the rabbi serving as a predictor of who would join Bayt Emett and who would stay at Temple Am Israel.

But just how strong of a predictor was it? Not very. True, the Rosefskys and the Fishs had had personal falling-outs with Moishe prior to their embracement of Orthodox Judaism. But what about the others who joined Bayt Emett? When considering the other leaders of the Orthodox camp, the causal link dwindles considerably.

Abe Shibel was the man who first facilitated the growth of Bayt Emett. He was not necessarily a leader; he did not go out and deliberate- ly acquire a following. However, it was his Talmud class that became the forum where disgruntled members of Temple Am Israel could gather, and he was the man who served as a role model for a more conservative brand of Judaism than that exhibited by Rabbi Moishe Kohner. Abe Shibel certainly didn't have a good relationship with Moishe. As discussed earlier, when Moishe first came to Willamette he had studied with Abe, but they had a falling-out—Yohanna claimed that Abe became irate when Moishe had to miss a Talmud class. But what is significant is that Abe Shibel was an Orthodox Jew before he ever met Rabbi Moishe Kohner. Thus, we cannot claim Abe Shibel's involvement with Bayt Emett resulted from his poor personal relationship with Moishe.

The same holds true for Lenny Levitan. Lenny had mentioned during his interview that he had never clicked with Moishe. However, Lenny had been an Orthodox Jew before he had ever met the Kohners.

And what about the other leaders of Bayt Emett? Jeff Bronner always had a good relationship with Moishe. And as for Bruce and Amanda Wallin, Irv Mendel, and Camille Vigeland—their relationships with Moishe only turned ugly in the midst of the schism, not prior to it.

At best, I was able to discern that a few of those who were significant members of Bayt Emett (Josh and Lynn Rosefsky, primarily) were people whose relationship with Rabbi Moishe Kohner was either poor or downright bad prior to the schismatic division. And nearly every member who remained loyal to Temple Am Israel had a relatively positive relationship to Moishe prior to the schism; not a single member who had a decidedly negative relationship with Moishe remained at Temple Am Israel.

Still Primarily Ideological

It would be impossible, however, to argue that the personal relationship each congregant had with Rabbi Moishe Kohner was an absolute, completely consistent predictor of who would join which camp. Some had been Orthodox before they had ever met Moishe, and most of those who joined the Orthodox camp only fell out with Moishe in the wake of the schism, not prior to it. Yes, in the case of the Rosefskys and the Fishes, their negative personal relationship with Moishe may have significantly affected their decision to join Bayt Emett. But they are only two couples, among over thirty.

Indeed, it would be incorrect and inaccurate to suggest that members' relationship to Rabbi Moishe Kohner caused the schism, or that members' choice of congregation was an absolute and inevitable outgrowth of their relationship to Moishe—that clearly wasn't the case. I had to tell my mentor that my hunting for social determinants in this case of religious schism—even considering the possible significance of members' prior relationship to the rabbi—was essentially fruitless.

What I found was that this was an unabashed case of differences of opinion. Nothing so clearly and absolutely divided the community, and predicted who would join which camp, as much as their disagreements over religious and ideological issues.

Dean Hoge (1976) came up with similar findings in his study of intrareligious conflict within mainline North American Protestantism in the 1970s. Hoge didn't study schism specifically, but his data are relevant for this discussion. He found that Protestant congregants were divided over such issues as literal inerrancy of the Bible, free will versus social determinism of people's behavior, questions concerning life after death—all of which are issues of belief, opinion, or ideology. And these ideological disagreements could not be correlated with any significant social variables. Hence, Hoge's conclusion about the source of contention within contemporary mainline Protestantism was that "theological causes account for more of the divisions than do any other factors" (p.73). In short, Hoge asserted, "What people believe about the nature of God and human nature and society—rather than age, economic class, clergy-laity differences, or psychological variations—underlies the formation of conflicting parties" (p.74).

I came to a similar conclusion in this case of religious schism. Those who formed Bayt Emett and those who remained in the Temple Am Israel camp disagreed over many things: Moishe's ability as rabbi, the rights of Palestinians, acceptance of homosexuals, the role of women, the wording of prayers, the physical separation of men and women during services, patrilineal descent, and so on. These issues divided the community. And what is theoretically significant is that these are *all matters of opinion, belief, or ideology*. In each instance, whether one supports or rejects the Middle East peace process, whether one accepts patrilineal descent, or whether one wants to refer to God as "he" or "she" or "it," is essentially a matter of individual ideology and belief. And since members of each camp appear to share no social characteristics, nor preexisting social ties, *divergence of opinion remains the ultimate source of this case of religious schism.*

This is theoretically problematic, because according to traditional sociological theory, religious schism is never simply ideological, never just the result of a divergence of opinion or belief alone, but always the result of preexisting social factors. In the words of sociologists of religion Kniss and Chaves (1995:174), "ideal factors have been given short shrift as causal influences in analyses of intradenominational conflict."

So how can we explain the schism of Willamette's Jewish community? Given the traditional sociological paradigm, we can't. Ultimately, what this case means for the general sociological study of religious schism can be summed up as follows: *While previous research has shown that religious schism is quite often the result of preexisting nonreligious or nonideological factors, there can be exceptions; sometimes ideological differences are the determining factors in a religious schism.*

Kniss and Chaves (1995) have rightly warned that broad theoretical propositions based upon one particular case study are dubious. However, while remaining cognizant of the fact that single case studies present theoretical limitations (in that generalizability can be problematic), I would still like to offer some insights based on my research suggesting new foci for future studies of religious schism.

I would like to briefly explore three areas of theoretical concern that came to occupy my sociological imagination while conducting this study, and that may enhance the future study of religious schism: 1) the necessity of taking the sociocultural context into account, 2) the possible effect of voluntary, "cost/benefit" congregational affiliation, and 3) the significance of the latent oppositional dynamic that is part of the "schismatic dance."

Ideologies in Sociocultural Context

To begin with, when claiming that a schism is primarily ideological in nature—as I have done for this case of Willamette's Jewish community—

it is essential to declare that this does not mean that social circumstances were not significant. In arguing that the only discernible "source" of the schism of Willamette's Jewish community was a division of ideology, and that clashing opinions and beliefs were the deciding factors in splitting apart the congregation and in determining who would join which faction, it is still essential to *take into account the sociocultural environment in which the schism took place*. No schism—indeed, no human undertaking—is ever purely ideological. After all, ideas, opinions, and beliefs, do not exist in a vacuum. Ideas and beliefs are not independent, free-floating, cloudlike objects that arbitrarily enshroud people's minds. Nor are they encoded in our DNA. Rather—and this is one of sociology's greatest insights—ideas, opinions, and beliefs are always and inevitably constructed in a given social context (Mannheim, 1936). Thus, while the schism can most explicitly be attributed to ideological factors in the immediate sense, social factors were still at play in the more generalized, abstract sense. Peter Takayama (1980), in his discussion of religious schism and "environmental permeability," has addressed the importance of recognizing that religious organizations are always and inevitably tied to their social surroundings. As he has explained, "Because they [religious organizations] serve culture-oriented goals, they are highly sensitive as well as vulnerable to moral climates and social issues of the society (and the world)"(p. 301).

Earlier, I discussed the extent to which the schism of Willamette's Jewish community could be understood as one manifestation of a "culture war," a general sociocultural trend in American society discussed at length by Hunter (1991) and Wuthnow (1988). This "culture war" perspective holds that American society in general, and American religions in particular, are becoming increasingly internally divided between those with an impulse toward progressivism (liberals) and those with an impulse towards orthodoxy (conservatives). This particular case of Temple Am Israel's schism is clearly enmeshed in this broad American sociocultural division.

I have also gone to lengths to expose the manner in which this division was affected by the permeating social significance of feminism in our culture. From disagreements over the gender-neutral wording of traditional prayers to the final battle over the *mehitzah*, feminism as a sociocultural contextual factor greatly shaped and informed the ideological nature of this case of religious schism.

But in addition to discussing the relevance of the "culture war" and the impact of feminism on Willamette's Jewish community, I would like to highlight two additionally pertinent elements of the sociocultural context: the predominance of baby boomers in the community and the decidedly voluntary nature of contemporary Jewish affiliation.

Baby boomers are generally defined as those Americans who were born between 1946 and 1964 (Roof, 1994). Of my entire sample, 80% were baby boomers (75% of the Temple Am Israel sample, 85% of the Bayt Emett sample). The shared sociocultural experiences of the baby-boom generation clearly informed the personal and ideological elements of this schism. While baby boomers defy monolithic generalizations and are a diverse and varied generation, there is much my sample of baby boomers shared: they are the generation immediately after the Holocaust, the generation that reaped the wealth and affluence that most Jews experienced during the 1950s, the generation that came of age in the 1960s, and the most educated generation in American history, and so on.

As baby boomers, perhaps all involved had a greater tendency to eagerly take up causes. This applies to both groups, the Orthodox as well as the feminist-minded. Both exhibited a willingness to stand for ideals, to fight for ideals, in short, to consciously and actively create an ideal communal identity based on a sense of intense moral purpose, regardless of the divisive consequences. As baby boomers, these individuals may have had a heightened sense of rebelliousness, of radical action, of self-righteousness, and less of a desire to seek "middle-of-the-road" compromise, communal rapprochement, or self-sacrifice for the sake of others.

Wade Clark Roof (1994) has commented on the idiosyncratic religiosity of the baby boomers during the late eighties and early nineties (the time period of Temple Am Israel's fragmentation). It was a time when baby boomers were entering mid-life, which Roof aptly describes as a "critical juncture of affirming life's meanings and fundamental values and of dealing with spiritual voids . . . " (p.6). Furthermore, "how they see themselves in relation to others is undergoing revision, new vistas of self-understanding and of commitment are opening up—in short, it is a time of soul stirrings . . . for boomers it is a time of growing and maturing, or refocusing life" (p.27).

Of course, exactly how the predominance of baby boomers influenced the schism can remain only speculative. But it is possible to suggest that as a community dominated by baby boomers, there were certain personal/generational propensities (suggested above) that decisively helped to shape the fabric of this particular schism.

Another important aspect of the sociocultural context that informed the schism of Willamette's Jewish community is the decidedly voluntary nature of contemporary American Jewish communal identity. It is quite possible to argue that being Jewish is more of a choice now, in late 20th-century America, than it has ever been in the history of Jewish civilization.

In the past, Jews, by and large, lived in tightly-knit, segregated, self-sufficient communities, and anti-Semitism was a constant presence. Individual Jewish identity was thus largely mandatory, as a result of both internal and external pressures. However, in the contemporary United States, with its plurality and diversity of religious, ethnic, and racial elements, and with anti-Semitism comparatively nonexistent, Judaism is no longer ghettoized; individual Jews are no longer bound to a given Jewish community. Being Jewish is optional, here and now more than in any other place or at any other time. As Michael Lerner (1994:20) succinctly acknowledges, "Jews don't *have* to remain Jews today. Every Jew is to some extent a Jew by choice."

Daniel Elazar (1980:133-135) has summed up the significance of this situation:

> The American Jewish community is built upon an associational base to a far greater extent than any other in Jewish history. That is to say, not only is there no inescapable compulsion, external or internal, to affiliate with organized Jewry . . . all connections with organized Jewish life are based on voluntary associations . . .
>
> . . . As the decision to be involved in Jewish life became increasingly a voluntary one, the new voluntarism extended itself into the internal life of the Jewish community as well, generating pluralism *even within* previously *free* but relatively homogenous and monolithic community structures. This pluralism was increased by the breakdown of the traditional

reasons for being Jewish and the rise of new and different incentives for Jewish association.

In a sociocultural context in which being affiliated with a Jewish organization is a voluntary act—a choice individuals make in an almost strictly cost/benefit manner—the texture of congregational life will surely be affected. When affiliation with the Jewish community is a choice individuals make—rather than some familial or cultural obligation, or reaction to persecution—we can expect significant consequences that will affect the form and nature of Jewish communal identity. We can speculate that given such a sociocultural Jewish context typified by choice, individual Jews who do volunteer to join a Jewish congregation will have a greater sense of personal authority and conscious responsibility in "getting what they want" out of their congregational affiliation. We can expect that there will be an increased motivation on the part of individuals to consciously, actively, and deliberately shape their community in a manner—and to a degree—hitherto unknown in Jewish history. Clearly this predominance of "Jews by choice" as congregational affiliates affected this particular schismatic dynamic.

Cost/Benefit Congregational Affiliation

Many, perhaps even most of the Jews of Willamette are not affiliated with Temple Am Israel or Bayt Emett. A large proportion of the Jews in this green nook of *Galut* are indifferent to religious practice and unconcerned with issues of Jewish identity. Without question, a sizable chunk of the Jews in Willamette are not affiliated congregationally; they are peacefully pursuing their professional goals, loving their non-Jewish spouses, and assimilating into WASP American culture with grace and ease.

But some Jews in Willamette want their Judaism to remain a significant aspect of their personal identity. They want to remain tied to other Jews in a structured Jewish communal environment. They want their children to go to Hebrew school. These are the Jews who choose to be affiliated congregationally. And "choose" is the key factor here. Being affiliated with other Jews in a congregational setting is a clear and definite choice these individuals make. As was discussed earlier, there are virtually no internal, external, societal or cultural pressures forcing any Jew in Willamette to affiliate with a Jewish congregation. That means that whoever joins the religious community does so as the result of an individual cost/benefit analysis. Those who choose to affiliate consciously want to "get" something out of their congregational ties, be it a spiritual connection, a sense of belonging to a group, a place to make friends or meet a potential mate, a place to feel a sense of heritage and tradition, a place to learn Hebrew, or something else. The reasons people choose to affiliate with a congregation are numerous—but what is consistent is that a definite choice is made.

This cost/benefit, voluntary aspect of congregational religiosity is certainly not limited to the Jewish community, but may be a growing phenomenon within American religious culture. Several sociologists have documented this "new voluntarism" among various Christian denominations in the United States (Roof and McKinney, 1987; Hammond, 1992; McNamara, 1992).

And what does this have to do with the sociology of religious schism? I would suggest that *the greater the proportion of members of a religious organization that is made up of people who join that organization from a decidedly cost/benefit vantage point, the greater the likelihood of religious schism.* It is my suspicion that extreme volunteerism in religious affiliation heightens the likelihood of divisiveness. This is because when affiliates of a congregation join in a decidedly cost/benefit manner, they are more likely to make sure the congregation meets their individual demands. They are more likely to expect an immediate and positive return for the cost of belonging. They are more likely to be insistent about "getting what they want" and making sure that their needs are being met. They are more likely to fight against and actively oppose trends or aspects of their congregation that they are unhappy with. They are less likely to be accommodating or accepting of aspects of the congregation with which they are dissatisfied. In a religious organization predominated by people who are members by choice—people who have made a conscious cost/benefit analysis prior to joining and have joined in order to receive anticipated benefits—tendency towards acquiescence, compromise, and passivity will be less salient when conflicts inevitably arise.

Throughout my study of Willamette's Jewish community, I was struck by the undisputed voluntary nature of my informants' congregational affiliation. These Jews did not *have* to be members. I couldn't help speculate about the affect this tendency of members, to weigh the costs against the benefits of membership, had on the inner struggle of Willamette's Jewish community that ended in schism.

The Oppositional Dynamic of the Schismatic Dance

And finally, it is important to recognize the ways in which the very schismatic process itself, through its inherent oppositional dynamic, serves to actually strengthen the individual and group identity of all parties involved. Whenever social groups exist, be they religious, political, or otherwise, little else so stimulates group cohesion and enlivens a sense of purpose among members as when there is someone or something to be against. Often, an oppositional dynamic strengthens group bonds, and increases individual members' sense of worth and meaning.

As Meredith McGuire (1997:173) notes, "The sectarian orientation thrives on a sense of opposition. Ironically, backlash movements often inadvertently contribute to the cohesion of the very groups they attack."

Throughout my study, I couldn't help notice how the schismatic process itself clearly served to strengthen both individual and group identity. It was my sense that being *in opposition* to someone or something, had positive latent results for all involved. Though the schism was viewed by my informants as an ugly, difficult, and a traumatic communal experience, the oppositional dynamic itself inevitably forced people to more clearly define themselves in terms of their Jewishness, and it fostered a strong sense of communal attachment on both sides.

Many of the people who became early members of the Orthodox group definitely experienced an exciting sense of rebelliousness when they first began meeting as a group. Their shared opposition to Temple Am Israel gave them a heightened sense of purpose and a bonding sense of a shared mission to defend "traditional" Judaism from the liberal desecration that was going on under Rabbi Moishe Kohner's tutelage. As Josh Rosefsky had fondly recalled, "We were the outlaws of the Jewish community."

There they were, this handful of Jews, gathering at Abe Shibel's Talmud class, joining together to valiantly resist the politically correct madness that was engulfing their congregation.

Bayt Emett clearly began in opposition. Bayt Emett began when a group of people became unhappy with Temple Am Israel's move toward liberalness, and all the pro-Palestinian activism, pro-gay rights activism, gender-equal rhetoric, rewording of prayers, and other random progressive innovations that went along with it. And in that opposition, this group felt a shared sense of purpose. They felt a shared sense of worth—they were standing up for "true" Judaism in the face of this liberal destruction. And since Temple Am Israel was becoming more and more extreme in its liberalness, these people would go in just the opposite extreme conservative direction: Orthodoxy. There is no doubt in my mind that the group's decision to become Orthodox was the result of this oppositional dynamic. These people didn't just decide to become Orthodox out of nowhere, in an isolated situation, in a purely self-reflective manner. Their embracing of Orthodoxy was in clear contradistinction to Temple Am Israel's liberal evolution. And then, as this Orthodox group became a presence to contend with, a strong segment of the liberal camp within Temple Am Israel mobilized in opposition to them. The anti-*mehitzah* group emerged. These were women and men who suddenly felt it was their duty to resist patriarchal Judaism, to defend the rights of women, to oppose fundamentalist Orthodoxy. In their opposition to the Orthodox group, these like-minded individuals were able to reaffirm their commitments to progressivism, to feminism, to Reconstructionism. They were able to clearly assert their ideals, and act upon them in a manner that felt both just and noble. The women and men who were opposed to the Bayt Emett group's use of Temple Am Israel's back room clearly experienced their own heightened sense of individual worth and group purpose in opposition to their Orthodox counterparts.

And once Bayt Emett successfully split and established its own congregation right across the street, Temple Am Israel quickly reaffiliated denominationally, becoming an official Reconstructionist synagogue. Reconstructionism is the most liberal, progressive Jewish denomination in existence. It is my belief that Temple Am Israel's motivation to finally affiliate as a Reconstructionist synagogue was in direct oppositional response to the establishment across the street of the Orthodox Bayt Emett.

In short, Bayt Emett had initially defined itself as Orthodox *in opposition* to the liberalness of Temple Am Israel, and Temple Am Israel redefined itself as Reconstructionist *in opposition* to Bayt Emett's Orthodoxy.

We're back to the Jewish man stranded on the desert island who had to build himself two bamboo synagogues, one to belong to, and one to be opposed to.

Sociologists of religious schism must always be aware of the fact that the schismatic process, while overtly one of division and apparent communal breakdown, is also one in which the personal and group identities of those involved are actually strengthened.

We must also recognize that the two oppositional groups in a given schism are always bound to one another in a dance—a dance of division, to be sure—but a dance none the less, in which almost every move by one group is in direct relation to the moves of the other. In the process of this schismatic dance, each group's motives and goals are directly related to the other group's, so that the outcome of the division is one in which each group's identity is to a large degree shaped in reaction to the other's.

THEY DROP OUT

Surprising as it may seem, most of the members of Willamette's Jewish community who had fought the hardest during the schism dropped out within a year after the break. The two congregations were neatly separated and doing relatively well on their own, and yet the key players on both sides—the leaders of the Bayt Emett group, as well as the leaders of Temple Am Israel's feminist, anti-*mehitzah* group—were all gone within a year after the actual schism occurred. Those who had exerted the most energy and had fought the hardest in securing their vision of Willamette's Jewish community withdrew from that community soon after the split and remain uninvolved and unaffiliated at the time of this writing.

Lynn Rosefsky was perhaps the only person to come up in virtually every single interview I conducted. Almost everyone described her as a decisive figure in the schism. She had lived at the house on University Street way back in the seventies, where she had been a brief devotee of Yakov Tish. She then fell out of that communal scene after marrying Josh, but the two of them went on to become major leaders within Temple Am Israel. In addition to serving on the key committees and the board of directors, they were important financial donors. But Lynn had never liked Rabbi Moishe Kohner. After his arrival in Willamette she had challenged his authority, questioned his politics, doubted his religious vision, and eventually led an unsuccessful (successful?) attempt to oust him. She was one of the early leaders of Bayt Emett, and once she and Josh became Orthodox, their energies were channeled into that community.

However, within six months after the schism and the successful establishment of the Bayt Emett congregation across the street, Lynn suddenly dropped out. She had a fight with Abe Shibel that permanently soured their relationship. She also had immediate differences with Rabbi Sapperstein. And then she soon decided that the whole Orthodox religious trip was hogwash. She quit Bayt Emett and completely gave up on her attempt to live an Orthodox lifestyle.

Though her marriage to Josh remains strong, he is now alone in his commitment to Orthodox Judaism, as well as Bayt Emett. As Lynn explained:

It just got too—the demands of just—you know, this is your social group, this is where you are gonna focus. You can only deal with other Jews. And all these—it made me uncomfortable. It wasn't the way I was raised . . . I started feeling less and less true to myself. You know, covering my hair on Shabbes and stuff. I don't know. There were some really great services and some really great people to meet. But I was—I was starting to God-wrestle again. I couldn't get it. It just wasn't coming naturally. I couldn't daven. I wasn't interested in it . . . it just didn't feel like a fit . . . and it was feeling more and more like—like something that was very fulfilling to Josh, and less so for me, on a spiritual level . . . and basically, I'm not a religious person. I just am not . . . I just think life is a pretty random experience.

According to Josh:

She found that she just couldn't maintain this new set of beliefs. It just was—it didn't make sense to her. She didn't have the faith. She had questions about the existence of God and the whole idea of Jewish law.

For over twenty years Lynn had been part of Willamette's Jewish community, from the house on University Street, to Temple Am Israel, to Bayt Emett. And she left all three.

"So now you don't have a synagogue," I remarked.

I don't need a synagogue. I don't need a rabbi and I don't need a synagogue. I take care of those needs myself. I do a lot of—I spend a lot of time alone. I walk. I get up between four and five every morning and I go out, all year round, unless it's too icy, and I spend an hour and a half and sort of—either listening to NPR . . . or thinking.

Lynn had been in the eye of the storm for a long time and had assumed a leadership role in the formation of Bayt Emett. She had fought against Temple Am Israel and to some degree won—at least in terms of creating

an alternative congregation. Yet, in the process, she had made many enemies. And now that she no longer affiliates with either congregation, she
is somewhat of an outcast. I wondered how she felt about her choices.

*What troubles me in retrospect . . . you sort of hope when you're acting
something out . . . that you're not going to feel embarrassed. I don't feel
embarrassed. I feel that we did what we had to do. But I hope that not a lot
of it was just horribly petty. And I do worry that this—that I was motivated, in part, by never having liked or respected Moishe Kohner. Maybe what
that gave me—I'd like to think—is just the incentive to be the most vocal,
and the most vitriolic—which the movement needed. I think. I don't—I
would hate to realistically look and think: that was wrong; what you did was
horrible and wrong. I would feel bad. I don't think it was. But I, you know,
so . . . I don't know. It's okay if you write that it was [sad laughter].*

But Lynn wasn't the only one to drop out.

Four months after Bayt Emett was firmly established and had hired its
own rabbi, Abe Shibel left town. Abe had lived in Willamette for over
twenty-five years. And all the while, he had persistently refused to join
Temple Am Israel because it wasn't traditional enough for him. His only
Jewish connection was his weekly Talmud study class, the initial arena
out of which the nucleus of the Bayt Emett group grew. He had served as
a visionary for that early Orthodox group, urging them on towards greater
religious observance and continually pointing out the weaknesses of
Rabbi Moishe Kohner. However, once an official Orthodox congregation
actually emerged in Willamette, Abe Shibel would have nothing to do
with it. He retired from his teaching job at the University and moved to
Cincinnati.

Aside from Abe Shibel, the first Jews to really embrace Orthodoxy in
Willamette were the Levitans. Lenny had been raised Orthodox, but after
he and his wife, Ginger, moved to Willamette, they had slacked off.
However, when they became disenchanted with Temple Am Israel and
came under the influence of Abe Shibel, Lenny's Orthodoxy kicked in
again. He and Ginger embraced the rituals and practices of Orthodox
Judaism, and Lenny was decisive in organizing the first separate Saturday
morning Bayt Emett services out in the Oliff house. However, less than

one year after Bayt Emett became its own functioning *shule*, the Levitans moved away from Willamette to find a place where they could raise their two children in a more Orthodox environment. Although they had devoted so much of their time, money, and energy into founding Bayt Emett, once it was established, it wasn't enough. They moved to Seattle.

Jeff Bronner had first become involved with the Jewish community in Willamette through his friend and fellow political activist, Julie Horowitz. Over the years he had grown from a liberal Jew without much Jewish education to a devout, fully observant Orthodox Jew. Though he loved Bayt Emett and had poured his heart into making it happen, less than a year after it was firmly rooted in Willamette, he moved to San Francisco to find himself an Orthodox wife.

Lynn Rosefsky, Abe Shibel, the Levitans, and Jeff Bronner: some of the most active founders of Bayt Emett, who had struggled within—and then against—Temple Am Israel, throwing their hearts into the Jewish community of Willamette, battling over its shape and destiny, were no longer members of that community once the dust cleared.

And just about the same held true for the other side as well.

Moishe and Yohanna Kohner had left town immediately after the split. They had fought to keep a *mehitzah* out of Temple Am Israel and had successfully driven out those who had wanted a *mehitzah*, and yet once the battle was over, they departed. Moishe soon died from a heart attack, and then Yohanna moved to Portland to live with her sister.

Many people had characterized Yohanna Kohner as Lynn Rosefsky's counterpart/nemesis. They were both strong, staunch women, and they had been on opposite sides of every single issue. They had antagonized each other for nearly two decades, ostensibly for the purpose of steering Willamette's Jewish community in the proper direction. Lynn had wanted an alternative to Moishe Kohner and Temple Am Israel. Yohanna had wanted a congregation free from Orthodoxy's treatment of women. Both of these were actualized with the realization of the schism. And yet, once each had what they wanted, they didn't want it anymore. Yohanna expressed to me little desire to return to Willamette. Like Lynn, there was nothing left for her in this community.

Second to Yohanna in the movement to evict the Bayt Emett group was Rhoda Fogel. Rhoda's husband, John Cohen, had been present at the

Talmud study class when derogatory remarks were supposedly made about women. Rhoda had led the fight to ban the _mehitzah_ from Temple Am Israel property. She and her husband were the ones who drafted up and circulated the petition to make sure no services that included a _mehitzah_ would be possible on Temple Am Israel property. Rhoda had fought with all her heart and soul, while serving on the board of directors and the Religious Affairs Committee, to maintain the principles of egalitarianism at Temple Am Israel. And yet, when the storm was over, and Bayt Emett was its own congregation and Temple Am Israel had further committed itself to the ideals of egalitarian Judaism by affiliating with the Reconstructionist movement, Rhoda Fogel and John Cohen dropped out. They disaffiliated from the congregation completely. Rhoda said that without Moishe, it just didn't feel like her synagogue anymore. As she explained:

> _After Moishe left, I resigned . . . he was a tower of strength, you know, and when he wasn't here I really didn't feel safe anymore._

Rhoda's close friend, Miriam Shimmel, also dropped out. She had been one of the women who had "attacked" Ginger Levitan at that Hanukkah party for being Orthodox, and she had assisted Rhoda and Yohanna in forming and leading the anti-_mehitzah_ group. However, in the immediate aftermath of the schism she got married and had a baby and decided that she no longer wanted to be part of Temple Am Israel either.

Yohanna, Rhoda and John, and Miriam. Four of those who had fought so hard to make sure their visions of Willamette's Jewish community were carried through, who had struggled so hard against the Orthodox camp, and then were no longer part of the community within a year after its division.

I wondered how people could fight so hard, supposedly on behalf of the Jewish community, only to drop out of that community once the battle was over. I wondered how people could put themselves out like that, withstanding personal attacks, being the focus of rumors, even losing friends, all in the name of the Jewish community—all in the name of furthering their concept of Jewish values—only to suddenly withdraw once the struggle was over.

There are many possible explanations as to why these people dropped out. Perhaps the trauma of the schism had taken its toll on them personally; the several years of rumors, arguments, and personal battles may have left them tired, wounded, and sick of the whole community, just wanting step away from it all. Or perhaps it had to do with the oppositional dynamic. That is, maybe the divisive struggle had been a somewhat rewarding experience in and of itself for these people, and once there was nothing to fight for, or nothing to defend, or nothing to attack or oppose, being part of the Jewish community suddenly lost its meaning. Perhaps without immediate opposition, being part of the club lost its appeal.

Though Lynn Rosefsky, Abe Shibel, Jeff Bronner, Lenny and Ginger Levitan, Yohanna Kohner, Rhoda Fogel, John Cohen, and Miriam Shimmel have taken their leave from Willamette's Jewish community, the two congregations on opposite sides of the street are doing fine.

It is actually *Shabbes* morning right now, as I write this. It is raining. Over at Temple Am Israel at this very moment, Rabbi Yakov Tish is probably playing his guitar and singing a song about loving life. And across the street, at Bayt Emett, Rabbi Sapperstein is probably swaying somberly in prayer, contemplating the ancient words of the Ameedah.

Appendix I TEMPLE AM ISRAEL

GENDER	AGE	WHERE RAISED	OCCUPATION	EDUCATION	PARTY	FATHER'S OCCUPATION	MOTHER'S OCCUPATION	CAME TO WILLAMETTE	RELIGIOSITY OF FAMILY WHEN CHILD
1. F	49	Morocco	schoolteacher	MA	Democrat	govt. bureaucrat	technical secretary	1977	Orthodox/traditional Moroccan
2. M	48	Madison, WI	lawyer	Law	Democrat	business owner	homemaker	1977	Conservative
3. F	47	Milwaukee	college prof.	MA	Democrat	business owner	bookkeeper/homemaker	1977	Conservative
4. F	41	St. Louis	editor	BS	Democrat	business owner	[unclear]	1993	Reform
5. F	53	L.A.	childcare administrator	BA	Democrat	business owner	piano teacher	1977	Orthodox
6. F	49	N.Y.C.	community volunteer	some coll	Democrat	lawyer	high-school teacher	1979	Reconstructionist
7. F	49	"West Coast"	R.N.	some coll.	Democrat	army officer	homemaker	1976	Episcopalian
8. F	37	S.F.	human resource consultant	MA	Democrat	business owner	homemaker	1980	Reform
9. M	56	Chicago	psychiatrist	MD	Democrat	bookkeeper	homemaker	1971	Secular/"Identified as Jews"
10. F	46	Montreal	college prof.	PhD	Democrat	doctor	homemaker	1991	Conservative and Reform
11. F	37	New Haven, CT	college prof.	PhD	Democrat	made neckties	homemaker	1988	Conservative/"Did Hanukkah"
12. M	39	L.A.	therapist	MSW	Democrat	nursing home administrator	artist	1975	Agnostic Zionist/"Did Kiddush"
13. M	40	Connecticut	college prof.	PhD	Democrat	pharmacist	administrative assistant	1988	Conservative
14. F	41	Orange County, CA	writer	some coll.	Democrat	factory worker	homemaker	1985	Secular/No Affiliation
15. M	52	L.A.	management consultant	BA	Democrat	electrician	homemaker	1976	Conservative
16. F	52	S.F.	teacher	MA	Democrat	editor	librarian	1976	Reform
17. M	44	"Willamette"	photographer	BA	Democrat	college prof.	homemaker	born here	Conservative/Temple Am Israel
18. M	49	N.Y.C	college prof.	MA	Democrat	CPA	homemaker	1975	Conservative
19. M	44	New York	soy-foods manufacturer	BA	Independent	engineer	schoolteacher	1978	Presbyterian
20. F	34	"Willamette"	mother	almost MA	Democrat	college prof.	homemaker	born here	No affiliation/"Knew I was Jewish"
21. F	39	Chicago	professor	Law	Democrat	journalist	homemaker/lawyer	1982	Southern Baptist
22. M	54	Cape Town	psychiatrist	ND	Democrat	[unclear]	[unclear]	1976	Orthodox
23. F	55	L.A.	teacher	MA	Democrat	jeweler	homemaker	1976	Sephardic Traditional
24. M	43	Utah	V.P. of computer company	BS	none	business exec.	homemaker	1987	Mormon

Appendix 2 BAYT EMETT

GENDER	AGE	WHERE RAISED	OCCUPATION	EDUCATION	PARTY	FATHER'S OCCUPATION	MOTHER'S OCCUPATION	CAME TO WILLAMETTE	RELIGIOSITY OF FAMILY WHEN CHILD
1. F	42	Portland, OR	business owner	BA	Democrat	surgeon	homemaker	1975	totally secular/"Had X-mas tree"
2. M	48	Detroit	business owner	MSW	Democrat	dentist	homemaker	1974	Conservative
3. F	49	Massachusetts	homemaker	Law	Democrat	toolmaker	homemaker	1982	Methodist
4. M	39	N.Y.C.	computer technician	BA	Democrat	elect. engineer	homemaker	1979	Orthodox
5. M	45	Indiana	restaurateur	some coll.	Republican	dentist	homemaker	[unclear]	Presbyterian
6. F	42	Chicago	R.N.	BA	Democrat	insurance broker	worked at father's shop	[unclear]	Secular/"High Holidays only"
7. M	81	Baltimore	accountant	some coll.	Democrat	clerk	clerk	1982	Reform
8. M	40	Long Beach	schoolteacher	MA	Independent	doctor	schoolteacher	1979	Secular/"Cultural Jews"
9. M	45	Pittsburgh	writer	MA	Democrat	accountant	teacher	[unclear]	Reform/"Lit Shabbes candles"
10. M	53	Chicago	computer sales	PhD	Libertarian	ad agent	homemaker	1990	Orthodox/Conserv./Reform
11. F	38	Columbus, OH	schoolteacher	MA	Democrat	aerospace engineer	homemaker	1987	Conservative
12. M	53	Detroit	psychologist/professor	PhD	Democrat	salesman	homemaker	1984	Conservative
13. F	49	New Jersey	college prof.	PhD	Democrat	businessman	bookkeeper	1988	Orthodox
14. M	43	N.Y.C.	Social Security admin.	BA	Democrat	govt. employee	govt. employee	1989	Conservative
15. M	46	California	doctor	PhD	Democrat	lawyer	nurse	1985	Not affiliated/"Did Hanukkah"
16. F	25	Atlanta	student	some coll.	Democrat	sales rep.	[unclear]	1993	Reform/"Lit Shabbes candles"
17. F	40	Chicago	homemaker	BS	None	business manager	homemaker	1990	Orthodox/Conservative
18. F	43	LA	store owner	10th grade	Democrat	car business	homemaker	1989	Not affiliated/"Cultural Jews"
19. F	45	Chicago	teacher	MA	None	engineer/philosopher	secretary	1987	Secular

Glossary

The following words are transliterated from Hebrew, unless otherwise noted. As transliterations, I have spelled them in English so that an English-speaking person with no knowledge of Hebrew will pronounce them as closely as possible to the Hebrew word they are meant to reproduce. While my spelling is non-traditional, in my opinion, it is much more accurate, because it calls forth a more precise approximation to the origin word — the very goal of transliteration.

Adon. Sir. Master. "Mr."

Adonai. A substitute name for God. Translated literally as "My master."

Aleeyah. When one is called up to the Torah to offer a prayer during the reading of the Torah during congregational Sabbath worship. Literally "to go up" or "going up."

Am. People.

Ameedah. One of the central prayers within Judaism.

Bayt. House.

Beema. Pulpit; the podium or table in the synagogue on which the Torah is rested while being read from during congregational worship.

Bubkis. Best translated as "diddly-squat," or "peanuts," or "nothing," as in: "She doesn't know diddly-squat," or "He doesn't know peanuts." Literally means "goat turds."

Cholent. A pre-made stew, usually containing meat and potatoes, that is eaten by observant Jews on the Sabbath.

Daven/Davening. (Yiddish) Pray/Praying.

Emett. Truth.

Froom. (Yiddish) Pious, holy, religious, traditionally observant.

Galut. All places outside of Israel; literally "exile."

Gemara. Part of the Talmud (codified oral law).

Gevalt. (Yiddish) "Oh, no!" "Wow!" "Shit!" "Help!" "Oh, God."

Haag. Holiday, celebration.

Haftorah. Portion taken from the Prophets that is read after the Torah during Sabbath worship and on various holidays.

Halakhik. Of the law; lawful, moral.

Hallah. Special braided egg-bread loaf, traditionally served and eaten on the Sabbath.

Har Sinai. Mt. Sinai, where, according to Jewish mythology, Moses received the Ten Commandments from God.

Harraydeem. Ultra-religious or observant Jews. This term has a decidedly political connotation within Israel as a reference to various Hasidic groups.

Hashem. A substitute name for God. Translated literally as "The Name."

Havdalah(s). Ritual/prayer recognizing the end of the Sabbath and its separateness from the other days of the week.

Haymish. (Yiddish) Cozy, warm, comfortable, home-like.

Hazan. Cantor; musically trained singer within the congregation.

Humasch. Pentateuch or the Five Books of Moses.

Kashrut. The kosher laws that determine the dietary behavior of Orthodox Jews.

Kavode. Honor, respect.

Keepa (pl. Keepote). Head covering traditionally worn by men; usually looks like the little "beanie"-type cap that the Pope wears.

Kiddush. Ritual blessing over the wine said at the beginning of the Sabbath meal and other holidays.

Kishkes. (Yiddish) Guts. Intestines.

Klezmeer. East European Jewish jazz/folk music.

L'shon horah. Gossip; literally "evil tongue/language."

Mahkome Miriam. Miriam's space; place of Miriam.

Mehitzah. A physical divider or border placed in some synagogues to separate men and women.

Mellah. (Arabic) A Jewish community or ghetto in Arab countries.

Mikvah. Ritual bath used by Orthodox Jews for various purification rites.

Minkhah. Afternoon prayer service.

Minyan (pl. Minyaneem). The quorum of ten Jews (for Orthodox Jews, only men) needed to conduct a proper prayer service.

Mishnah. Part of the Talmud.

Mitzvah (pl. Mitzvote). Good deed, moral action, commandment.

Moshiakh ben David. The Messiah, son/descendant of David

Nigguneem. Wordless Yiddish folk melodies.

Nu. "So?" "Well?" "What's up?" "C'mon!" "Go on!"

Olam. World.

Payisses. Sidelocks; the curly strands of hair descending from the sides of the head.

Parsha. 1) Chapter; Section of the Torah that is read during the Sabbath service. 2) Speech on the Torah.

Sayder. Ritual dinner that is central to the holiday of Passover.

Shabbat. Sabbath (sundown Friday to sundown Saturday).

Shabbes. (Yiddish) Sabbath (sundown Friday to sundown Saturday).

Shaliakh Tzubbir. Leader of the prayer/worship service.

Sh'ma. Central prayer of Judaism affirming the oneness of God.

Shiddukh. 1) A great match. 2) An arranged marriage.

Shule. (Yiddish). Synagogue, house of prayer.

Shtetl. (Yiddish) A small, tightly-knit, ghetto-like community where Jews lived in pre-modern Eastern Europe.

Simkhah Torah. Jewish holiday commemorating the completion of the annual reading of the Torah.

Smeekha. Rabbinic ordination.

Tallis or Talleet (pl. Talliseem). Fringed prayer shawl.

Tikkun. Heal, mend, repair.

Treyf. Not kosher; dirty, unclean.

Tseet-Tseet. Tassles at the corners of the four-cornered undershirt worn by Orthodox men.

Yiddishkeit. (Yiddish) Jewish life, Jewish culture, Jewish way of life.

Zaydeh. (Yiddish) Grandfather.

References

Adler, R. 1973. The Jew who wasn't there. *Response* 18 (Summer):77-81.

Aidala, A. 1985. Social change, gender roles, and new religious movements. *Sociological Analysis* 46 (3): 287-314.

Ammerman, N. 1987. Schism: An overview. *The Encyclopedia of Religion*, vol.13, New York: Macmillan.

_____. 1990. *Baptist Battles: Social Change and Religious Conflict in the Southern Baptist Convention*. New Brunswick, NJ: Rutgers University Press.

Babbie, E. 1992. *The Practice of Social Research*. Belmont, CA: Wadsworth Publishing Co.

Balmer, R. 1994. American fundamentalism: The ideal femininity. In *Fundamentalism and Gender*, edited by J.S. Hawley, 47-62. New York: Oxford University Press.

Berger, P. 1954. The sociological study of sectarianism. *Social Research* 21:467-85.

Biale, R. 1984. *Women and Jewish Law*. New York: Schocken Books.

Brown, K.M. 1994. Fundamentalism and the control of women. In *Fundamentalism and Gender*, edited by J.S. Hawley, 175-201. New York: Oxford University Press.

Bynum, C. 1986. Introduction: The complexity of symbols. In *Gender and Religion: On the Complexity of Symbols*. Boston: Beacon Press.

Bynum, C., S. Harrell, and P. Richman. 1986. *Gender and Religion: On the Complexity of Symbols*. Boston: Beacon Press.

Cantor, A. 1995. *Jewish Women, Jewish Men*. San Francisco: HarperCollins.

Chaves, M. 1997. *Ordaining Women: Culture and Conflict in Religious Organizations*. Cambridge, MA: Harvard University Press.

Clifford, J. 1988. *The Predicament of Culture: Twentieth-Century Ethnography, Literature and Art*. Cambridge, MA:Harvard University Press.

Clifford, J. and G.E. Marcus, eds. 1986. *Writing Culture: The Poetics and Politics of Ethnography*. Berkeley, CA: University of California Press.

Cohen, S. 1980. American Jewish feminism: A study of conflicts and compromises. *American Behavioral Scientist* 23: 519-558.

Danzger, H. 1989. *Returning to Tradition: The Contemporary Revival of Orthodox Judaism*. New Haven, CT: Yale University Press.

Davidman, L. 1988. Gender and religious experience. Paper presented at the meetings of the American Sociological Association, Atlanta.

_____. 1991. *Tradition in a Rootless World: Women Turn to Orthodox Judaism*. Berkeley: University of California Press.

Doherty, R.W. 1967. *The Hicksite Separation*. New Brunwick, NJ: Rutgers University Press.

Durkheim, E. 1915. *The Elementary Forms of Religious Life*. New York: The Free Press.

Eilberg-Schwartz, H. 1994. *God's Phallus and Other Problems for Men and Monotheism*. Boston: Beacon Press.

Elazar, D. 1980. Patterns of Jewish organization in the United States. In *American Denominational Organization*, edited by R.P. Scherer. Pasadena, CA: William Carey Library.

Fishman, S.B. 1993. *A Breath of Life: Feminism in the American Jewish Community*. New York: The Free Press.

Frankiel, T. 1990. *The Voice of Sarah*. New York: Biblio Press.

Geertz, C. 1966. Religion as a cultural system. In *Anthropological Approaches to the Study of Religion*, edited by M. Banton, 1-46. London and New York: Tavistock Publications.

_____. 1973. *The Interpretation of Cultures*. New York: Basic Books, Inc.

Greenberg, B. 1981. *On Women and Judaism*. Philadelphia: Jewish Publication Society of America.

Grossman, S. and Haut, R. 1992. *Daughters of the King: Women and the Synagogue*. Philadelphia: The Jewish Publication Society of America.

Hammond, P. 1992. *Religion and Personal Autonomy: The Third Disestablishment in America*. Columbia, SC: University of South Carolina Press.

Harris, L. 1985. *Holy Days*. New York: Summit Books.

Haywood, C.L. 1983. Women's authority in spiritualist groups. *Journal for the Scientific Study of Religion* 22: 157-66.

Heilman, S. 1973. *Synagogue Life*. Chicago: University of Chicago Press.

Heschel, S., ed. 1983. *On Being a Jewish Feminist: A Reader*. New York: Schocken Books.

Hoge, D. 1976. *Division in the Protestant House*. Philadelphia: The Westminster Press.

Hunter, J.D. 1991. *Culture Wars*. New York: Basic Books.

Iadarola, A. 1985. The American Catholic bishops and woman: From the nineteenth amendment to the ERA. In *Women, Religion, and Social Change*, edited by Y.Y. Haddad and E.B. Findly, 457-476. Albany: State University of New York Press.

Jacobs, J. 1989. *Divine Disenchantment*. Bloomington, IN: Indiana University Press.

_____. 1991. Gender and power in new religious movements. *Religion* 21:345-356.

Joseph, N.B. 1992. Mehitzah: halakhic decisions and political conse-
quences. In *Daughters of the King: Women and the Synagogue*, edited by
S. Grossman and R. Haut. Phildelphia: The Jewish Publications
Society.

Kamenetz, R. 1994. *The Jew in the Lotus*. San Francisco: HarperCollins.

Kaufman, D. 1991. *Rachel's Daughters: Newly Orthodox Jewish Women*.
New Brunswick, NJ: Rutgers University Press.

Kniss, F. 1996. Ideas and symbols as resources in intrareligious conflict:
The case of American Mennonites. *Sociology of Religion* 57(1):7-23.

Kniss, F. and M. Chaves. 1995. Analyzing intradenominational conflict:
new directions. *Journal for the Scientific Study of Religion* 34:172-185.

Kugelmass, J., ed. 1988. *Between Two Worlds: Ethnographic Essays on
American Jewry*. Ithaca, NY: Cornell University Press.

Lawless, E. 1992. "I was afraid someone like you . . . an outsider . . . would
misunderstand": Negotiating interpretive differences between ethnographers and subjects. *Journal of American Folklore* 105:302-314.

Lehman, E. 1985. *Women Clergy: Breaking through Gender Barriers*. New
Brunswick, NJ: Transaction Books.

Lerner, M. 1994. *Jewish Renewal*. New York: HarperPerennial.

Liebman, R.C., J.R. Sutton, and R. Wuthnow. 1988. Exploring the social
sources of denominationalism: Schisms in American Protestant
denominations, 1890-1980. *American Sociological Review* 53:343-352.

Mannheim, K. 1936. *Ideology and Utopia*. New York: Harcourt, Brace, and
World, Inc.

Manning, C. 1997. Women in a divided church: Liberal and conservative
Catholic women negotiate changing gender roles. *Sociology of Religion*
58:4, 375-390.

Marcus, G. E. and M.J. Fischer. 1986. *Anthropology as Cultural Critique: An Experimental Moment in the Human Sciences.* Chicago: University of Chicago Press.

McGuire, M. 1997. *Religion in Social Context.* Belmont, CA: Wadsworth Publishing Co.

McNamara, P. 1992. *Conscience First, Tradition Second: A Study of Young American Catholics.* Albany: State University of New York Press.

Myerhoff, B. 1978. *Number Our Days.* New York: Simon and Schuster.

Neitz, M.J. and M.S. Goldman., eds. 1995. *Sex, Lies, and Sanctity: Religion and Deviance in Contemporary North America. Religion and the Social Order*, vol.5. Greenwich, CT: JAI Press, Inc.

Niebuhr, H. R. 1929. *The Social Sources of Denominationalism..* Cleveland: World Publishing Co.

Plaskow, J. 1990. *Standing Again at Sinai: Judaism from a Feminist Perspective.* San Francisco, CA: HarperCollins.

Pope, L. 1942. *Millhands and Preachers.* New Haven, CT: Yale University Press.

Prelinger, C., ed. 1992. *Episcopal Women.* New York: Oxford University Press.

Ranke-Heinemann, U. 1988. *Eunuchs for Heaven: The Catholic Church and Sexuality.* London: Andre Deutsch Limited.

———. 1992. *Putting Away Childish Things.* San Francisco, CA: HarperCollins.

Ricoeur, P. 1972. The symbol gives rise to thought. In *Ways of Understanding Religion*, edited by W. Kapps. New York: Macmillan.

Roberts, K. 1984. *Religion in Sociological Perspective.* Homewood, IL: The Dorsey Press.

Rochford, E. Burke. 1989. Factionalism, group defection, and schism in the Hare Krishna movement. *Journal for the Scientific Study of Religion* 28:162-179.

Roof, W.C. 1994. *A Generation of Seekers*. New York: HarperCollins.

Roof, W.C. and W. McKinney. 1987. *American Mainline Religion: Its Changing Shape and Future*. New Brunswick, NJ: Rutgers University Press.

Rosaldo, R.I. 1986. When natives talk back. *Renato Rosaldo Lecture Series Monograph*, vol.2, Spring.

Schneider, S.W. 1984. *Jewish and Female: Choices and Changes in Our Lives Today*. New York: Simon and Schuster.

Sered, S. 1992. *Women as Ritual Experts: The Religious Lives of Elderly Jewish Women in Jerusalem*. New York: Oxford University Press.

_____. 1997. Women and religious change in Israel: Rebellion or revolution. *Sociology of Religion*, 58: 1-24.

Shepherd, N. 1993. *A Price Below Rubies: Jewish Women as Rebels and Radicals*. Cambridge, MA: Harvard University Press.

Shin, E.H. and H. Park. 1988. An analysis of causes of schisms in ethnic churches: The case of Korean-American churches. *Sociological Analysis* 49:234-248.

Sklare, M. 1993. *Observing America's Jews*. Hanover, MA: Brandeis University Press.

Stacey, J. 1990. *Brave New Families*. New York: Basic Books, Inc.

Stark, R. and W.S. Bainbridge. 1985. *The Future of Religion*. Berkeley, CA: University of California Press.

Swatos, W.H., ed. 1998. *Encyclopedia of Religion and Society*. Walnut Creek, CA: AltaMira Press.

Takayama, K.P. 1980. Strains, conflicts, and schisms in Protestant denominations. In *American Denominational Organization*, edited by R.P. Sherer. Pasadena, CA: William Carey Library.

Titon, J. 1988. *Powerhouse for God: Speech, Chant, and Song in an Appalachian Baptist Church*. Austin, TX: University of Texas Press.

Tubeville, G. 1949. Religious schism in the Methodist church: A sociological analysis of the Pine Grove Case. *Rural Sociology* 14:29-39.

Turner, V. 1967. *The Forest of Symbols: Aspects of Ndembu Ritual*. Ithaca, NY: Cornell University Press.

_____. 1974. *Dramas, Fields, and Metaphors*. Ithaca, NY: Cornell University Press.

Vrga, D. and F.J. Fahey. 1970. The relationship of religious practices and beliefs to schism. *Sociological Analysis* 31:46-55.

Wallace, R. 1993. The social contruction of a new leadership role: Catholic women pastors. *Sociology of Religion* 54:31-42

Warner, R.S. 1988. *New Wine in Old Wineskins*. Berkeley: University of California Press.

Wegner, J.R. 1988. *Chattel or Person?* New York: Oxford University Press.

Wertheimer, J. 1993. *A People Divided*. New York: Basic Books.

Wilson, B. 1990. *The Social Dimensions of Sectarianism*. Oxford: Clarendon Press.

Wilson, J. 1971. The sociology of schism. *A Sociological Yearbook of Religion in Britain*, 1-20.

Wuthnow, R. 1988. *The Restructuring of American Religion*. Princeton, NJ: Princeton University Press.

Zuckerman, P. 1997. Gender regulation as a source of religious schism. *Sociology of Religion* 58:4, 353-373.

References Not Cited

Biale, R. 1995. *Women and Jewish Law*, 2nd edition. New York: Schocken Books.

Cohen, S. 1983. *American Modernity and Jewish Identity*. New York: Tavistock Publications.

_____. 1988. *American Assimilation or Jewish Revival?* Bloomington, IN: Indiana University Press.

Daum, A. 1992. Language and liturgy. In *Daughters of the King: Women and the Synagogue*, edited by S. Grossman and R. Haut, 183-202. Philadelphia, PA: Jewish Publication Society.

Eister, A.W. 1973. H. Richard Niebuhr and the paradox of religious organizations: a radical critique. In *Beyond the Classics?*, edited by C.Y. Glock and P.E. Hammond, 355-408. New York: Harper and Row.

Fein, L. 1988. *Where Are We? The Inner Life of America's Jews*. New York: Harper and Row.

Herberg, W. 1955. *Protestant Catholic Jew*. New York: Anchor Books.

Hoge, D., B. Johnson, and D. Luidens. 1994. *Vanishing Boundaries*. Louisville: Westminster/John Knox Press.

Isaacson, L. 1995. Rule making and rule breaking in a Jesus community. In *Religion and the Social Order*, vol. 5., edited by M. Nietz and M. Goldman. Greenwich, CT: JAI Press, Inc.

Kaplan, M. 1981 [1934]. *Judaism as a Civilization*. Philadelphia: Jewish Publication Society of America.

Kosmin, B. and S. Lachman. 1993. *One Nation Under God*. New York: Crown Publishers.

Legge, J.S., Jr. 1996. Traditional Judaism: Assessing the potential for the emergence of a new denomination. Paper presented at the Annual Meeting for the Society for the Scientific Study of Religion in Society and the Religious Research Association, Nashville.

Neusner, J. 1974. *The Life of Torah*. Encino, CA: Dickenson Pubishing Company, Inc.

Sachar, H. 1958. *The Course of Modern Jewish History*. New York: Vintage Books.

Wagner, J. 1982. *Sex Roles in Contemporary American Communes.* Bloomington, IN: Indiana University Press.

White, H. and R. Breiger. 1975. Patterns across networks. *Society* (July-August):68-73.

Index